Passion for Travel

Romania

AD LIBRI

text
MARIANA PASCARU

English translation
MARIA DUMITRU
ALISTAIR IAN BLYTH ("Bucharest", pp. 19-37)

Proofreading
ALISTAIR IAN BLYTH

photographs
FLORIN ANDREESCU

Romania / trad. eng.:Maria Dumitru; versiune originală: Mariana Pascaru;
foto: Florin Andreescu
Bucureşti; Ad Libri, 2015
ISBN 978-606-8050-67-6
913(498)(084)

Published by AD LIBRI
tel./fax: 021-212.35.67, 021-210.88.64; tel: 021-610.37.92
e-mail: adlibri@adlibri.ro
www.adlibri.ro
www.calator-pe-mapamond.ro

The publisher endeavours to provide readers with complete and
up-to-date factual information. We are nevertheless aware that,
between the date this guide is published and that in which it is
purchased, various modifications may appear in the information
offered herein. We apologise for any eventual oversights and
shall be grateful to all of those who point them out. Any other
observation or new information regarding the subject matter of
the guide will be regarded as welcome.

KEY TO SYMBOLS

✉ address

☎ telephone number

🕐 opening times

Ⓢ admission charge

🚍 nearest bus/tram route

➤ indicates the page where you will find a fuller description

Contents

Welcome to Romania!

Previous page: *Between working their land and doing housework, the elders find time to read the Book of Hours*

Introduction

Romania is becoming more and more well known in Europe. While before its EU accession (2007), it came as a surprise for some to look at a map of Europe and discover a place called Romania, others admitted to having been won over by this country full of life and colour, which had not become just another standard product for tourists. A trip to Romania will produce thrilling sensations, strong impressions and feelings that can suddenly shift from enthusiasm to astonishment, from trust to suspicion and from empathy to outrage. But leave your preconceptions behind and you will be able to enjoy one of the least conventional journeys through the European continent. Time moves at its own pace depending on your location – spinning out of control in the frantic capital city or slowing to a gentle crawl in the sleepy country villages, where you are under the impression that life comes to a halt or barely moves along.

To arrive in Romania just follow the ancient and sacred Danube River (Dunărea, in Romanian) which runs 1,075km along the border of the country before flowing into the Black Sea. The Roman army crossed the Danube on their way to Dacia, the land of the "immortal" Getae (Dacians) – the Romanians' ancestors – who worshipped Zalmoxis. Still extant today are the pylon of the bridge built on the orders of the Roman Emperor Trajan by the architect Apollodorus of Damascus between 103 and 105 at Drobeta-Turnu Severin, the Roman baths at Băile Herculane, the remains of Roman castra, traces of ancient roads, such as the one built along the Danube, as attested by a Roman memorial plaque (Tabula Traiana) carved deep into the rock where the Danube exits the Small Kazan Gorge. After the Romans conquered the Dacians, Southern Dacia became a Roman province, called *Dacia Felix* (meaning, "Fertile Dacia"). This ethnic mixture formed the basis for the Romanian people, who are said to represent "an island of Latin culture in the midst of a sea of Slav tribes". Romanian so closely resembles Italian, French or Spanish that some have wondered how it was possible for this Latin language to emerge in a corner of Europe considered the realm of the Slav languages par excellence.

The outline of Romania as it currently stands is lent by its provinces, formerly known as mediaeval "states" – small voivodeships and independent knezates, each with its particularities and evolution. In the 12th century, King Géza II of Hungary sent Saxon colonists to the Romanian province of Transylvania, who founded traditional fortified settlements (Sighişoara, Sibiu, Bistriţa). Transylvania was later annexed to the Austrian and the Austro-Hungarian Empire. Dobruja, settled by

Greeks in the 7th century B.C., was part of the Roman Empire and later came under Turkish rule between 1417 and 1878. The rulers of Moldavia, a province strewn with remnants of citadels and princely courts, were tireless fighters against the invading Turks; rumour has it that after each of his many victories, Stephen the Great erected a church; in fact here we can find churches with glorious exterior murals, which have earned them great renown. Phanariote rule (18th century) put Greek rulers at the helm of Muntenia and Moldavia, originating from the Phanar neighbourhood in Constantinople and appointed by the Sublime Porte; it was a period when the Romanian space became imbued with the Orient. During the Russo-Turkish conflict in 1828-1829, the Russian army, led by Pavel Kiseleff, occupied Moldavia and Wallachia (until 1834).

So, before we set out on our journey, let us become a little more familiar with the regions of the country. There is Transylvania in the centre, to the south – Wallachia (with Muntenia and Oltenia), to the south-east – Dobruja, to the north-east – Moldavia, to the north-west – Maramureș, and to the west – the Banat. Their inhabitants can be easily told apart by their Romanian accents and the regionalisms they use – some of them quite delightful and often misunderstood even by Romanians. A person living in Ardeal can be as easily identified as a person living in Moldavia after only a few minutes' conversation. Depending on how they have evolved in time, the inhabitants of each region have acquired specific characteristics associated with them as either shortcomings or strengths. Those living in Oltenia are impatient, hasty, always managing things and talkative, those living in Moldavia – slow, funny and welcoming, people from Ardeal – calm and hard-working, those in the Banat – penny-wise and proud, in Bucharest people are crafty and feisty. These patterns and labels have been the inspiration of many jokes which you will definitely hear (though they do lose much of their flavour when translated) if ever at a Romanian party.

Background information

- **Location:** *South-Eastern Europe, having as natural borders the Danube River (to the south), the Prut River (to the east) and the Tisza River (to the north along a short section.)*

- **Neighbouring countries:** *Ukraine and the Republic of Moldova (to the north and east), Hungary (to the west and north-west), Serbia (to the south and south-west) and Bulgaria (to the south)*

- **Area:** *238,391km²*

- **Population:** *21,733,556 inhabitants (2003), 89% of whom are Romanian. The main ethnic groups are made up of Hungarians and Szeklers (7.1%) and Roma (1.7%)*

- **Main religion:** *Greek Orthodox (86.8% of the population). Other denominations: Roman Catholics (5%), Protestants (3.5%), Greek Catholics (1%).*

Located in the Lower Danube, in the northern Balkan Peninsula, Romania is often said to be a Balkan country, although where exactly Balkans end is a rather controversial issue. If the Balkans overlap South-Eastern Europe, then it is safe to say that Romania is part of this colourful region. Some Balkan elements are certainly felt, but do not expect to find here a land in stark contrast to Western Europe.

Historical Landmarks

The 2nd Millennium B.C.
On the territory of modern Romania the presence of Thracian tribes, of Indo-European origin is attested.

The 6th Century B.C.
Greek documents tell of the existence of Getae in the Lower Danube and south of the Carpathians.

1st Century B.C. - 1st Century A.D.
The Dacian Empire flourishes, with its centre in the Orăştie Mountains (➤133), south-west of Transylvania, with fortresses and strategically-placed buildings covering 200km².

8-18
The poet Publius Ovidius Naso is exiled to Tomis, present-day Constanţa (➤74), where he writes *Epistulae ex Ponto*.

101-102, 105-106
The wars between Dacian king Decebalus and Roman emperor Trajan break out. Dacia is conquered by the Romans.

106-271
The Romans rule for approximately 165 years over central and south-western Dacia. They build roads, castra and towns (the Ulpia Traiana Sarmizegetusa settlement, Apulum) and engage in mining. The Dacian-Roman population adopts the Latin language which forms the basis for today's Romanian language, the only language of Latin origin in Eastern Europe. In 271 the Roman legions withdraw under Emperor Aurelius.

The 4th-6th Centuries
A series of barbarian peoples invade the present-day Romanian territory: Goths, Huns, Gepids, Avars, Slavs, Pechenegs, Cumans etc. The Slavs will be assimilated, as evidenced by the numerous Slavic words in Romanian.

The end of the 9th Century
The Hungarians, of the Finno-Ugric tribes originating from Asia, around the Altai Mountains, settle in Pannonia. In the 9th-13th centuries they establish their rule over the early Romanian statelets, and Transylvania is included as an autonomous voivodeship within the Kingdom of Hungary.

The 12th-13th Centuries
Saxons and Szeklers settle in Transylvania.

1241
The Tartars invade Europe, arriving in these parts as well.

1247
The *Charter of the Knights Hospitaller*, granted by King Béla IV of Hungary, mentions the existence of several knezates, voivodeships and "lands" (*ţara* in Romanian): Ţara Severinului, the Voivodeship of Litovoi, Ţara Haţegului, the Voivodeship of Seneslau etc.

1330
Wallachia (*Ţara Românească* in Romanian) is created as an independent state, in the aftermath of the Battle of Posada.

1359
Moldavia is founded ("the dismounting") by Voivode Bogdan who crosses the mountains accompanied by people from Maramureş.

October 1394
The Battle of Rovine which sees Bayezid's army defeated by Mircea the Elder.

January 1475
Stephen the Great defeats the Turks led by Soliman Pasha during the Podul Înalt battle, near Vaslui.

July 1514
The peasant uprising led by Gheorghe Doja against the Hungarian elite is crushed with great bloodshed.

1600
The first and, alas, short-lived attempt to unify the Romanian principalities, under Michael the Brave, proclaimed "the Prince of Wallachia, Transylvania and the whole of Moldavia". In 1593, he joins the Holy League – an anti-Ottoman Christian alliance orga-nised by the Pope and the Holy Roman Empire – and manages to regain independence for Wallachia following the Battles of Călugăreni and Giurgiu.

1699
After the peace Treaty of Karlowitz between the Turks and the Austrians, Transylvania is annexed to the Austrian Empire under whose "protectorate" it remains until 1867. Between 1867 and 1918 it is part of the Austro-Hungarian Empire.

1716-1821
Wallachia is under the rule of Phanariote Greeks (from the Phanar district of Constantinople) appointed by the Sublime Porte. Moldavia shares the same fate, between 1711 and 1821. After Tudor Vladimirescu's revolt (1821) local rulers are appointed.

The 18th-19th Centuries
Principalities frequently find them-selves caught in the middle of the wars between Austria, Russia and the Ottoman Empire. Between 1718 and 1793, Austria temporarily occupies Oltenia, a Romanian province and, between 1775 and 1918, Bukowina.

1812-1918
Bessarabia, a Moldovan province is annexed by Russia.

1828-1834
During the Russo-Turkish war of 1828-1829, the Russian army led by Pavel Kiseleff occupies Moldavia and Wallachia (until 1834). The Organic Statutes (a sort of Constitution) adopted during that period may be regarded as the first step towards the modern organisation of the Romanian principalities; they introduce for the first time the principle of the separation of powers.

1848
The revolutionary ideas of 1848 arrive in the Romanian provinces, but the uprisings are quickly suppressed.

1856
After the defeat of Russia in the Crimean War (1853-1856), the Romanian principalities come under the protection of the seven powers signatory to the Peace Treaty of Paris.

1859
Alexandru Ioan Cuza is appointed sole ruler of Moldavia and Wallachia, which take the name of the United Principalities and, from 1862, Romania, with the Capital City in Bucharest. Along with Mihail Kogălniceanu, Alexandru Ioan Cuza initiates a series of reforms which contribute to the modernisation of the country.

1866
After deposing Cuza (1866), Carol of Hohenzollern-Sigmanringen (Carol I) becomes the ruler of Romania. A new democratic constitution is adopted on this occasion, inspired by the Belgian constitution.

1877
After the Russo-Turkish War of 1877,

Romania gains full independence. At the same time Dobruja, under Turkish rule since 1417, is restored to Romania.

1881
In March 1881, Romania proclaims itself a Monarchy and Carol I is appointed King. The long and beneficial rule of Carol I (1866-1914) is followed by those of his successors: Ferdinand I (1914-1927), Michael I (1927-1930; 1940-1947) and Carol II (1930-1940), the last of whom imposes a royal dictatorship in 1938.

18/28 November 1918
The unification of Bukowina with Romania.

1 December 1918
The unification of Transylvania, the Banat, Maramureş and Crişana with Romania, following the Great National Assembly vote at Alba Iulia.

1944-1958
The Soviet occupation of Romania. During the World War II, the Soviet army occupies Romanian territory and withdraws only in 1958. The Government is taken over by Communists who arrest the members of the historical parties.

1947
The Treaty of Paris acknowledges the annulment of the Second Vienna Award and the annexation of Bessarabia and Northern Bukowina by the USSR.

30 December 1947
King Michael I abdicates and the People's Republic of Romania and the communist regime are established under pressure from the Red Army.

1948
Businesses are nationalised.

1949-1962
Collectivisation of agriculture.

1953
Gheorghe Gheorghiu-Dej becomes Secretary General of the Communist Party and the leader of the country.

1965-1989
Nicolae Ceauşescu becomes the head of state and after a short period of political thaw marked by his anti-Soviet stand during the Warsaw Pact invasion of Czechoslovakia (1968) when Romania refuses to get involved, he establishes a dictatorship and commences his megalomaniac projects.

December 1989
The fall of the communist regime following widespread street protests. Democracy, the multi-party system and the free market are re-established.

2007
Romania joins the European Union.

Photo: *Statue of Carol I of Romania, at Peleş Castle (Sinaia resort)*

The Ten Best Places to Go in Romania

Bucharest, the Capital City of Romania ➤19-41

A vibrant city with more on offer than ever before! The Old City's scintillating night life has turned Bucharest into a European destination for clubbing, with urban festivals and less conventional events never in short supply in summer, earning it the reputation of a Little Berlin. The explosion of alternative "urban hubs", independent theatres, art galleries and industrial space conversions has created a cultural scene to be envied by any capital city.

Braşov ➤112

Braşov seems to have discovered the secret of indefinitely extending the tourist season. Come summer, or winter, the Old City of this mediaeval burg buzzes with tourists from every corner of the earth. Statistics show that the city annually attracts more visitors than any other region in Romania. They all admire the city layout so specific to old Saxon burgs and architecture featuring Gothic, Renaissance and Baroque elements, making the best of the amazing location of the city, in the foothills of the Tâmpa Mountains, from the top of which there are spectacular views.

Sighişoara ➤119

Sighişoara, one of the few inhabited citadels in the world is a textbook example of mediaeval town planning. The features of the mediaeval world have been preserved intact: curtain walls with bastions and nine artillery towers which run for almost a kilometre around the Citadel Hill, the main square where the pillory once stood and public executions took place, Gothic churches, narrow cobbled streets, old craftsmen's houses with brightly coloured facades and geraniums adorning their windows. Sighişoara, a citadel founded by the Saxons in 1191 on a hilltop on the left shore of Târnava Mare River, is still alive…

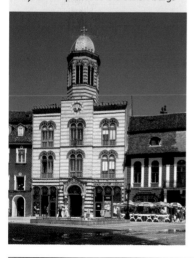

Left: *Church of the Dormition of the Theotokos, Braşov*

Right: *Clock Tower, Sighişoara*

Sibiu ➤123

Miraculously, Sibiu's Old City, the old citadel on the Cibin River, has managed to preserve most of its original features. The architecture typical of a German mediaeval burg and Baroque Vienna-style architecture merge into a single style. Here you discover narrow streets flanked by the old houses of the Saxon craftsmen, broad squares whose glory is reminiscent of the times when they played a central role in the community life, curtain walls, bastions and towers coming together to form a formidable defense system, stairs and bridges which take you back to the Middle Ages.

Timişoara ➤147

The administrative seat of the Banat, Timişoara can boast several "firsts" for Romania: the horse-drawn tram was first introduced here, followed by the electric tram, electric street lighting, as well as telephone services. It was from here that the spark of the December 1989 Revolution spread, leading to the fall of communism. Locals call their city on the Bega River "the leading light" with good reason! Furthermore, its centre is home to the most remarkable 18th-century Baroque complex in Romania, Union Square, Victory Square and Freedom Square being good examples.

Danube Delta ➤85

A delta has formed where the Danube meets the Black Sea, unanimously recognised as one of the most amazing places in Europe. Covering 2,681km^2, the Danube Delta represents the continent's largest wetland reserve and the largest expanse of reed beds in the world. This "Noah's Ark", where 1,200 species of plants and trees have been

identified, along with 320 bird species and 100 fish species, has been declared a Biosphere Reserve and listed as a UNESCO Natural World Heritage site. Under the RAMSAR Convention, it is a Wetland of International Importance. Scattered along the sandbars stretching between the three main channels of the delta – Chilia, Sulina and Sfântu Gheorghe – lie centuries-old fishing villages, completely cut off by the waters from the rest of the world.

Transylvania's Fortified Churches ➤116, 117, 122, 130

Right in the heart of each old rural settlement founded in the 12th century by the Saxon colonists of Transylvania stands a fortified church which used to serve as a retreat in days of peril. Of the more than 300 fortress churches (13th-16th century) mostly built in the wake of the Tartar invasion of 1241, around 150 have been preserved to this day, 7 of which – Biertan, Câlnic, Dârjiu, Prejmer, Saschiz, Valea Viilor and Viscri – have been included on the UNESCO World Heritage list.

The wooden churches of Maramureș ➤162

Woodcarving saw its heyday in Maramureș, where wooden churches with their tall, slender spires soaring boldly towards heavens and absolute harmony of proportions, seem to have transcended the perishable nature of the matter from which they are made. Impressive examples of peasant craftsmanship, expressions of rural spirituality, the wooden places of worship differ from weightier brick and mortar churches in their spatial organisation. Eight of the one hundred wooden churches in Maramureș – from Ieud Hill (14th century), Bârsana (1720), Budești (1643), Poienile Izei (1604), Rogoz (1663), Desești (1717), Plopiș (1792) and Șurdești (1767) – have been included on the UNESCO World Heritage list.

The Painted Churches of Bukowina ➤100

Nowhere in Romania are there so many churches, monasteries and hermitages clustered in such a small area than in Bukowina. Most of them are centuries-old and constitute unique illustrations of mediaeval architecture. The splendor of the murals, painted in inimitable hues of blue, red, yellow and green, covering the exterior walls of the Voroneț (1488), Humor (1530), Suceviţa (1591), Moldoviţa (1532) and Probota (1530) monasteries is overwhelming. They have also been declared UNESCO World Heritage sites.

Jassy (Iași) ➤94

The sweet city of Jassy, stretching over seven hills like Rome, started to develop in the 15th century, when the Moldovan rulers moved their capital here. The superb places of worship (the churches of the Three Hierarchs, Galata, Golia, Cetăţuia and Frumoasa monasteries) date back to the time when it was the capital of Moldavia. The Neogothic building of the Palace of Culture, erected on the site of the old princely court between 1907 and 1926, has been converted into a vast museum compound. Jassy can be regarded as the Capital City of literature, as it is home to an impressive number of museums and memorial houses.

Left: *Ieud Hill wooden church in Maramureș*

Right: The Siege of Constantinople – *mural on the walls of the Moldoviţa Monastery, Bukowina*

The Ten Most Interesting Romanian Experiences

Conquer the most dramatic peaks of Romania's Carpathian Mountains

Of the 1,600-km total length of the Carpathian Mountains, half lies on Romanian soil, forming an arc covering one third of the country's territory. A heaven for mountain climbers, skiers, extreme sports and hiking enthusiasts, who can enjoy hundreds of waymarked trails with varying degrees of difficulty and dozens of cabins along the route, Romania's Carpathians are remarkable for their steep ridges which, once you are on top, reward you with magnificent views. Twelve peaks in the Carpathians exceed 2,500m. The record is held by Moldoveanu Peak at 2,544m, in the Făgăraş Massif, a challenge for mountain climbers bold enough to tackle the Transylvanian Alps. Piatra Craiului (The Knight's Rock) appears as a jagged ridge of greyish white lime, with tall walls, footpaths, flat and abrupt

rocks and scree. The Retezat Massif, with 80 glacial lakes, is home to a 54,400-hectare nature reserve, and has been declared a Biosphere Reserve. "The Stone Fortress" of the Apuseni Mountains is the realm of karst: the Ponor Fortresses, the Live Fire Glacier, Padiş Plateau and the gorges of the Galbena River, Someş Cald River and Râmeţi River. The strange-looking Lady's Rocks offer the most spectacular panoramic views of the Rarău Massif.

Behold the clash of water and rock in spectacular ravines carved out by mountain rivers

The Carpathians have been likened to a "castle of water", since it is here that hundreds of streams and springs start their journey through Romania. They carve out 98% of the hydrographic network of the country. In many cases these rivers made their way through the mountain in a head-to-head battle, a spectacle in which the mountain has yet to emerge the victor. The Danube Canyon (►69), the most monumental portion of the Danube Gorge, is currently listed as one of the best Romanian tourist destinations. Forty-seven kilometres long, the Olt River Gorge, carved out between the Lotru Mountains and Căpăţâna Mountains, is the longest in Romania. The Mureş River Gorge, formed between Harghita Mountains and Gurghiu Mountains and the Jiu River Gorge, hollowed out between Parâng Mountains and Vâlcan Mountains, are ideal for trips that last several days. Along the Nera Gorges, running for 22km between Anina Mountains and Locva Mountains, lies the 15-metre-high Beuşniţa Waterfall, the Ochiul Beiului Lake (The Bey's Eye Lake), of greenish blue, and Bigăr Waterfall, chosen by the *The World Geography* website as the most spectacular waterfall in the world.

Photo: *Retezat Massif*

Follow in the footsteps of bloodthirsty Dracula, associated today with Vlad Țepeș (Vlad the Impaler) thanks to Bram Stoker's novel

For many foreign visitors, Romania is synonymous with Dracula. It was Bram Stoker who came up with the idea of identifying his bloodthirsty character with the notoriously cruel Romanian prince Vlad the Impaler (1431-1476), a case of mistaken identity that has proven lucrative for the tourist industry, however. Despite the throngs of tourists eager to walk in Dracula's footsteps at Bran Castle (➤60), built around 1212 by the Teutonic Knights, the truth is that his story has nothing to do with that of a possessed vampire, as many wrongly imagine. Having said that, in the beautiful mediaeval citadel of Sighișoara (➤119) you can find the house where Vlad the Impaler was born, nowadays a restaurant. The Chindia Tower (➤50) of the old princely court of Tîrgoviște was built by Vlad the Impaler, and today it hosts an exhibition dedicated to him. The Poenari Fortress (➤54) was also rebuilt under his reign. Around 1459, Vlad the Impaler built on the Dîmbovița Riverbank Bucharest's first princely court (➤25). It is rumoured that after he died in a battle against the Turks and the Dănești dynasty in 1476, his head was sent to Constantinople and his body secretly buried near Snagov Monastery (➤39).

Take a steam train ride along the Vaser Valley ➤165

The Maramureș Mountains are crossed by Vaser Valley (42km), along which one can hear the Steam Train (*Mocănița*) puffing and huffing – an old train pulled by a steam engine

along a narrow-gauge forest railway built in 1932 – one of the few still running in Europe. The train departs from Vișeu de Sus, generally around 9 in the morning, and runs up the hill for about two hours as far as Paltin station (Km21,6) where it stops for two hours. The scenic steam train is the only one in the country still used for hauling logs.

Sample traditional Romanian cuisine

Try traditional country dishes that use fresh and healthy ingredients: tripe soup, fish borscht, bean and smoked meat soup, stuffed cabbage rolls with polenta and sour cream on the side, chicken stew, Moldavian meatballs, minced meat rolls, Pleșcoi sausages, lamb meat pie, pan-fried cubed pork, Shepherd's baked polenta with Romanian sheep cheese and sour cream, or *zacuscă* (a roasted vegetable spread). And for dessert, you can choose *brașovence* (stuffed crêpes with meat and Bechamel sauce), jam and cream cheese dumplings, homemade panetone, roasted pumpkin, *mucenici* (sweet cookies shaped like an "8") or *poale-n*

Photo: *The steam train that runs along the Vaser Valley*

brâu pies (sweet or salty cheese pies). Wash down the food with a glass of wine from the Cotnari, Dealu Mare, Murfatlar and Niculiţel Vineyards, ideally to the accompaniment of lively Romanian folk music.

Enjoy the vibrant atmosphere of local festivals

On the first Sunday after Easter, seven groups of young men (➤115) parade through the centre of Braşov to the Solomon's Rocks where a lively outdoor celebration is held. On Meatfare Sunday, the Hungarian and Saxon communities of Transylvania celebrate *Fărşang* (➤138), a sort of carnival revolving around the Nichita doll (or Johann), the embodiment of that year's evil, which is carried around the village and then buried. At the end of December, the Saxons from the Valea Hârtibaciului villages (Sibiu) hold the Parade of the *Lole* (funny masked characters) (➤131), clad in black who chase away the winter and the evil spirits with cowbells and whips. In summer, the mediaeval festivals at Sighişoara (➤119) and Hunedoara (➤135) attract people who dress up in mediaeval costumes, demonstrations of mediaeval cooking, craft workshops, gigs, mediaeval dancing and so on. In August, Roşia Montană, a village in the Apuseni Mountains threatened with extinction by a mining project using cyanide, is home to a three-day Hay Feast, a cultural festival showing documentaries, theatre performances, hosting debates, workshops, exhibitions, concerts, guided tours, activities for children, etc.

Spend a holiday in true Romanian style, staying with locals in the country

Romanian villages have discovered in recent years the amazing opportunities that rural tourism has to offer. Communities in Maramureş (➤159-167) or from the Rucăr-Bran Pass (➤58) have led the way. Old traditions and crafts can be admired in the fishing villages of the Danube Delta (➤85), the shepherd villages of Mărginimea Sibiului (➤128), the villages of master coopers in Bukowina (Pleşa, Bogata) and the villages of potters (Horezu, Vama, Marginea), which look like large open-air pottery workshops. At Axente Sever you can find accommodation within the compound of a 14th-century fortified church, and at Viscri you can stay in one of the 18th-century Saxon houses converted into guesthouses after Prince Charles set the tone for their restoration. The Romanian countryside is dressed up in festive garb at Easter or Christmas while the homemade panetone and the sweet cheese pies are baking in the oven, the eggs are being painted and the children are going door-to-door singing Christmas carols. A community such as Ciocăneşti

Photo: *Folk dances from Ţara Oaşului*

in Bukowina with small houses decorated with carved wood panels looks like it is straight out of a fairy tale. And in the Delta, a fishing village such as Sfântu Gheorghe (➤87) – located where the Danube flows into the Black Sea – is flooded mid-August with movie lovers from around the world coming to this secluded place to be part of the International Independent Film Festival.

Experience the Transfăgărăşan and Transalpina highways, two high-altitude passes through the Făgăraş and Parîng Mountains, at more than 2,000m above sea level
The Transfăgărăşan or DN7C (➤55), dotted with many waterfalls and glacial lakes (Capra, Bâlea) on the way, is very popular with tourists who use it as a connecting road between Transylvania and Muntenia. The Transalpina or DN67C, the highest road in Romania, is even more spectacular, with its highest point in the Urdele Pass (2,145m). Both roads are closed from November to June due to weather conditions.

Party the night away in Bucharest's old quarter, one of Europe's hottest new clubbing destinations ➤23-26
Bucharest has such a vibrant night life that it is now on tourists' lists of clubbing destinations. Many come all this way for a night of no-limits fun in the bustling Old City with its dozens of bars that organise wild parties.

Be part of the George Enescu International Music Festival, held every two years in Bucharest, the Transylvania International Film Festival, held every June in Cluj, and the Gărîna Jazz Festival
Every other year Bucharest is home to the prestigious George Enescu Festival (➤176), which invites the best-known orchestras in the world to perform under the baton of celebrated conductors. Every year at the beginning of summer the popular Transylvania International Film Festival (TIFF) takes place at Cluj-Napoca (➤138) screening around 200 films over a span of 10 days. Every August during the International Jazz Festival, Gârâna (➤144), an old town near Semenic National Park, becomes the capital of jazz.

Photo: *Late autumn on Transfăgărăşan Highway*

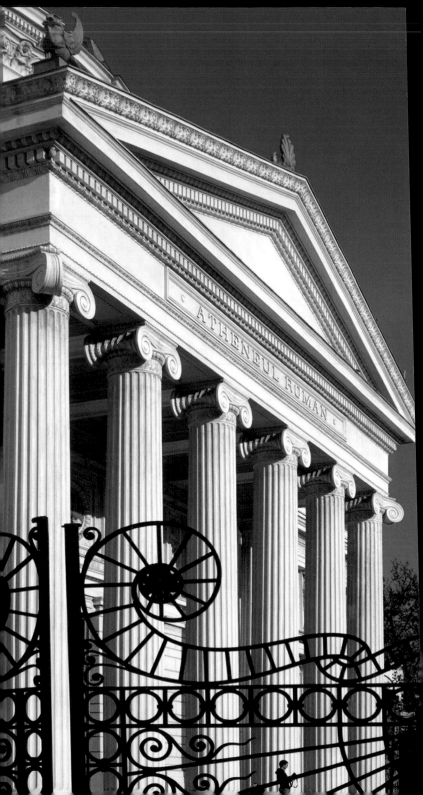

Bucharest, the Capital City

Previous page: *The Romanian Athenaeum*

Bucharest

In the last few years, the younger generation, the much-mocked hipsters, have found a way to avoid the pitfalls of nostalgic hankering after the Little Paris of the Belle Époque and the dead end of fatalistic post-communist victimhood, reinventing Bucharest as a place of experimentation and unconventional events. It is a kind of Little Berlin, some say, a place whose nightlife is just as exciting, that has once more gained a reputation as a European clubbing destination.

If you pause to think about what Bucharest looked like before 2007, the year when Romania joined the EU, and what it looks like now, then you will be surprised to discover that it is in fact a completely different city in many respects. And the change can best be seen in the old centre, which used to be deserted and desolate, but is now busy and bursting with life at every hour of the day and night. Colțea Square had been renovated and now plays host to concerts of classical music every weekend. The statues area of Piața Universității has been freed up by the opening of an underground car park and is now a public space once more. The National Theatre has been reshaped. Examples of street art have multiplied and it is already a tradition to close the Kiseleff Boulevard to traffic at weekends in summer as a way of encouraging the inhabitants of Bucharest to take part in sports. There has been an explosion of independent theatre, thanks to increasing numbers of small companies and spaces to host experiment (Godot, Mignon, În Culise, Teatrul de Artă, Teatrul de Sufragerie, Unteatru), and the idea of converting industrial spaces into cultural centres (ARK, Anexa MNAC, WASP, Atelierul de Producție, Halele Carol, Turnul de Apă Pantelimon, TurboHalle) has begun to make inroads in Romania.

For full information
see the Bucharest
travel guide
published by
Ad Libri.

PALATUL PARLAMENTULUI
(PALACE OF PARLIAMENT)

www.cdep.ro/cic
✉ *2-4 Izvor St.* ☎ *021.3113611,*
021.4141426 🖥 *Daily: 10am-4pm (last tour*
starts at 3:30pm). Telephone in advance for
guided tours or send an e-mail to cic.vizite@
cdep.ro 🕐 *Standard tour: 25 lei. Tour of the*
terrace and belvedere (lift access): 15 lei.
Tour of the basements (stair access): 10 lei.
Standard tour + terrace: 35 lei.
Standard tour + basements: 30 lei.
Standard tour + terrace + basements: 45 lei.
Free entry for children under the age of 7 and
schoolchildren under the age of 18.
Photo charge: 30 lei. Video charge: 30 lei.

Bucharest was once a city of hills, with numerous gardens and green spaces. This changed drastically as a result of the grandiose urbanisation plans set underway in the "golden age" of the Ceaușescu regime. The Spirii, Uranus and Mihai Vodă hills of Bucharest's historic centre fell victim to communist systematisation. An entire district of old houses, churches, monasteries and other institutions (including the Brîncoveanu Hospital, the Unirii Covered Markets, the National Archives, the Republic Stadium, the Central Military Museum, and the Queen Maria Theatre) was demolished and the hills were levelled. The eighteenth-century Burnt Court of Alexander Ipsilanti and an archaeological site dating back to the Palaeolithic were likewise destroyed. In their place were built the Civic Centre and the gargantuan Palace of Parliament, which remain symbols of Ceaușescu's megalomania.

The Palace of Parliament, which the people of Bucharest still refer to by its original name, the House of the People, is a colossal structure, the second largest in the world after the Pentagon. Built between 1984 and 1989 on what had once been Spirii Hill, it is 84m tall (12 storeys) and 92m deep (8 underground levels). It has twenty-one wings and covers a surface area of 330,000m^2. Dictator Nicolae Ceaușescu intended the building to house the Presidency, the Central Committee of the Communist Party and a number of ministries. The excessive size, the opulence of its interior decorations and the lack of a unitary style have drawn no small amount of criticism. Ironically, it is now one of the Capital's most visited tourist attractions.

Photo: *Palace of Parliament*

Work on the building stopped after the 1989 Revolution and the Palace of Parliament is still only 85-90% complete.

At present, the building houses the Chamber of Deputies, the Senate, an International Conference Centre, the South-east Europe Co-operation Initiative, the Secretariat of the Stability Pact for the Fight against Organised Crime, the National Museum of Contemporary Art (➤right) and the Museum of Romanian Folk Costumes. It has more than four hundred offices, dozens of conference rooms (two with a surface area of more than two thousand square metres), and reception rooms. The interiors are replete with marble, gold, sculptures, mosaics, tapestries, crystal lamps and huge carpets decorated with gold thread. The most splendid room is the Hall of the Union ($2,200m^2$), which seats one thousand and is lit by a three-tonne, seven-thousand-bulb chandelier. The carpet alone weighs fourteen tonnes. The rooms and salons of the Palace of Parliament can be hired and are the venue for numerous conferences, symposia, seminars and exhibitions.

Part of the colossal palace is accessible to tourists, who can join guided tours given in the world's major languages. It is important to remember that you must bring your passport or identity card when visiting the palace and it is advisable to book in advance, since access is available only to guided tours of up to twenty-five persons.

In front of the Palace of Parliament stretches the vast **Piaţa Constituţiei**, where concerts, parades and trade fairs are held, as well as New Year's Eve celebrations. The square leads into **Unirii Boulevard** (formerly Victory of Socialism Boulevard), modelled on the Champs Elysées in Paris. The grandiose boulevard, along the middle of which there is a series of fountains, examples of communist-era kitsch, intersects with Piaţa Unirii.

THE NATIONAL MUSEUM OF CONTEMPORARY ART (PALACE OF PARLIAMENT)

> www.mnac.ro
> ✉ 2-4 Izvor Street, Entrance E4 – Palace of Parliament. Access from Calea 13 Septembrie (third entrance).
> ☎ 021.3139115, 021.3189137
> 🕐 Wed-Sun: 10am-6pm
> 💲 10 Lei (5 Lei, children)

Since 2004, the National Museum of Contemporary Art has occupied the west wing of the Palace of Parliament (➤21), and has been at the forefront of Bucharest's cultural life. Making use of a space that had entered the collective mind as a symbol of totalitarianism, the National Museum of Contemporary Art has set an example of "post-communist habitation." Artists, curators and art critics have paved the way to partnerships with other institutions around the world that promote and support contemporary art. Conceived as a work in progress, the museum has rapidly become a space for dialogue between the arts, encouraging dynamism, interactivity, and greater public participation in the multimedia projects (including experimental video works, photography, art installations, art digital art) hosted in its spacious four-storey premises.

Photo: *Human Rights Hall, Palace of Parliament*

PIAŢA UNIRII (UNIRII SQUARE)

🚋 Trams 15, 27 and 30; buses 104, 123, 124, 312 and 385; metro (Piaţa Unirii station)

Flanked by eight- to ten-storey Soviet-style housing blocks and the drab Unirea Department Store (recently re-launched as the Unirea Shopping Centre), the monotony is broken only by one side of Hanul Manuc. With its numerous fountains, examples of communist kitsch, the broad Unirii Boulevard (formerly the Victory of Socialism Boulevard) cuts a swathe along one side of the square on its way to the Palace of Parliament, whose megalomaniacal Ceauşescu-era outline can be glimpsed from Piaţa Unirii.

Belying the name of plaza, Piaţa Unirii is sooner a vast, chaotic, noisy open space that is anything but welcoming to pedestrians. The green spaces by the fountains might seem inviting, but given the surrounding of traffic, you will not be tempted to linger for long.

THE HISTORIC CENTRE

The city sprang up around the Old Court (▶24), built by Vlad the Impaler on the bank of the Dîmboviţa. It was here that merchants and craftsmen established their shops and ateliers, founding the city's old commercial quarter, known generically as Lipscani, after one of its most

important streets (▶24-25). Bucharest rapidly became a centre of trade, situated as it was at the intersection of routes between East and West, which led to an unprecedented burgeoning of the trades and crafts. Huge sums were made from domestic and foreign commerce. Given the large number of foreign merchants who came to Bucharest to sell their wares, dozens of inns were built, mainly in the area of the Old Court. The laying out of Podul Mogoşoaiei (Calea Victoriei ▶27) in 1792, during the reign of Constantine Brîncoveanu, and the development of the western outskirts of the district surrounding this major thoroughfare, where rich boyars built themselves residences and the first department store opened (La Fayette), likewise contributed to reviving the area.

Around the turn of the century, the commercial district underwent a major transformation, making it a financial and banking centre. The Palace of the Savings and Loans Palace (CEC) was built on Calea Victoriei, and the Palace of the Dacia Insurance Company near Strada Lipscani. Magnificent banks were designed by the best architects of the time, clustering around the French neoclassical National Bank of Romania (1884-90): the Sconto Bank (1898), the Agricola Bank (1894), the Bercovitz Bank (1903), the Marmorosch Blank Bank (1905), the Romanian Commercial Bank (1906), the Franco-Romanian Bank (1914), the Chrissoveloni Bank (1920). By 1913, there were two hundred banks in Bucharest.

After the advent of the communist regime, the district decayed. Private properties and businesses were nationalised, and banks and insurance companies were abolished. The owners of private shops, restaurants and cafés were forced out of business. Everything was centralised, becoming the property of the state, under the control of the communist party. The most unusual, picturesque and beautiful part of Bucharest vanished. Names such as At the Sea Eagle with the Fish in its Claws evoke the memory of this vanished Bucharest. The buildings of the historic centre were converted into social housing for families of gypsies, with the obvious intention of hastening the demise of any memory of the bourgeois past. At the last moment, they were saved, declared historic monuments and restored to their former glory after extensive work to revitalise the area, which commenced in 2007. They are typical merchant houses, with the ground floors serving as shops and the upper floors as residences. The façades, although forming a whole, reflect this dual status: the lower storey is reserved in its ornamentation, while the upper floor is thrown into relief. Today, only a few families of gypsies remain in the old centre, squatting in houses that are in stark contrast with the renovated buildings, which have been converted into bars, cafés and clubs. Day and night, all week round, the area hotches with swarms tourists and revellers. Whereas a decade ago it was a place to avoid after nightfall, today Lipscani seems to be the city's biggest hotspot.

Curtea Veche (The Old Court)

www.muzeulbucurestiului.ro
21-23 Franceză Street 021.3140375
Daily: 9am-5pm 3 Lei

Since 1972, the remains of the Old Court have been preserved as part of a museum,

where you can see the ruins of the fifteenth-century fortress, a fragment of wall made from boulders dating from the time of Vlad the Impaler, and walls built using a Roman-Byzantine technique, by setting boulders or stone flags between rows of bricks.

DID YOU KNOW?
In the final decades of the eighteenth century, the Princely Court, which had been abandoned after the fire of 1718 and the earthquake of 1738, was the equivalent of the Cour des Miracles in Paris. The capital's vagabonds, thieves and ne'er-do-wells lived among the ruins. The inhabitants of Bucharest mockingly called them the Kings of the Old Court, an expression that came to refer to any rascal or rake.

The old mercantile streets of the historic centre
The old centre of Bucharest forms a remarkable urban fabric, which has preserved many of the characteristic features of its original function as a commercial centre. The buildings are L-, U- or I-shaped, with a narrow (three-metre) front to save space, with the rest of the building extending lengthwise back from the street. They had a dual function: the lower storey was a shop or atelier, and the

Photo: *The ruins of the Old Court*

upper floor was a dwelling space. Of course, few of the buildings have preserved this dual function to the present day (Smîrdan no. 30, Franceză no. 17, Franceză no. 30). The façades have been altered in various ways, according to the fashions of the times, with the upper storeys being decorated richly in various styles to distinguish them from the shop storey: Lipscani no. 21 (neoclassical), nos. 63-65, 72-74 (Art Nouveau), Şelari no. 22, Franceză nos. 40, 68, Covaci no. 4, etc.

Strada Lipscani – known as the "Large Lane by the Princely Court" – preserves the shops of merchants who imported wares from Leipzig (which in Romanian was called Lipsca, whence "Lipscani").

Strada Smîrdan – formerly known as "Germans' Lane" or "German Street", because it was here that German and Austrian merchants sold their wares – was first paved with cobbles in 1860, at the same time as Strada Franceză. It was renamed after 1878 in honour of a Romanian victory in the War of Independence, the same as Calea Victoriei (formerly Podul Mogoşoaiei), Rahova and Călăraşi.

În **Strada Gabroveni** – "the Lane that runs past the wall of the Princely Court" – was where the merchants who imported cloth from Gabrovo in Bulgaria kept their shops.

Strada Franceză – known as "Işlik makers' lane," "Princely Lane", and "the Lane that leads to the upper gate of the Princely Court" – has conserved a remarkable architectural fabric, with examples of the French eclectic style, the neo-Gothic, the Renaissance style, and the Art Nouveau.

Stavropoleos Monastery

> *www.stavropoleos.ro*
> ✉ *4 Stavropoleos Street* 📞 *021.3134747*
> 🕐 *Service: Mon-Fri: 8am, 5pm, 9pm (midnight mass according to the Byzantine rite), Sat: 8am, 9:30am, 11am, 5pm, 7pm, 9pm (midnight service), Sun: 9:30am, 10:15am, 5pm, 9pm (midnight service)* Ⓢ *Free*

The small Stavropoleos Church, hidden away behind the National History Museum, near Strada Lipscani, is reckoned to be the most beautiful and representative monument of late Brîncoveanu period art. It was built in 1724 to serve the inn of Greek archimandrite Ioannikios Stratonikeas, originally from the Epirus, who two years later was appointed Metropolitan of Stavropolis ("City Cross"), a title derived from the name of the newly built church. The same as elsewhere, the inn was a source of income for the monastery within whose precincts it stood. The porch, added in 1730, has four columns, five poly-lobe arches and a balustrade, decorated with carved floral motifs and tendrils and a scene of *Samson wrestling the lion*.

The founder died in 1741 and by the late-nineteenth century the monastery complex had fallen into ruin. The monastery

Left: *The Linden Inn links Strada Lipscani and Strada Blănari*

Right: *Stavropoleos Church*

buildings were demolished in 1886. In 1904, architect Ion Mincu restored the church and designed new precincts for the old inn of the Greek Quarter. Today, the buildings house a library (which preserves old manuscripts and books in Romanian, Greek and Slavonic, and old Byzantine musical scores), a refectory, an exhibition and conference room, and the cells of the nuns of the Stavropoleos Monastery, who restore old books and icons. There is also a collection of icons and old ecclesiastical objects (telephone to make an appointment if you wish to visit). The church is famous for is Byzantine chant, sung by the Stavropoleos Psaltic Group during services. The music is completely different from what you will hear nowadays in most Romanian Orthodox churches: the chant is *monodic* and accompanied by a vocal drone (*ison*). In 2008, the church was restored to its former status of monastery and is now home to a community of six nuns,

You should also take the time to look at the garden of the inner courtyard, where there is a collection of eighteenth-century funerary slabs, fragments of fresco, and remains salvaged from the churches that were demolished in central Bucharest during the communist period. It is an oasis of almost preternatural tranquillity.

Caru' cu Bere (The Beer Dray)

www.carucubere.ro
✉ 5 Stavropoleos Street
📞 01.3137560, 0726-282373
🕐 Mon-Thu, Sun: 8am-12am, Fri-Sat: 8am-2am

One of the few neo-Gothic buildings in Bucharest, the Beer Dray was built between 1875 and 1879 and was designed by Polish architect Zigrid Kofczincky. The massive revolving door at the entrance will whisk you back in time, and you will emerge in the midst of a dining room of astonishing refinement and elegance, which recreates the ambience of an old German beer cellar. The interior is decorated in the Romantic style, with murals, stained glass, stuccowork, oak panelling, ironwork, candelabras, etc. The atmosphere is

enlivened almost every night of the week by ensembles of folk musicians. The restaurant was once frequented by writers Eminescu and Caragiale, and in the late-nineteenth and early-twentieth centuries it was here that poet George Coşbuc presided over the meetings of a famous literary cenacle. In the basement there is a traditional Romanian style wine cellar.

The Vilacrosse-Macca Arcade

This elegant horseshoe-shaped shopping arcade, roofed with yellow glass and decorated with bas-reliefs and ornamental stuccowork, was built in 1891 by Felix Xenopol on the site of the former Cîmpineanu Inn. It was designed to connect nos. 16-20 Calea Victoriei and Strada Eugeniu Carada, on which the grand edifice of the National Bank was constructed. On the ground floor of the arcade are shops, and there are private homes on the upper floor. It has two wings, one named after Catalan Xavier Vilacrosse, the architect-in-chief of Bucharest between 1840 and 1850, and the other after his brother-in-law, Mihalache Macca. It was here that the city's first stock exchange was housed. In the communist period it was renamed the *Bijuteria Arcade,* after a bijouterie shop on Calea Victoriei.

Photo: *Caru' cu Bere (the Beer Dray)*

CALEA VICTORIEI (VICTORY AVENUE)

Calea Victoriei is Bucharest's main avenue, stretching 2.7km between Piața Națiunilor Unite, to the south, and Piața Victoriei, to the north. Along the avenue, almost in a row, can be found some of the city's most beautiful buildings, dating from the nineteenth and twentieth centuries: the National Museum of History (formerly the Post Office Palace), the Savings Bank Palace, the Military Club, Casa Capșa, the Odeon Theatre, the Krețulescu Church, the Central University Library, the Romanian Athenaeum, Casa Monteoru, the Cantacuzino Palace (the Georges Enesco Museum), and the Știrbey Palace. It was on Calea Victoriei that Bucharest's first theatre was built (the Novotel Hotel, built on the site, recreates the portico of the old theatre), as well as the Royal Palace, which is now home to the National Museum of Art.

Calea Victoriei was originally a "deck" (Romanian: pod), in other words a street surfaced with wooden beams. Podul Mogoșoaiei, as it was called, was carved out in 1692, when Constantine Brîncoveanu decided to build a road from the Old Court to his estate in Mogoșoaia, where he erected a palace in 1702. The section between Piața Victoriei and the Military Club used to be called Brașov Road, and that between the Military Club (built on the site of the Sărindar Church) and the Dîmbovița embankment was called the Ulița Mare (Big Lane). Boyar residences, churches, inns, shops and summer gardens quickly sprang up along the new road.

In 1878, after the victorious Romanian army returned from the War of Independence (the Russo-Romanian-Turkish War) and marched in triumph down Podul Mogoșoaiei, the avenue was renamed Calea Victoriei.

Piața Palatului, situated roughly in the middle of the avenue, was renamed Piața Revoluției in memory of the demonstrations that led to the overthrow of the communist regime in December 1989.

Walking along Calea Victoriei, you will be able to admire beautiful boyar houses and palaces, silent witnesses of the Belle Époque, deluxe shops, theatres, splendid hotels, and cafés. Every building tells its own story, stories that are sometimes long and tangled, connected by dozens of threads to the tumultuous history of the city itself, stories that stretch back as long as this 320-year-old street.

THE NATIONAL MUSEUM OF ROMANIAN HISTORY

> www.mnir.ro
> ✉ 12 Victory Avenue ☎ 021.3158207
> 🕐 Thu-Sun: 10am-6pm (summer), 9am-5pm (winter) 🎫 25 Lei (adults), 7 Lei (children)

The National Museum of History is opposite the C.E.C. building. Up until 1970 it was the Post Office Palace. The building, in the neo-classical style, was designed by architect Alexandru Săvulescu and constructed between 1894 and 1900. The monumental entrance has a portico of ten Doric columns.

With a total surface area of eight thousand square metres, the museum's sixty rooms house exhibits and documents that record the human settlement of what is now the territory of Romania from the earliest times to the present day.

The **Lapidarium** on the ground floor includes Greek and Roman monuments (funerary steles, altars, seven statues from

Photo: *The Savings Bank Palace on Calea Victoriei*

Lower Moesia, a decorative frieze from the temple of Aphrodite in Histria, Corinthian capitals from buildings in Tomis and Callatis), as well as mediaeval tombstones and sarcophagi (the tombstone of the Lady Elina, wife of Matei Bassarab, the sarcophagus of Bălaşa Cantacuzino).

The basement houses the **Historic Treasury**, which includes the priceless hoards of Getic princes found at Agighiol, Surcea, Poroina and Craiova (fourth century B.C.), the Dacian hoards from Sîncrăieni, Surcea, Coada Malului, Herăstrău and Senereuş (second to first century B.C.), and the archaeological discoveries made at Coşoveni (fifth to seventh centuries A.D.). Do not miss: the statue known as *The Thinker* (Hamangia culture, sixth millennium B.C.), discovered at Cernavodă (the ancient Axiopolis), the copy of Trajan's Column and the *Pietroasa hoard* (known at *the Hen with the Golden Chicks*), made up of 12 gold items weighing 19kg, which probably belonged to Visigoth King Athanaric (fourth century A.D.), discovered in 1837 by two peasants quarrying stone from Istriţa Hill in Buzău. Also of note are the tomb treasures from Cucuteni (Jassy) and the royal helmet from Coţofeneşti (Prahova). Also exhibited are the Steel Crown of the Kings of Romania, forged in 1881 (the year the Kingdom of Romania was proclaimed) from the steel of a Krupp cannon captured by Romanian soldiers from the Ottoman army in 1877 during the War of Independence, the crowns of the queens of Romania, the royal sceptre of King Ferdinand, and the swords of King Carol I.

In 1939, the Romanian State commissioned master craftsmen from the Vatican to make a copy of *Trajan's Column* (113 A.D.), the work of the famous Apollodorus of Damascus. The copy was finished in 1943, during the Second World War, and was not delivered to Romania until 1967. Visitors to the National Museum of Romanian History can now admire the 125 reliefs depicting episodes from the Dacian wars, which are also exhibited in the basement.

Ever since it was unveiled in 2012, the *Trajan and the She-wolf* statue that stands on the steps of the museum, the work of sculptor Vasile Gorduz (1931-2008), has been labelled ridiculous and unsightly by many people, unleashing a torrent of criticism, indignation, and parodies. And no wonder: the naked emperor stands in a stiff and awkward position, cradling a bizarre-looking wolf with a Dacian flag billowing from the back of its head. The controversy shows no signs of fading away and the same as in other similar cases, the sculpture has become a photo opportunity.

REVOLUTION SQUARE AND GEORGE ENESCU SQUARE

The vast Piaţa Revoluţiei, formerly known as Piaţa Palatului, is dominated by the old Royal Palace (now the National Museum of Art ➤29), the Ministry of the Interior, the Central University Library, the Romanian Athenaeum and Kretzulescu Church (1722). Unfortunately, the constant flow of traffic along Calea Victoriei and the car park that occupies a large part of the square rather spoil the atmosphere.

In 2010, the **equestrian statue of King Carol I** was restored to its former place in the square, albeit a rather unfaithful copy of the original made by Croat sculptor Ivan Meštrović in 1939, which the communists melted down in 1948, later using the bronze to cast the statue of Lenin in front of the House of the Spark. Controversies were not long in coming, with Meštrović's descendants complaining that sculptor Florin Codre did not have the right to make a copy without their permission, while Bucharest's more aesthetically minded citizens have pointed out anomalies such as the King's rigid posture, the horse's unnaturally raised tail, and other amusing anatomical details. The sculpture has remained, however, having become a landmark.

The same thing happened with the controversial **Memorial of Rebirth**, erected in honour of the heroes of the December 1989 Revolution. The work of Alexandru Ghilduş and costing one and a half million Euros, it has been given a wide range of nicknames since its inauguration in 2005: *Ghilduş's Stake, The Potato on a Stick, The*

Impaled Potato, The Brain on a Stick, The Olive on a Toothpick, The Potato of the Revolution, and so on. The monument consists of the Wall of Remembrance, inscribed with the names of the 1,058 victims of the Revolution, the Plaza of Recollection, in the centre of which rises the Pyramid of Victory, and the log Path of Triumph, a symbol of the road to democracy.

There are another two monuments in the square, commemorating two of Romania's most prestigious political leaders: **Iuliu Maniu** (1873-1953), prime-minister of Romania (1928-30, 1932-33), president of the National Peasants Party, and a political prisoner from 1947 until his death, and **Corneliu Coposu** (1914-1995), president of the National Christian Democratic Peasants Party and a political prisoner during the communist regime. The bust of Corneliu Coposu, by sculptor Mihai Buculei, was unveiled next to the Kretzulescu Church in 1996, and the monument to Iuliu Maniu, by sculptor Mircea Corneliu Spătaru, was inaugurated in 1998, on the other side of Calea Victoriei, in front of the former **Central Committee of the Romanian Communist Party**, from whose balcony Nicolae Ceaușescu gave his last speech on 21 December 1989, before fleeing a few hours later by helicopter from the roof. After 1990, the Romanian Senate moved into the building, constructed in 1938 to house the Council of Ministers. Although the Senate moved to the Palace of Parliament in 2004 (➤21), the building continues to be known as the Palace of the Senate. It now houses the Ministry of the Interior, the Ministry of Health, and the Ministry of Labour.

Piața Revoluției stretches northward to join **Piața George Enescu**, next to the Athenaeum, a space that is likewise used as a car park for most of the time. However, the space also provides the venue for a number of important cultural events: the Georges Enesco Festival, the Bucharest Music Film Festival, Bucharest Jazz Festival and New Year's Eve parties, celebrated with fireworks and concerts.

THE ROMANIAN NATIONAL MUSEUM OF ART (THE FORMER ROYAL PALACE)

> www.mnar.arts.ro
> ✉ 49-53 Victory Avenue ☎ 021.3133030
> 🕐 Wed-Sun: 11am-7pm (May-Sept), 10am-6pm
> (Oct-Apr) 💲 8 Lei (Gallery of European Art),
> 10 Lei (National Gallery and Treasury), 15 Lei
> (Gallery of European Art and National Gallery),
> 20 Lei (National Museum of Art and Museum
> of Art Collections). Entrance free on the first
> Wednesday of the month.

Piața Revoluției is dominated by the former Royal Palace, which is now the Romanian National Museum of Art. The U-shaped neoclassical building, consisting of a

---

Photo: *Piața Revoluției, with the Central University Library, the Union of Romanian Architects headquarters and the former Central Committee of the Romanian Communist Party (from left to right)*

central corpus and two wings, was built between 1928 and 1937 and was designed by architect Nicolae Nenciulescu.

In the early-nineteenth century the houses of Dinicu Golescu the Stolnik stood on the site. His heirs sold the houses to the state, which, between 1834 and 1837 altered and extended them to provide a residence for ruler Alexandru Dimitrie Ghika. Alexander John Cuza also resided here between 1859 and 1866, when he was deposed. On 10 May 1866, Carol I moved into a house on the site of what is now the Krețulescu wing of the palace. Between 1882 and 1885 the central corpus of the Royal Palace was built to the designs of French architect Paul Gottereau. It was destroyed in a fire in 1926. The original boyar house of Dinicu Golescu was demolished in 1936 to make way for the Krețulescu wing.

The palace in which it is housed has two entrances: one on the left, which was originally for the King and his guests, and one on the right, originally for visiting dignitaries. Both entrances lead to large halls with marble staircases. The first-floor rooms are richly decorated in the neo-Byzantine and English styles. The left wing is impressive for its ceiling friezes and medallions, the work of sculptor Cornel Medrea, and its panels, painted by Cecilia Cuțescu-Storck, Arthur Verona and Nicolae Tonitza.

Since 2014, there have been guided tours of the historic rooms of the central corpus of the Royal Palace (the Royal Dining Room, the Throne Room, and the Voievodes' Stair) every third weekend of the month (🕐 starting at 11:30am, 2pm and 4:30pm). The tours cost 20 Lei and also provide an opportunity to see the *Fragments of Memory: Royal Portraits, The Royal Palace* exhibition in the annex to the Throne Room and the annex to the Royal Dining Room.

The Collections of the Romanian National Museum of Art

The gallery of Romanian mediaeval art (first floor of the Ştirbey wing) has 9,500 items, including the *Cozia Epitaph* (1396) and *Dobrovăț Epitrachelion* (1504) embroideries, the manuscript of Gavriil Uric (1436), fragments of a mural from the Curtea de Argeş cathedral, icons from the sixteenth to eighteenth centuries, two thousand pieces of silverware fashioned in Sibiu, Braşov, Suceava and Tîrgovişte, carved wooden doors from the monasteries of Cotmeana and Snagov and remains of the Enei Church, Cotroceni Monastery, Văcăreşti Monastery and Şerban Inn church.

The gallery of modern Romanian art (second floor of the Ştirbei wing) has an impressive collection of works

Photo: *The Romanian National Museum of Art (the former Royal Palace)*

(8,794 paintings and 2,118 sculptures) by Romanian artists: Theodor Aman (*Evening*), Nicolae Grigorescu (*Girls Working by a Gate*), Ştefan Luchian (*Anemone*), Theodor Pallady (*Toujours du Baudelaire*), Nicolae Tonitza (*The Forester's Daughter*), Ion Andreescu (*Rocks and Beeches*), Camil Ressu (*Reapers Resting*), Ion Ţuculescu (*Moods of the Plain*), Victor Brauner (*Passivité courtoise*), Arthur Segal (*Woman Reading*), Marcel Janco (*Peasant Woman with Eggs*), Max Hermann Maxy (*Electric Madonna*), Cecilia Cuţescu-Storck (*Nude with Fruit*), Frederick Storck (*Mystery*), Constantin Brâncuşi (*Prayer, The Mindfulness of the Earth*), Dimitrie Paciurea (*Chimaeras*) and Corneliu Baba (*Venetian Landscape*).

The gallery of European art (first and second floors of the Kretzulescu wing) houses 2,223 paintings, 578 sculptures, and 9,189 works of decorative art from the fourteenth to twentieth centuries. Here you can view works by Lucas Cranach the Elder (*Venus and Amor*), Pieter Bruegel the Younger (*Spring, Summer, Autumn, Winter*), Tintoretto (*Annunciation, Portrait of Marc Antonio Barbaro*), Rubens (*Hercules and the Nemaean Lion*), Francesco Raibolini (*Virgin and Child*), Hans von Aachen (*The Three Graces*), Rembrandt (*Aman begging Esther's Forgiveness*), El Greco (*The Adoration of the Shepherds*), Anton van Dyck (*Jesus and the Repentant Sinners*), Émile Antoine Bourdelle (*Hercules drawing a Bow*), August Rodin (*The Age of Bronze*), Claude Monet (Fishing Boats at Honfleur), and Camille Pissarro (*Orchard in Bloom*).

THE ROMANIAN ATHENAEUM

www.fge.org.ro
✉ 1-3 Benjamin Franklin Street
☎ 021.3152567

With its portico of Ionic columns, the Romanian Athenaeum is Bucharest's most beautiful classical music concert venue. It was built between 1886 and 1888, following a subscription campaign that raised 500,000 lei selling 1-leu tickets to the

public. The man behind the campaign was naturalist Constantin Esarcu (1836-1898), the founder of the Romanian Athenaeum Society. The neoclassical building capped with a baroque cupola was designed by architect Albert Galleron, to the indications of Alexandru Odobescu. Its circular plan is due to the fact that it was built on the foundations of a manège. The portico is 48 metres wide, consists of six twelve-metre-high columns, and is capped with a triangular fronton. The mosaic medallions of the peristyle depict rulers Neagoe Bassarab, Alexander the Good, Vasile Lupu and Matei Bassarb, and King Carol I. From the main lobby, a monumental Stair of Honour and four spiral staircases of Carrara marble lead to the one-thousand-seat circular auditorium, which rests on twelve Doric columns on the ground floor. The auditorium has a seventy-five-metre-long frieze depicting twenty-five scenes from the history of the Romanians (from the Roman conquest of Dacia to the Great Union of 1918), created by Costin Petrescu between 1933 and 1938. The baroque cupola and circular seating lend the auditorium perfect acoustics, rather like those of a Greek amphitheatre.

Today, the Romanian Athenaeum is home to the Georges Enesco Philharmonic and, with the Palace Concert Hall, is one of the two venues for the International Georges Enesco Festival.

Photo: *The Romanian Athenaeum*

PIAȚA UNIVERSITĂȚII/ 21 DECEMBRIE 1989

> 🚍 Trolleybuses: 61, 66, 69, 70, 85, 90 and 91; buses: 122, 137, 138, 268, 336, 381, 601, 783, N110, N116, N117 and N119; metro

Far from being a plaza in the usual sense of the word, Piața Universității (University Square) is a busy traffic intersection. It is thus named because the main building of Bucharest University can be found on one side of the intersection, which is the node of the city's most important thoroughfares. The corners of the intersection form four distinct enclaves, standing apart from the busy traffic in the centre of the "plaza".

It was in Piața Revoluției that the most significant events of the December 1989 Revolution took place, leading to the overthrow of dictator Nicolae Ceaușescu. The crosses in the small traffic island commemorate the violent upheaval. During the revolution, Piața Revoluției acquired the symbolic status of the city's Kilometre 0: the spot is marked by a milestone painted red, yellow and blue in the middle of the intersection. Bucharest's real Kilometre 0 is in Piața Sfîntul Gheorghe, however. The small square between the University and the Faculty of Architecture, known as **Piața 21 Decembrie 1989**, has a fountain, which is a popular meeting place. Opposite

the square is the Hotel Intercontinental and Bucharest's principal theatre: the Ion Luca Caragiale National Theatre. In front of the theatre there is a small green space, the National Theatre Park, which on the side adjacent to the intersection is girdled with a flight of steps. Since 2010, the park has been home to a group of sculptures named The Clown Cart. Seven metres high and weighing twenty-five tonnes, the work was created by Ioan Bolborea, inspired by characters from the plays of Ion Luca Caragiale (1852-1912).

Opposite the University there is a row of four statues portraying important figures from Romanian history and culture. The bronze equestrian statue of Michael the Brave, who briefly united the three Romanian provinces of Wallachia, Moldavia and Transylvania in 1600, was created by Albert Ernest Carrière de Belleuse in 1876. The three marble statues are of leading figures in the history of Romanian education: Gheorghe Lazăr (1779-1823), sculpted by Ion Georgescu in 1885; Ion Heliade Rădulescu (1802-1872), created by Italian sculptor Ettore Ferrari in 1870; and Spiru Haret (1851-1912), sculpted by Ion Jalea in 1935. For many years, the so-called **Statues Esplanade** was occupied by parked cars, but since the construction of an underground car park

Photo: *I. C. Brătianu/ Nicolae Bălcescu Boulevard and Piața Universității (University Square)*

beneath it in 2012, it has become a space for open-air events, including a traditional Christmas Market, the International Street Theatre Festival, concerts, and various exhibitions. During excavation work for the car park, the ruins of the St Sava Monastery complex were unearthed. The St Sava Church stood between what is now a bus stop and the statue of Michael the Brave; its outline is marked in the paving stones, but so unobtrusively that most passers-by miss it.

On the other side of the intersection, between the Palace of the Ministry of Agriculture and the Colţea Hospital, the 3,200m² **Colţea Square** was laid out in 2007. Between May and October, concerts are given here every weekend, part of a series called *Summer Symphonies*. As a space dedicated to classical music, the square has a fitting work of monumental art: The Broken Violin Fountain (Violino Spaccato), cast in bronze by Ioan Bolborea, based on a drawing by artist Domenica Regazzoni, who wished to convey music's transformative power.

CIŞMIGIU GARDEN

Access points: *Regina Elisabeta Bd., Schitu Măgureanu Bd., Ştirbei Vodă street, Walter Mărăcineanu Square*

The sixteen-hectare Cişmigiu Garden in the centre of Bucharest is the city's oldest park. It was laid out in 1845, on a swampy piece of land mentioned in documents dating back to the reign of Matei Bassarab. In 1779, Prince Alexander Ypsilanti had had a drinking fountain (*cişmea*) installed there for the people of Bucharest. Nearby, the drinking fountain superintendent (*cişmigiu*) built himself a house, whence the name of the later park.

The present layout of the garden was designed by German landscape architects Karl Wilhelm Meyer and Friedrich Rebhuhn. After the land was drained, thirty thousand trees and shrubs were planted, including plane trees, hazel trees, ash trees, and magnolias. Floral arrangements, rare trees

and shrubs (ginkgo biloba, red spruce, Japanese red pine, Turkish hazel trees), winding paths, the lake in the middle of the park, fountains, and a children's playground all lend Cişmigiu its special charm. It is no wonder that it is a favourite spot for the city's inhabitants.

Arranged around a lake that is used as a skating rink in winter, the park is divided into sections, each with its own evocative name: Lovers' Lane, Chess Players' Corner, the Rose Garden, the Japanese Garden. The Writers' Round section can be found on the side of the park adjacent to Boulevard Schitu Măgureanu and is in the style of an ancient Roman garden, with twelve statues of Romania's most important writers.

COTROCENI PALACE

www.muzeulcotroceni.ro
✉ *1 Geniului Bd.* ☎ *021.3173107*
🕐 *Tue-Sun: 9:30am-5:30pm* 💲 *12 Lei (Roumanian tourists), 27 Lei (foreign tourists), 4-6 Lei (children). Church: free access*
🚌 *Buses and trolleybuses: 61, 62, 136, 139, 180 and 336*

Photo: *Hall in Cotroceni Palace*

At the end of Eroilor Sanitari Boulevard, Cotroceni Palace stands on a gentle slope. Built between 1893 and 1895, it was designed by Paul Gottereau, the architect to the Royal House, and is located within the precincts of a monastery founded by Șerban Cantacuzino in 1679. King Carol I of Hohenzollern-Sigmaringen had the palace built as a residence for the Crown Prince Ferdinand and Princess Maria.

At the beginning of the twentieth century, the Cotroceni Palace was renovated in the neo-Romanian style. The southern wing, which is now the Romanian Presidency, was built in the 1980s. The Cotroceni Museum, which is open to visitors, is housed in the other two wings and dates from 1991.

Even today, the interiors of the Cotroceni Palace bear witness to the grandeur of the original princely residence: the neoclassical Hall of Honour, the neo-Renaissance German Dining Room, the Italian Renaissance Hunting Salon, the Flowers Salon, the Library, the neo-Romanian Reception Room, the Norwegian Salon with its astonishing neo-Gothic wood carvings, and the second-floor apartments, which are variously in the Henri II, Louis XV, Louis XVI, Tudor, rococo, Empire, Biedermeier, and Art Nouveau styles.

Cotroceni Monastery – one of the most significant monuments of Romanian mediaeval art, was demolished at the orders of Nicolae Ceaușescu in 1984. In 2004, the church was rebuilt and the remains of Șerban Cantacuzino and his descendants were re-inhumed there.

The museum includes a number of vaulted mediaeval chambers: the kitchen, refectory, cellar, and a few monastic cells.

Guided visits to the Cotroceni National Museum must be pre-booked, in groups of a maximum of fifteen persons. You can join a tour group without booking if there are free places still available. To book, telephone: ☎ 021.3173107(🕐 Mon-Fri: 9:30am-4:30pm) or e-mail: vizitare@ muzeulcotroceni.ro at least a day in advance.

THE MUSEUM OF THE ROMANIAN PEASANT

> www.muzeultaranuluiroman.ro
> ✉ 3 Chaussée Kiseleff ☎ 021.3179661
> 🕐 Tue-Sun: 10am-6pm Ⓢ 8 Lei (2 Lei, children)
> 🚇 Metro (Piața Victoriei); Buses 122, 182, 205, 300, 361, 381, 783, N 118, Bucharest City Tour; trams: 1, 34 and 46

The Museum of the Romanian Peasant, which locals call simply MȚR (Muzeul Țăranului Român), is an unforgettable living museum, as its thousands of visitors would be the first to agree. The items on display here succeed in creating a fresh look at the world of the everyday and bring to life the spiritual world of the Romanian peasant. The museum's highly original discourse, one dotted with signs that the visitor is invited to decipher, was conceived in 1990 by painter Horia Bernea. At the MȚR you will find objects that you will have seen when visiting Romanian villages: there, perhaps they did not have much to say, but here they become interconnected and imbued with meanings, they give rise to dialogue, provoke questions, emanate light.

One room of the museum is dedicated to the sign of the cross, another to icons on glass and wood. In one room, a wayside cross from Burluș (Argeș) is exhibited, in another a village classroom has been reconstructed. Debates and film showings are regularly held in the Village School. Every

Photo: *Museum of the Romanian Peasant*

Tuesday, Wednesday, Thursday and Friday afternoon, between twelve o'clock and two o'clock you can consult the visual memory archive to find out more about Romanian peasant traditions. There is a room with all kinds of rustic chairs, another with rustic windows. One room is a treasure trove of folk costumes; others explore themes such as "simple splendour" and "grandmother's kitchen." In the museum you will also find the relics of a church saved from destruction. On the first floor you will find "the hall of triumph" and "the halls of labour," where there are installations of machinery driven by water, wind and fire, and an exhibition of painted terracotta stove tiles. In the *House in a House* room you can admire the wooden house of Antonie Mogoș from Ceauru (Gorj), built in 1875-79 and purchased in 1908 by Alexandru Tzigara-Samurcaș, the director of the Carol I Museum of National Art, the predecessor of the present-day Museum of the Romanian Peasant.

Horia Bernea said that he intended the museum to be an "initiatory journey." Here and there, you will find reading places, which provide materials such as you will not find in many other museums: handwritten by Horia Bernea's team of researchers (Irina Nicolau, Ioana Popescu, Anca Manolescu, et al.), these texts, bound in cardboard tied with string, tell the stories of Romanian folk beliefs, rituals and customs; they collect stories about the sun and moon, the stars and the sky, spells against the evil eye, proverbs about fire, notes about iconographic subjects, and much more.

The museum's collection also includes four wooden churches, conserved in situ, including the church at Lunca Moților (Hunedoara) and the one at Troaș (Arad). The seventeenth-century Udriște Năsturel House in Herești village (Hotarele commune, Giurgiu County), 35km from Bucharest, is also a section of the MȚR.

In 1996, the European Museum Forum declared the Museum of the Romanian Peasant European Museum of the Year, the first time a museum from south-eastern Europe had been granted the title.

On important feast days, the MȚR holds folk markets and festivals: the Feast of the Cross (14 September), Easter, the Feast of the Archangels Michael and Gabriel, etc. On most weekends, there are craft fairs in the museum courtyard.

THE TRIUMPHAL ARCH

Situated at the intersection of Chaussée Kiseleff and the Constantin Prezan, Alexandru Aversescu and Alexandru Constantinescu boulevards, near Herăstrău Park, the Triumphal Arch was built in 1922 to celebrate the Romanian Army's victories in the First World War. Originally made of wood clad in stucco, the arch was rebuilt in 1935-36, using reinforced concrete and granite, under the supervision of architect Petre Antonescu. The carvings and other stone decorations were created by Ion Jalea, Corneliu Medrea, Frederick Storck, Dimitrie Paciurea, Constantin Baraschi and Mac Constantinescu.

The Triumphal Arch houses a museum with exhibits relating to the Great War for National Reunification and the heraldry of the great boyar families. There are also period images of the monument and the Great Union of 1918. Access is only on national holidays, including Romania's National Day and Army Day. When the museum is open, the top of the twenty-seven-metre arch provides splendid views of the surrounding area.

Photo: *The Triumphal Arch*

HERĂSTRĂU PARK

www.herastrauparc.ro
✉ 1 Chaussée Kiseleff ⑤ Free
🚇 Metro (Aviatorilor station); busses: 105, 131, 149, 205, 261, 282, 301, 304, 330, 331, 335, 449, 783, Bucharest City Tour; trams 41 and 42

At 110 hectares, Herăstrău Park is Bucharest's largest. In the middle of the park there is a 74-hectare lake, part of the chain of lakes formed by the Colentina River in the north of the city. For the people of Bucharest, Herăstrău is a favourite spot for walks, water sports and outdoor recreation.

The park is delimited by Boulevard Aviatorilor, Chaussée Kiseleff, Boulevard Beijing, Chaussée Nordului, Strada Elena Văcărescu, the Bucureşti-Ploieşti highway, and Boulevard Constantin Prezan. It was laid out in 1936-39 to mark the *Bucharest Month Exhibition* and was designed by architects Emil Pinard and Friedrich Rebhun. Originally named the Carol II National Park, it was renamed Herăstrău in 1948 (the word means "sawmill"; there

was once a sawmill on the shore of the lake). Later, in the communist period, it was renamed Stalin Park.

The main entrance to the park is in Piaţa Charles de Gaulle, by the Aviatorilor metro station, and is guarded by bronze statue of the French general. There is another entrance on Chaussée Kiseleff, opposite the Triumphal Arch (➤35).

In the oldest section of the park there are two theatres, one of which is for children, two exhibition pavilions, libraries, reading booths, and chess tables. Here too you will find Rose Island, designed by Austrian landscape gardener Friedrich Rebhun, and the Japanese Garden, which was planted in 1998 in partnership with the Japanese Embassy. At the jetty you can hire pedalos and rowing boats or take a ride on the steamboat.

Caryatids Lane, which leads to the Modura Fountain at the entrance to the park on Piaţa Charles de Gaulle, is flanked by twenty statues designed by Constantin Baraschi. The original sculptures were destroyed, but have been recreated using a period copy now found in the Bellu Cemetery. Around Herăstrău Park you will find numerous other monuments: *The Sleeping Nymph* (1906), *Hercules' Battle with the Centaur* (1925), by Ion Jalea, *Prometheus* (1960), by Marie Thomas Lambeaux, and *The Monument to the Fathers of the EU* on Rose Island, which consists of twelve sculptures depicting the politicians who made significant contributions to the founding of the EU.

In summer and at weekends, there is an open-air cinema in the meadow near the entrance to the park on Piaţa Charles de Gaulle, a CreArT project. The Summer Garden is the venue for summer performances by the Constantin Tănase Revue Theatre.

The other half of the park is set aside for sports and recreation. Here you will find a base for kayaking, canoeing and yachting; tennis, basketball and volleyball courts; a bowling alley; and roller-skate rinks. There are also restaurants and beer gardens on the shore of the lake in this area.

Photo: *Herăstrău Park*

In the area by Chaussée Nordului you will find Children's Island.

In 2011, in the area of the Seagull Meadow (Pajiştea Pescăruş), at the intersection of Boulevard Aviatorilor and Boulevard Beijing, the Green Revolution Association created **Cultural Wheelbarrow (Roaba de cultură)**, which in summer serves as a venue for concerts, film showings, theatre performances, exhibitions, painting and pottery workshops, dance lessons, sports activities, and an open-air library. Entrance is free. You can find a programme of events at www.roabadecultura.ro

The park is the ideal place for walks, rollerskating and cycling. There is a path surrounding Lake Herăstrău, stretching for 5.9km.

At the Piaţa Charles de Gaulle and Triumphal Arch entrances there are two **I'Velo** cycle hire centres (www.ivelo.ro ☏ 021.3106397 🕐 Mon-Fri: 11am-7pm, Sat-Sun: 10am-7pm). At the entrance near the Aviatorilor metro station there is a free bicycle hire centre – **La Pedale** (www.la-pedale.ro ☏ 0730 620 516 🕐 Daily: 10am-8:30pm), with 700 bicycles to share.

THE MUSEUM OF THE VILLAGE

> www.muzeul-satului.ro
> ✉ 28-30 Kiseleff Chausée ☏ 021.3179103
> 🕐 Tue-Sun: 9am-7pm (summer), 9am-5pm
> (winter) Mon: 9am-5pm. Closed: 1, 2 Jan, Easter,
> 25, 26 Dec. 💲 10 Lei 🚌 Busses 131, 205, 282, 301,
> 330, 331, 335, 783, N113; tram 14

The Museum of the Village was founded in 1936 by Dimitrie Gusti, the father of the Romanian sociology. This "village in the heart of the capital," surrounded by greenery, is one of Bucharest's most impressive museums and is a must-see attraction. It is the ideal place to get away from the hustle and bustle of the city for a few hours.

The open-air ethnographic museum stretches along the shore of Lake Herăstrău and covers fifteen hectares. Here you will find around three hundred traditional peasant houses and outbuildings dating from the seventeenth to the twentieth centuries, grouped by historical region. Seventy-two of them have been declared historic monuments. None are copies of originals; all are authentic, having been acquired from peasants in their home villages, dismantled piece by piece, transported to Bucharest, and then reassembled in the museum. There are houses, wooden churches, watermills, windmills, wells, wayside crosses, various machines (for making woollen fabrics and for pressing grapes and seeds for oil), workshops, and eighty thousand items of folk art (furniture, fabrics, carpets, crockery, icons).

Throughout the year, the Museum of the Village is the venue for numerous festivals and crafts fairs. Every summer there is an arts camp for children, called Summer on the Village Lane. The children are invited to immerse themselves in the world of folk crafts, learning to paint icons on glass, to carve wood, to weave, to make folk masks, dolls and pottery, and to paint Easter eggs.

At the entrance to the museum there is a shop selling souvenirs, folk costumes, icons on glass, pottery and books.

Photo: *Village Museum*

small cruise ships and speedboats stop here too. You can dive in the lake or cycle all around it. The lake is transformed at the end of summer when Indian water lilies acclimatised here are in bloom.

Outside Snagov Village, **Artha Park** (www.artha.ro ☎ 0735-868986) covers seven hectares, with sports fields, a recreation area with garden kiosks, a bar and grill, and two marquees for weddings and luxury parties. Besides the off road routes for cycling and horse riding lessons, the main attraction is kayaking through the white and scarlet water lilies along the water channel flowing into the Snagov Lake.

The church of the old **Snagov Monastery** stands on an island in the northern part of the lake, probably built in the 14th century by Mircea the Elder and rebuilt by Wladyslaw II and Vlad the Impaler. It was considered one of the largest and most beautiful monasteries in Vlad the Impaler's time. There are still legends about the treasure possibly hidden in its underground labyrinths. It is said that after fighting the Ottomans and the Dănescu dynasty in 1476, his head was cut off and sent to Constantinople. Vlad the Impaler's body was secretly buried near the monastery, which is enclosed by walls like a fortress.

Today's church of the Snagov Monastery, of the Presentation of the Blessed Virgin Mary, was built between 1517 and 1521 by Neagoe Basarab. It was an important cultural centre; in 1643, during Matei Basarab's reign, a printing press was brought to Snagov. Under Constantine Brîncoveanu, the abbot of the monastery was the scholar Anthim the Iberian, who founded the first press in Romania.

OUTSIDE BUCHAREST

SNAGOV

> www.snagov.ro
> 🚌 Minibuses 444 and 446 from the Piaţa Presei Libere, terminus of tramway 41

Snagov Lake covering 576ha and 16.5km long, is located 35km north of the Capital city, and is considered one of the largest lateral lakes in the Romanian Plain. It is ideal for fishing (one can fish common bream, asp, catfish, carp, zander, marbled goby) and for nautical sports lovers.

The forest (1,470ha) – declared a nature reserve – surrounding Snagov Lake is a remnant of the Vlăsia Woods. It is made up of oak, ash and centuries-old linden trees, some over 30m high. The area has been developed into a park. **Snagov Park**, on the western shore of the lake, may be regarded as a mini resort, with its cobbled or paved lanes, shady places to rest, children's playgrounds, sports fields, restaurants, picnic spots and gift shops. The Snagov public pool has a long fine sandy beach, along with green areas shaded by trees; the grounds include cabins and locker rooms, showers, a pier where you can hire rowboats, speedboats, pedalos and water skiing equipment;

CĂLDĂRUŞANI LAKE AND MONASTERY

> 🚌 Minibus from the Piaţa Presei Libere, terminal station of tramway 41, or from the Cora-Pantelimon shopping mall, terminus of tramways 14 and 55

Photo: *Snagov Monastery*

Forty kilometres north-east of Bucharest, the 6-km-long Căldărușani Lake is surrounded by the forest of the same name (a remnant of the Vlăsia Woods), ideal for bike rides and animal watching. It is home to rare species of birds, reptiles (the snake-eyed skink), animals (pheasants, hares, bucks, deer) and fish (zander, catfish, perch, asp, carp, common bream). A pheasant farm has been set up to the west of the forest. The Grădiștea – Căldărușani – Dridu area has been declared a protected area for wild birds and animals, with 20,000 migratory birds stopping here on their way from North Europe to Africa. The lake with its wide reed beds and floating islands might remind one of a miniature delta.

The church of the Căldărușani Monastery was built by Neagoe Basarab between 1637 and 1638, on the Curtea de Argeș and Dealu Monasteries model. The monastery museum houses one of the richest collections of church artefacts, paintings, icons (some of them signed by Nicolae Grigorescu) and books.

CERNICA LAKE AND MONASTERY

✉ 16 Pantelimon Road (DJ301)
🚌 Minibuses 410, 459 and 461 from the Cora – Pantelimon shopping mall, terminus of tramways 14 and 55

The southern part of the Cernica Lake (341ha), located 14km east of Bucharest, is covered by reed beds and has been declared a nature reserve.

In 1608, Cernica Știrbei, Mihai Viteazul's *vornic* (a high-ranking official in charge of justice and internal affairs), built the Cernica Monastery on the shore of this lake. The monastery grounds are divided into two: Saint Nicholas Church on a lake island (1815), and on another – Saint George Church (1831-1842). Gala Galaction, Ion Țuculescu and Dumitru Stăniloae are buried in the graveyard; look for the white marble vault of Metropolitan Nifon, with interior murals painted in 1875 by Gheorghe Tattarescu. The graveyard chapel, of Saint Lazarus, was built in 1804.

Within the monastery precincts there is a museum in the house where St Calinic (1787-1868) lived. In the Church of St George, which he founded, there is a casket with his relics. He was the abbot of the monastery for 31 years. In the monastery museum we can admire 17th- to 19th-century icons, casings and embroidery, manuscripts, paintings, silver artefacts and pottery.

PASĂREA LAKE AND MONASTERY

🚌 Minibuses 401 and 503 from the Cora – Pantelimon shopping mall, terminus of tramways 14 and 55; minibus 503 from Bucur Obor

Pasărea Lake, formed at the junction of Pasărea and Șindrilița streams, is surrounded by Pustnicu Forest, which was part of the Vlăsia Woods. Cut off on the shore of the lake, 19km east of Bucharest

Photo: *Pasărea Lake and Monastery*

(DN3bis), there is a beautiful convent, organised according to the idiorrhythmic form of monastic life: the nuns here (around 170) lead a self-regulated life, and live in beautiful country houses with front porches in the monastic village. The convent was founded in 1813, when Abbot Timothei of Cernica built a wooden church, which collapsed during the 1838 earthquake. Saint Calinic, the abbot of the Cernica Monastery, built a new church in 1846; the graveyard church was erected by the same, in 1834.

The convent's museum features an impressive collection of old religious items, along with plaster casts by Gheorghe D. Anghel, the sculptor, author of the Eminescu statue outside the Atheneum (➤31), who spent his last years here and was buried in the convent graveyard.

On the opposite side of the lake you will find the Pustnicu tourist complex and restaurant; you can take a short boat trip from there. To get there, take the road which branches off DN3 near the railway overpass next to Brănești.

MOGOȘOAIA

www.palatebrancovenesti.ro
✉ 1 Valea Parcului Street, Mogoșoaia
📞 021.3506619 🕐 Tue-Sun: 10am-7pm (Mar-Oct), 9am-5pm (Nov-Febr) 💲 5 Lei 🚐 Maxi-taxi from 1 Mai metro station

On Lake Mogoșoaia (66ha), 15km from Bucharest, stands one of the most beautiful Brîncoveanu-era buildings – the Mogoșoaia Palace (1702). The edifice, rectangular in shape, built on the Potlogi Palace model (Dîmbovița County, 40km from Bucharest), combines elements of Wallachian, Byzantine, Oriental (Ottoman) and Italian Renaissance styles; due to its decorative richness, the Brîncoveanu style (or Romanian Renaisssance) was said to be the Romanian Baroque.

The facades of the palace show clear Venetian architectural influences (for instance, the loggia with five trefoil arches resting on six neo-Corinthian pillars on the facade looking out on the lake). An exterior stone staircase leads to the balcony located in the middle of the facade towards the palace courtyard. The servants' quarters were found on the ground floor, and the large chambers of the royal family and the reception halls were on the upper floor. A Lapidarium has been set up in the basement, where a vaulted cellar is now to be found.

To reach the Palace Courtyard you go under an arched gate, on top of which there is a watch tower – a wonderful vantage point. In this vast courtyard, with its gravelled paths, lawns and ornamental trees, open-air shows, concerts and festivals are organised. Along the sides there is the royal kitchen – which hosts exhibitions, conferences and film projections, the ice house and the guest house. On the shore of the lake, guarded by two stone lions, the restored Brîncoveanu-style columns stand next to a hedge maze, in the French garden style.

Outside the Palace Courtyard, next to the English park, stands Saint George Church, the first to be built on the grounds (1688), as a chapel for the court; it retains its original interior painting from 1705 (the votive painting in the narthex is especially valuable).

After 1714 (when Brîncoveanu and his four sons were beheaded by the Turks for having refused to convert to Islam), the palace remained uninhabited and was plundered, being later turned into an inn by the Turks. Later on, in the 19th century, it was taken over by the Bibescu family, scions of the Brînoveanu family. On the east side of the courtyard, Prince Nicolae Bibescu built the Elchingen Villa for his wife, Hélène d'Elchingen. The Elchingen Villa is currently home to a modern conference and accommodation centre, a restaurant seating 120 people and a hotel.

Martha Bibescu, George Valentin Bibescu's wife, restored the estate after 1912, making radical changes, with the help of the architects Domenico Rupolo and George Matei Cantacuzino. The funeral monument of the Bibescu family is found in the palace park, not far from the flower greenhouses.

Nowadays, the grounds have been turned into the Brîncoveanu Palaces at the Gates of Bucharest Cultural Centre. The rooms host a permanent display of the art collection donated by Liana and Dan Nasta, as well as temporary exhibitions by Romanian artists.

It is an ideal destination for a day trip, particularly given that the palace park, with its many creeks, green and picnic areas, offers a pleasant breeze in summer. The complex also includes a cycle hire centre and water sports centre.

Do not miss out in April-May on the purple blanket of irises in Princess Martha Bibescu's garden, which alongside the blooming chestnut trees make the place otherworldly.

COMANA

On the road from Bucharest to Giurgiu, a section which is in very bad repair, before Comana village (35km to the south) there is a structure built by Vlad the Impaler in 1461. This fortress-monastery cut off in the middle of marshes was also called the Neajlov Stronghold. It is reflected today, as in the days of yore, in the waters of a very wide pond (1,200ha) on the Neajlov River, in the middle of a plain. The church, later rebuilt by Radu Șerban (1588) and Șerban Cantacuzino (1700),

who also erected a tower on the northen side, became the burial place of the Cantacuzino family.

Part of the Comana Forest has been declared a forest and wildlife reserve. The Comana Pond, which looks like a delta formed between the Neajlov and Argeș rivers, is a protected area for wild birds and animals (140 bird species have been identified). Also in the Comana Nature Park (25,000ha) there are nature reserves of prickly burweed and Lily of the Valley and a well-known peony reserve (*Peonia peregrina*): in the second Sunday of May, each year, it hosts the Peony Festival (➤176). The forest is an ideal place for bycicle rides and it includes a popular adventure park (➤172). The Comana Nature Park Office (www.comanaparc.ro) has a boat hire centre.

The surrealist Romanian poet Gellu Naum (1915-2001) had a retreat in Comana village; here, in the "magical garden" on the "blue shore", he wrote part of his poems and here he was visited by his friends and literary followers. After his death, Lyggia Naum, his wife, founded a memorial house in Comana.

Nearby is Călugăreni, the town where Michael the Brave won a battle against Sinan Pasha's Turks in August 1595.

Photo: *Mogoșoaia Palace*

Muntenia
and Oltenia

previous page: *Rucăr-Bran Pass*

Muntenia and Oltenia

There was a time when the corridors of power were not in Bucharest. The capital was finally established in the fortress on the shores of the Dîmbovița River relatively late, in 1659. Wallachia (made up of Muntenia and Oltenia) – which along with the other Romanian provinces, Moldavia, Transylvania, Dobruja, Crişana and the Banat, form today's Romania – had previously had its princely capital at: Câmpulung, Curtea de Argeş and Tîrgovişte. The first capital was Câmpulung, where Basarab I (1310-1352) established his court after defeating King Carol Robert de Anjou of Hungary in the Battle of Loviştea (1330) when he won Wallachia's independence. Forty years on, in 1369, Vladislav I Vlaicu established the capital in the old princely city of Curtea de Argeş. Under Mircea the Elder (1355-1418), Tîrgovişte made its mark as the main princely court. In the 15th century, Vlad the Impaler set up a second capital in Bucharest. The former Wallachian capitals, today backwaters sunk into oblivion, lag well behind Bucharest. Having said that, many corners of these towns continue to bear witness to times long passed if you are patient enough to explore.

Many sacred buildings – churches and monasteries – have been handed down by the rulers of this "land": Neagoe Basarab (1512-1521), who built the Curtea de Argeş Monastery, Matei Basarab (1632-1654), a true "patron of the Church", who built over 30 places of worship, and Constantine Brîncoveanu (1688-1714), during whose reign culture burgeoned as never before.

Muntenia is also synonymous with the Bucegi Mountains, and their Sphinx and "Old Ladies" rock formations, with the Sinaia, Buşteni and Predeal mountain resorts, the spectacular mud volcanoes near Buzău and the underground "salt castle" in Slănic where the temperature is a constant 12°C.

Off the beaten tourist track, Oltenia hides away remnants of fortresses and Roman castra, the health resorts at Călimăneşti-Căciulata, Voineasa, Olăneşti and Govora, the monasteries at Cozia, Tismana, Bistriţa, Govora and Arnota, the concretions at Costeşti, unique caves, *cule* (tower-like fortified boyar residences) of the 18th century, centuries-old traditions (*Căluşul* – the horseman dance) and long-forgotten harbours, one of them fortunate enough to have been turned into an art colony by poet Mircea Dinescu.

MUNTENIA

PRAHOVA VALLEY

The Prahova Valley, one of the areas most visited by tourists, is guarded by the Bucegi Mountains to the west and Baiului Mountains to the east. It is the ideal spot to spend a weekend outside Bucharest. Five resorts (Sinaia, Poiana Ţapului, Buşteni, Azuga and Predeal) lie within a 25km distance, from where you can hike to the cabins on top of the surrounding mountains (Babele, Omu, Valea Dorului, Valea cu Brazi, Scropoasa, Cuibul Dorului, Caraiman, Diham, Mălăieşti, Padina, Gura Diham, Piatra Arsă). The resorts started to thrive after King Carol I of Romania established his summer house at Sinaia in 1866 and an international railway track was built in the area.

The stylish **Sinaia** resort (120km from Bucharest) sprang up around the Sinaia Monastery built between 1690 and 1695 by Prince Mihail Cantacuzino, after a pilgrimage to the Holy Land (Mount Sinai). Captivated by the surroundings of Sinaia, Carol I of Hohenzollern-Sigmaringen, the first king of Romania, decided to set up his summer house here and built between 1875 and 1883 the **Peleş Castle** (🏛 Tue: 11:15am-4:15pm, Wed-Sun: 9:15am-4:15pm

Photo: *Peleş Castle, Sinaia*

(mid-May to mid-Sept), Wed: 11:15am-4:15pm, Thu-Sun: 9:15am-4:15pm (the rest of the year) 🔵 20-70 Lei, depending on the castle tour). It shows the influences of the German neo-Renaissance style. It is easily accessible to tourists and it showcases collections of engravings and prints (Rembrandt, El Greco, Rafael, Correggio, Murillo, Velázquez, Bruegel), sculptures, armour, medals, Oriental rugs, furniture, vintage costumes, Flemish and French tapestry, Swiss and German stained glass from the 15th-18th centuries, rare books, Japanese pottery, English silver etc. The **Pelişor Castle** (🏛 Wed: 11:15am-5:15pm, Thu-Sun: 10:15am-5:15pm (mid-May to mid-Sept), Wed: 11:15am-4:15pm, Thu-Sun: 9:15am-4:15pm (the rest of the year) 🔵 20 Lei), nearby was the home of the royal couple Ferdinand and Maria. The Villa Luminiş in the Cumpătu district, which once belonged to famous composer George Enescu, is now the **George Enescu Memorial Museum** (✉ 2 Yehudi Menuhin Street 🏛 Tue-Sun: 10am-5p, 🔵 6 Lei).

Buşteni is known as "The Gateway to the Bucegi", as it is from here that most of the trails up into the Bucegi Mountains of "Eastern Alps" lead. Mountain climbers can tackle around 250 climbing routes up the steep mountain walls, each with its degree of difficulty. Kalinderu ski slope (1,500m long), located on one of the Caraiman Massif sides, 1km away from downtown Buşteni, boasts a gondola lift, snow machine and floodlights. In 1990, an area of 35,700 hectares in the Bucegi Mountains was declared a National Park Reserve. At an altitude of 1,800-2,000m there is an eroded platform covered by alpine pastures (Bucegi Plateau), covering approximately 10km. On this plateau weathering (wind, freeze-thaw) has caused some strange-looking rocks to be formed – *The Old Ladies, the Sphinx, the Mushrooms, Hermes, Zalmoxis*, which attract hundreds of visitors in summer. In 1978, Buşteni was linked to the Bucegi Plateau by a funicular. The Buşteni – Babele Cableway (🏛 Mon, Wed-Sun: 7:30am-5:45pm (mid-

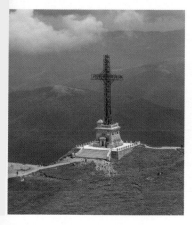

Jun-mid-Sept), 8:30am-3:45pm (the rest of the year) Ⓢ 35 Lei), 4,350m long, is the longest in the country and the third longest in Europe. The Babele (Old Ladies) Cabin is connected to the Peștera Hotel near the Ialomița Cave by a cableway (🅿 Mon, Wed-Sun: 9am-5:15pm Ⓢ 20 Lei), 2,611m long. On the Șaua Mare platform of the Caraiman Mountain, 2,291m above sea level, stands the impressive Heroes' Cross, 33m high. Built between 1926 and 1928, on Queen Maria's initiative, in memory of the soldiers who had died during the Prahova Valley battles in World War I, the cross is mounted on a 7.5m high stone-clad base of rebar shaped in the form of a pyramid. It has an electric generator which powers the 120 500W light bulbs outlining the cross.

Azuga, located 895-950m above sea level, is known as the "skier's paradise". The winter sports Azuga complex includes: the Cazacu slope, the only one in Romania certified by FIS, the Sorica slope, cross-country and nordic skiing routes (18km), snowboarding slope and ski-lifts.

Predeal, towered over by Piatra Mare, Postăvaru and Clăbucet Peaks, developed as resort after 1918. Located 1,020-1,160m above sea level it has numerous ski slopes (10km), two chairlifts and three ski lifts. Predeal is an ideal place for winter sports lovers; snow cover lasts approximately 100 days per year.

Also in the Prahova Valley, in the Subcarpathian region, lies **Breaza**, with a much sought after golf course (Lac de Verde), and **Posada**, Martha Bibescu's house (1934), which now hosts the Carpathian Wildlife Museum.

SLĂNIC

Built close to the salt deposits mined here for over three centuries (1685), this health resort is located in Prahova County, 40km from Ploiești and around 100km from Bucharest. Despite the lack of infrastructure, the town does have potential and a definite touristic vocation. Here lies the deepest salt mine in Europe, currently open to visitors (🅿 Wed-Fri: 8am-3:30pm, Sat-Sun: 8:30am-4pm Ⓢ 20 Lei). The old Unirea salt mine (1938-1970), 210m deep, is made up of fourteen 54-metre-high galleries covering 80,000m^2. The temperature is kept at a constant 12^{0}C, irrespective of the time of the year. Visitors can enjoy sports grounds, volleyball, handball, tennis and minifootball facilities, playgrounds, kart races, slot machines, a buffet and a sanatorium to treat respiratory conditions. In the Genesis Chamber one can admire the monumental salt sculptures portraying Burebista, Trajan, Decebalus and Michael the Brave. Unlike the Turda and Praid salt mines, the one in Slănic has yet to be refurbished but this only increases its authenticity.

Left: *Heroes' Cross, on the Caraiman Mountain*

Right: Sphinx *on the Bucegi Plateau*

The Mihai salt mine, a vertically excavated mine, separated by a 40-metre-thick slab from the Unirea mine, hosts national and international aeromodelling competitions, open to the public.

Since 1982 the Treasury House in Slănic – built in the early 18th century to serve as the residence of the court clerk in charge of collecting salt taxes – houses the **Salt Museum** (☎ 0244.240961 ⏰ Tue-Sun: 9am-5pm).

Another attraction in Slănic is the Baia Baciului (the Shepherd's Lake) Complex made up of the Bride's Lake, the Great Lake (the Shepherd's Lake) and the Pigs' Lake, saltwater lakes formed when salt mines collapsed. Their water, much like the waters of the Green Lake or Baia Roşie (Red Lake) is recommended for the treatment of various conditions, which is why in summer the bathing area around the lakes is crowded. Unfortunately, in 2006 most of the Salt Mountain (2ha), declared a geological and geomorphological nature reserve in 1954, collapsed into the Bride's Cave which is starting to disintegrate.

The resort also has springs containing chlorine and sodium, sulphur and calcium – Fântâna Rece-Sub cetate, Fântâna lui Duşman, Fântâna Gogon, located around a 30-minute walking distance from the resort.

There is also a choice of many hiking trails on the nearby oak forest-covered hills, e.g. up to Piatra Verde (5km), a volcanic rock, or up to **Crasna Monastery** (12km).

There are waymarked trails up to the Grohotiş Mountains too.

CHEIA

Unjustly passed over for the more popular resorts in the Prahova Valley, Cheia, nestling in the Teleajen Valley, at the foot of the Ciucaş Mountains, 125km from Bucharest, is still a well-kept secret. At an elevation of 871m, the resort has a climate specific to intramontane depressions and highly oxygenated air due to the endless pine and beech forests all around.

The resort is dominated by the spectacular jagged ridge of the Gropşoarele-Zăganu Mountain and it developed around Cheia Monastery, built in 1770 and rebuilt with bricks between 1835 and 1839. The complex, in the south-east of the town, preserves the murals painted by Gheorghe Tattarascu in 1837.

What sets Cheia apart are the many trails on the Ciucaş Mountain, one of the mountains close to the hearts of hiking lovers. The trails set out from the Muntele Roşu Cabin, located 1,280m above sea level, about 5.5km away from the Cheia resort, which can be reached either by foot or by car along a bumpy road, left unpaved for years. From here you can continue to the Ciucaş Peak and Ciucaş Hut (marking: red triangle; duration: 5-6h), Tigăile Mari, Babele la Sfat, Bratocea Pass or Bratocea's Sphinx, listed as a natural monument.

If you are just passing through Cheia, we recommend a light 1-1.5h stroll along the Cheiţa Gorge (marking: blue triangle), up to the Teleajen springs. Although not spectacular, some portions of the gorge may prove a challenge and force you to keep your balance by holding on to the rocks to keep out of the water. It is worth it: you will enjoy some small charming waterfalls and a thick carpet of greater burdock all along Cheiţa's banks.

Photo: *Salt Mountain, Slănic*

URLAŢI

The **Bellu Manor House** (✉ 12 Orzoaia de Sus Street, Urlaţi 🕐 Tue-Sun: 9am-5pm), located in the Subcarpathian foothills, 80km from Bucharest and 22km from Ploieşti, was the last home of Baron Alexandru Bellu (1850-1921) who retired here during the last years of his life with his seven children. Lawyer, numismatist, a great collector and photographer (his snapshots of the local peasants were included in a photo album dedicated to Romania, printed in Paris in 1919), he was born to an Aromanian-speaking family originating from Macedonia who settled in Wallachia at the end of the 18th century, where they amassed vast estates. Later on, Eliza Bellu, née Ştirbey, donated the Urlaţi property and vineyard to the Romanian Academy. The Bellu Cemetery, built on a piece of land donated by Barbu Bellu, Minister of Religious Denominations and Justice in the mid-19th century, is the only place in Bucharest to mention this old family name.

The Urlaţi manor house is typical of the local architecture of the mid-19th century. The wooden veranda, shingle roof and the impeccable whitewash on the facade adorned with Balkan-style woodwork were again restored to their previous glory after the restoration work begun in 2004. And the interior is even more surprising... Turned into a museum in 1954, the house holds an art collection (including an Oriental artefacts collection), a library of rare books, wood furniture, icons, ceramics, clothes, 19th-century Romanian rugs, china, metalwork, 18th- and 19th-century weapons, as well as carved stone windows and door frames dating back to the 17th-18th centuries.

Urlaţi, located on the *Wine Road*, passing through Filipeştii de Târg, Floreşti, Băicoi, Plopeni, Zamfira, Boldeştii-Scăeni, Bucov, Valea Călugărească, Vărbila, Jercălăi, Ceptura, Mizil and Tohani, is bordered by extensive vineyards. In October 2014 the first Wine Cellar half-marathon took place here – with two routes (of 7 and 17km) across the scenic vineyard covered hills surrounding the town.

The **Vineyard Manor House** (www.conaculdintrevii.ro 🕐 Valea Bobului Street (18 Filitiş) ☎ 021.2125262), outside the town, is a former manor house from 1930, restored and turned into a deluxe tourist facility in 2006. It offers diverse services, from accommodation to events (weddings, teambuilding sessions etc.). The estate includes a restaurant and a wine cellar which organise tastings of local wines. The prices match the renown of the location.

On the other side of the town there is the Jercălăi Monastery (or the Sf. Maria-Cricov Hermitage), with an old wooden church dating back to 1731. In 1932 it was donated by the community of the Luieriu-Reghin village (Mureş County) to the Bran Castle estate (➤60), being relocated in 1956 in order to prevent its deterioration. Beside the harmony of its structure, the interior paintings are impressive by themselves: they date back to 1731 (egg tempera paintings, on the iconostasis and vault) and 1838 (oil paintings on lateral walls).

To reach Urlaţi take the Ploieşti – Buzău road, then the road branching off at Albeşti-Paleologu.

We suggest you take two detours from Urlaţi to the former **Vărbila Monastery** (1536) in the commune of Iordăcheanu, 8km away, and **Apostolache Monastery** (1645-1652), 17km away, both fortified and surrounded with thick defensive walls and both recently restored to their former glory with EU funds. They used to be part of the former Saac County (Săcuieni), inhabited by Romanian-born Hungarians and Szeklers who crossed the mountains to settle in Wallachia. Not many people have heard of these remarkable pieces of architecture, which is a shame! From here here it is just 7km to **Sângeru** village, where poet Lucian Avramescu founded in his grandparents' house an interesting **Stone Museum**, with over 1,000 carved stone exhibits fashioned by craftsmen of the Dealul Istriței and the surrounding area, highly typical of naive peasant art. The vast inner courtyard was laid out differently the better to capture the value of the sculptures and to host a summer sculpture camp for children. Right across the street there is the Village Museum, located in the family mansion of Andrei Bozianu from 1793, head of the treasury and later on *stolnic* (a high-official in charge of the voivode's table) in the Court Council; his complex includes an old church dating from the end of the 18th century.

TÎRGOVIȘTE

Tîrgoviște (75km south-east of Bucharest), former capital of Wallachia (1396-1714), preserves the vestiges of the **Princely Court** (🕐 Tue-Sun: 9am-6:30pm (summer),

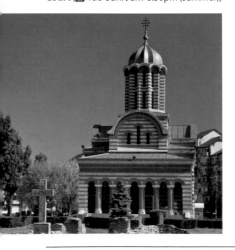

9am-5pm (winter) 🎫 10 Lei). It was built consecutively by Mircea the Elder, Petru Cercel, Matei Basarab, Radu the Great and Constantine Brîncoveanu. It is possible to get a panoramic view if you climb up to the top of the 27-metre-high **Chindia Tower**. The novelty of this tower – now the landmark of Tîrgoviște – lies in its pyramid-shaped stone-clad base, while the tower itself (9m in diameter), built with bricks, is a cylinder. The construction was built by Vlad the Impaler in the 15th century, on top of the porch of a chapel from the time of Mircea the Elder. Archdeacon Paul of Aleppo, who visited the principalities between 1653 and 1658, wrote that the tower was used as the town's "clock", most likely signalling at dusk (close to sunset) that it was time for the gates to close. The **Royal Church** (1584) is of remarkable beauty, a Greek cross in plan, and was built by Petru Cercel and painted during the reign of Brîncoveanu (1696-1698). It is no exaggeration to say that its architecture lives up to the great architectural achievements in Europe at that time. The walls are covered in 17th century paintings featuring a large array of Muntenian rulers. Please take a moment to look at the tombstone (17th century) of Lady Elina, Matei Basarab's wife, made by master Elias Nicolai of Sibiu; it has one of the most beautiful engraved epitaphs in the country, a lament for the transience of mortal man: *The man begotten by woman lives but a short while, overwhelmed by troubles and as a flower he blossoms, withers and fades away like a shadow.* Further up stands the Church of St. Friday which is less impressive despite its long history (15th century).

The old city is a true reserve of old architecture; along the narrow streets flanked by merchant houses you will come across numerous centuries-old churches. No other Romanian town has so many 15th- to 17th-century churches in such a confined space. Everywhere you turn you are reminded that the town was once the most important economic, military and cultural centre of Wallachia.

Photo: *Metropolitan Church, Tîrgoviște*

The **Metropolitan Church,** built between 1515 and 1518 by Neagoe Basarab, painted in 1708, during the reign of Constantine Brîncoveanu, was pulled down and reconstructed from its foundations between 1890 şi 1923, by the French architect André Lecomte du Noüy. He drew on the original church but never managed to achieve its initial glory.

The **Stelea Monastery** contains the church built in 1645 by Vasile Lupu on the model of the famous Three Hierarchs Church in Jassy, the cells (16th century) and the abbot's house (1645). The two octagonal church towers have quite an effect: they are supported by star-shaped bases and decorated with green enamelled ceramic plates and buttons. The church stands out for its original mixture of Moldavian and Wallachian elements. Beyond its walls, in the county hall park near Freedom Avenue the ruins of the Stelea-Veche church (14th-15th century) demolished in 1864, are still visible. Right next door there is the **Stelea Gallery**. This original building, the exterior of which is more reminiscent of an Italian church than of a museum, was designed in 1938 by architect Nicolae Ghika-Budeşti to serve as a community museum; it is currently used as an exhibition space. Go in and take a look at the central hallway where a lapidarium has been set up. It contains inscriptions and other historical artefacts from local monuments long since vanished.

The area between the Revolution street and Ion Heliade Rădulescu street, flanked with the shops of long-gone merchants, exudes some of the atmosphere of Lipscani street in Bucharest.

Take a walk around the town to discover its old churches, hidden away here and there: *St. George Church*, built between 1512 and 1521 by Neagoe Basarab, the *Ss. Constantine and Elena Church*, built in 1650 by Matei Basarab and his wife Elina, *Archangels Michael and Gabriel*, built in the 15th-17th centuries on 14th-century ruins, *St. Nicolae Androneşti* (1527; 1625), the *Town Church* (1654), *St. Dumitru Buzinca* (1639), *St. Nicolae Simuleasa*

(1654), *St. Nicolae Geartoglu* (15th century, rebuilt in 1638). The truly curious visitor is advised to head for the edge of the town and look for Valul Cetăţii street, along a good portion of which the defensive city ditch and embankment are still standing. The ditch, not impressive by modern standards, once played a crucial role in defending the town. The first fortifications, built during the mid-15th, were rebuilt towards the mid-17th by Matei Basarab, most likely along the initial route.

Tîrgovişte is an old cultural mediaeval centre, proud to have been the home of Macarie, who in 1508 published here the first book to be printed in Wallachia (*The Liturgy*). The **Museum of Printing and Old Romanian Books** (🏛 Tue-Sun: 9am-5pm (summer), 8am-4pm (winter) 🎫7 Lei) was founded in a neo-Romanian style house during the mid-19th century by architect Ion Mincu, over the 17th-century cellars belonging to the mansion of Stolnic Constantin Cantacuzino.

Painter Gheorghe Petraşcu (1872-1949) was so captivated by the special charms of this historic town in the Ialomiţa Valley, that in 1922 he built here an unassuming house which he used as his workshop for 20 years. It has been the **Gheorghe Petraşcu Museum** (🏛 Tue-Sun: 9am-5pm (summer), 8am-4pm (winter) 🎫 7 Lei) since 1970 and the paintings of his favourite flowers – zinnias, which used to fill up the entire front garden – can still be admired here.

Dumitru Bucureşteanu House (18th century), on 300 Calea Domnească street, which used to be owned by a wine merchant, is probably the oldest example of secular architecture in Tîrgovişte. The old heritage house representative of Balkan architecture, with opened verandas, is now a restaurant

Take a short trip 4km from Tîrgovişte, up to the **Dealu Monastery**, perched on top of a hill near the Viforîta village. The head of Mircea the Brave, the author of the short-lived Union of Wallachia, Moldavia and Transylvania in 1600, was buried in the church with walls clad in stone, built between 1499 and 1501 by Radu the Great.

THE COURT OF THE GOLESCU FAMILY AND THE VITICULTURE AND ORCHARD MUSEUM MUSEUM – GOLEŞTI

✉ 1 Banul Radu Golescu Street, Ştefăneşti
📞 0248.266364 🕐 Tue-Sun: 9am-6pm(summer), 8am-4pm (winter) 🎟 7 Lei (2 Lei, for children)

The Golescu family's feudal complex at Ştefăneşti, 10km from Piteşti and 110km from Bucharest, was built in the year 1640 by Stroe Leurdeanu, who enclosed it with tall, thick brick walls with buttresses and four cylinder towers equipped with cannons, located at the four corners of the rectangle. Later it was inherited by the Great Ban (the Prime-Minister) Radu Golescu who expanded it. The manor house is a typical example of pre-Brîncoveanu architecture.

The entry into the complex is through Tudor Vladimirescu Gate, which served as a watchtower. Tudor Vladimirescu established his camp here, between 18 and 21 May, 1821, before falling victim to an Eteria plot. Its members assassinated him with the connivance of some of his militiamen. The tower is right next to the monastery hospital for the elderly, the sick and the poor, founded by the Great Ban Radu Golescu and maintained at his own expense; today, the building is used as a room for temporary exhibitions.

The free community school (1826-1830), established by the scholar Dinicu Golescu, was the first modern school to teach in Romanian. The children of the poor studied alongside those of the rich, the textbooks were free of charge and what is more, girls were accepted alongside boys.

The main alley takes us to the manor house – a fortified lay house unique in the country, which comprises the Oriental Hall, Anica Golescu and her husband's chambers, the room of the French physician Carol Davila, and Zoe's chambers (Zinca), the wife of Dinicu Golescu (1777-1830), the first to keep a travel diary in Romanian literature. A spiral wooden staircase leads from the main hall to the upper floor, which is currently not open to visitors. The chambers preserve the original furniture; note the upright piano on which Franz Liszt played during his two-week stay at Goleşti, at the invitation of Carol Davila. The family portraits are displayed on the walls, copies of those done by C.D. Rosenthal. A secret door leads from the house directly to the 250m² caves and the almost 1m-thick walls hiding a "priest hole", a room where the family could take refuge in times of danger.

The hammam (18th century), or the Turkish bath, the only one in the country preserved in its original form, has 80cm-thick walls lined with ceramic pipes to allow the circulation of steam and a domed ceiling with air holes.

The church of the complex, erected in 1646, combines architectural elements from Muntenia, Moldavia, Armenia and Turkey. It holds the remains of the Golescu family.

The mansion is encircled by Golescu Park, which used to have a pond spanned by a birchwood bridge. It has now been transformed into the splendid **Viticulture and Orchard Museum**, covering 10 hectares dotted with 35 cottages brought from the main vineyard and orchard areas in the country, grouped within a village. Each homestead has a farmhouse, outbuildings, facilities and the implements needed to carry out various tasks. There is also a horse riding centre offering pony rides for children.

THE VILLA FLORICA (BRĂTIANU CULTURAL CENTRE)

✉ 37 Staţiunii Street, Ştefăneşti
🕐 Mon-Fri: 8am-4pm, Sat-Sun: 9am-5pm

The Brătianu family estate at Ştefăneşti, 5km from the city of Piteşti, is made up of a manor house, a farm, a chapel, a wine cellar, a train station, and even an astronomy observatory in the middle of a park surrounded by vineyards. Considered one of the most beautiful boyar estates in Romania, the Ştefăneşti complex is the work of Ion C. Brătianu (1821-1891) and of his son, Ion (Ionel) I. C. Brătianu (1864-1927), two of the most prominent Romanian politicians, both of them leaders of the Liberal Party; the former was Prime-Minister for 12 years, and the latter served five terms as Prime-Minister. The old and ordinary-looking administrative building was converted in the second half of the 19th century into a glorious neo-Romanian style house, with one floor and 20 rooms, named the Villa Florica, in the memory of Ion C. Brătianu's first daughter, who died before the age of three.

Visited by kings Carol I, Ferdinand I and Carol II, and queens Elizabeth and Maria, Marshal Averescu, the Golescu brothers, C.A. Rosetti, D.A. Sturdza, I.G. Duca, Constantin Argetoianu and Barbu Știrbey, the mansion was the setting of historic decisions crucial for the country during the last half of the 19th century and the beginning of the 20th century.

The house held an impressive library with a book collection deemed the largest in the country, larger than that of the Romanian Academy. Unfortunately, under the communist regime, when the house was nationalised, the books vanished, much like many of the valuable pieces of furniture inside.

The tombs of the most prominent members of the Bratianu family – Ion C. Brătianu, Ionel Brătianu, Vintilă Brătianu, Dinu Brătianu and Gheorghe Brătianu, the last two dead in the Sighet prison during the communist persecution, are housed in St. John the Baptist Church (1898).

The complex has become the Brătianu Cultural Centre, and is open to visitors.

DID YOU KNOW?
In addition to the country's political and administrative capital, some of Wallachia's rulers also saw fit to have temporary capitals for when they were travelling. It seems that the court travelled around the country, which would explain the multiple capitals. Wallachia always had dual capitals, in Cîmpulung and Curtea de Argeș, or in Curtea de Argeș and Tîrgoviște, or in Tîrgoviște and Bucharest.

CURTEA DE ARGEȘ

Curtea de Argeș, 150km from Bucharest, is one of the three former voivodeship capitals of Wallachia together with Câmpulung (➤56) and Tîrgoviște (➤50). Of the first princely court only the ruins on top of the plateau of Sân Nicoară Church (13th-14th century) survive. It was probably used as a chapel and was connected through a tunnel to the **Saint Nicholas Royal Church** (before 1352), built by Basarab I, considered to be one of the most important feudal monuments in the area. The building in the form of a Greek cross, with walls in faux brick panels preserves the interior murals painted between 1364 and 1369 in the Byzantine style.

The city is famous for the beautiful church of the **Curtea de Argeș Monastery** (✉ Bd. Basarabilor 🕐 Daily: 7am-8pm), built by Neagoe Basarab between 1512 and 1517 and known as the Diocesan Church as it was the seat of the diocese between 1739 and 1748. This place of worship is closely linked with the Legend of Master builder Manole who walled his wife into its foundation alive so as to stop it from crumbling. And in order to keep the way the monastery was built forever a secret, Manole himself had to be sacrificed.

Photo: *Curtea de Argeș Monastery*

Left stranded on top of the church at the king's orders, Manole fashioned wings and tried to fly off the roof but he fell to the ground and turned into a spring. This is in short the story of Manole's Spring. In 1875, the beautiful stone church, which is a tri-conch in plan, was pulled down and rebuilt by the French architect André Lecomte du Noüy. It was consecrated in 1886. The monastery, visited annually by 100,000 pilgrims, is home to the tomb of its founder – Neagoe Basarab – and the tombs of the royal family (Kings Carol I and Ferdinand, Queens Elizabeth and Maria).

Although very few trains pass through it any more, the **Curtea de Argeş Train Station** (✉ 4, 1 Mai Street) has remained one of the most impressive monuments in the city. It was built in 1898 by the same André Lecomte du Noüy.

Despite their value, the exterior paintings of the **Olari** church built by the former potters guild, on the site of a women's hermitage from 1300, have been left to deteriorate. Note the death scene on the eastern wall. The shingle roof protecting the church is equally unusual.

The 18th-century house (✉ 1 Viorelelor Street) owned by the grandparents of the baritone opera singer Petre Ştefănescu Goangă, who performed in all the world's major opera houses, is now home to the city's library.

The house of the painter Dumitru Norocea, in charge of restoring the paintings at the Royal Church between 1914 and 1924, is now the **Ethnographic Museum**, housing an array of craft tools, folk costumes and art from around the Argeş region.

A narrow path leading from Căpăţâneni village (27km from Curtea de Argeş), on the Argeş Valley, upstream of Vidraru Lake, takes you up to the **Poenari Citadel**, which is rumoured to have been built in the 14th century by Radu I (Negru Vodă) and rebuilt during the reign of Vlad the Impaler. 1,480 concrete steps will take you to this fortress on the Cetăţuia Mountain plateau, 850m in altitude. Legend has it that on Easter Day 1459, Vlad the Impaler, seeking revenge against the boyars from Tîrgovişte who killed his brother and betrayed his father, had them walk all the way to Poenari for tens of miles, where they were forced to build the citadel.

Continuing from the Poenari Citadel on the road to Vidraru Lake, stop at the red cross before the first 180 degree bend and take the adventure road that runs along **Stan Valley**, dotted with waterfalls (one with a 35m drop), many rock-cut basins, called cauldrons, vertical walls and rocks which you can only climb using metal ladders, a test for the fainthearted. There are cables and handrails fastened in the

Photo: *The Saint Nicholas Royal Church, Curtea de Argeş*

rock. The route takes around 5-6 hours and it is a circular route, which means that you will return through a beech wood to the Vidraru Lake. Be properly equipped: it is a difficult enough trip and in some areas dangerous (although not as dangerous as it used to be a few years back before its development and the replacement of ladders and cables). It is not recommended for beginners and those with balance disorders. Ideally, you should go in the dry season, when you can make use of the parched riverbed.

TRANSFĂGĂRĂŞAN HIGHWAY

The high-altitude Transfăgărăşan highway (DN 7C), stretching more than 91.5km over the ridges of the Făgăraş Mountains at altitudes of over 2,000m, links Muntenia (Argeş County) to Transylvania (Sibiu County).

After exiting the city of Curtea de Argeş, the road follows the Argeşului Gorge (5km), then runs past the Vidraru Dam and Reservoir, constructed between 1961 and 1966 on the Argeş River. The reservoir, 14km long and 155m deep, is 850m above sea level and is surrounded by the sheer slopes of the Clăbucet, Vidraru, Pleşa, Călugăru, Paltinu and Lăcşoru Peaks. Building the 166m high dam took five years, and 42 kilometres of tunnels had to be dug beneath it. It was one of the "great achievements" of the communist era, one that communist officials liked to boast about when foreign heads of state came to visit. On top of Mount Pleşa there is a statue of Prometheus (or the Electricity Monument) victoriously raising a lightning bolt above his head. From a pier on the lake you can take boat trips. Those interested in bungee jumping can do so from a 166m-high platform. And those looking for accommodation can stay at the Vidraru floating Hotel: a 20-cabin boat.

After the reservoir and dam, the road through the mountains has long and spectacular bends, which are photographed by countless tourists.

Near the Capra (Goat) Waterfall you will find the Capra Chalet, where Nicolae Ceauşescu stayed during his chamois hunting parties. You will then pass through the longest road tunnel in Romania – Capra-Bâlea (887m), which needed 20 tonnes of dynamite. The tunnel takes you close to the Bâlea glacial lake, which is 360m long, 240m wide and 11m deep, and is 2,034m above sea level. The Bâlea Chalet was built on a lake peninsula, which receives hundreds of visitors every year. The land around the lake has been declared a nature reserve (180ha). In winter the lake turns into a skating rink and on the northern side of the Bâlea Depression there are ski slopes, recommended only for experienced skiers. In 2006 an ice

Photo: *The spectacular Transfăgărăşan highway*

church, the first of its kind in Romania, and a spectacular Ice Hotel opened here. There are numerous mountain trails leading from here to the peaks and cabins of the Făgăraș Mountains: Capra Saddle (2,315m), Vânătoarea lui Buteanu Peak (2,507m), the Văiuga Depression (2,390m), the Paltinul Saddle (2,044m), and Podragu, Negoiu, and Pârâul Caprei Cabins. After only a 40-minute climb, below the Capra Saddle at an altitude of 2,230m, you will find the Capra glacial lake.

The road descends to the 60m-high Bâlea Waterfall (altitude: 1,234m), the most spectacular in the Făgăraș Mountains. The trail ends in Cârțișoara, Sibiu County, an area of Transylvania where the Saxon villages have fortified churches.

? DID YOU KNOW?

The bends of the Transfăgărășan highway are a challenge for any motorist. The recommended top speed on this road is 40km/h. Bear in mind that the section between the Bâlea Waterfall and Negru Peak is closed from the end of October to June, because of the high risk of rockslides, landslides and avalanches. From the Bâlea Waterfall (1,234m) you can take a cable car, over a distance of 3,800m, to Bâlea Lake (altitude: 2,034m).

CÂMPULUNG MUSCEL

The old commercial road, which in the Middle Ages linked Transylvania and Wallachia, began in Brașov (➤112) and ended in Câmpulung, the capital of Basarab I (1330-1352), the first ruler of Wallachia. It was along this road that the *Letter of Neacșu of Câmpulung* (considered to be the oldest Romanian text to have been preserved) was taken to Brașov in 1521, where it was delivered to Mayor Johannes (Hans) Benckner.

In 1369, in the reign of Vladislav I, the capital of the country was moved from Curtea de Argeș (➤53) to Câmpulung (Campolongo – Longfield), thus named because of the field stretching through the high hills (Măţău, Cetăţuia, Hodor, Flămânda, Ciocanu, Măgura etc.), called *muscele* (rolling hills) by the locals. It is an area of idyllic scenery, overshadowed by the Iezer-Păpușa, Piatra Craiului and Leaota Mountains, whose snowy peaks dominate the skyline.

According to tradition, it was in this community on the Râul Târgului Valley that Negru Vodă is said to have built a monastery in 1215. Later, the **Negru Vodă Monastery** (✉ 64 Negru Vodă Street) was rebuilt by Basarab I, Nicolae Alexandru Basarab, Vlaicu Vodă, Matei Basarab, Grigorie Dimitrie Ghica, and others. The monastery, thought to be one of the oldest monuments of Romanian feudal art, consists of a 35m-high the bell tower, built in 1647 by Matei Basarab; the Princely House, built in 1650 by Matei Basarab, where the first book in Romanian was printed in 1642 in Wallachia (*Învățături pentru toate zilele* – *Everyday Teachings*); the 17th-18th-century abbot's house, refurbished in the Brîncoveanu style in 1745; the monastery inn (1647), demolished to make room for the Dinicu Golescu Highschool; the monastery hospital, dating from 1718, painted by Gheorghe Tattarescu in 1856; and the Royal Church – the only example of Gothic art in Wallachia – built of stone in 1567 at the behest of Lady Chiajna, the wife of ruler Mircea Ciobanu. At the entrance to the monastery complex, you will observe an unusual bas-relief depicting a deer, most likely originating from the no longer extant Catholic Cloașter monastery.

Also remarkable is the feudal complex around the Catholic Church of St. Jacob, part of the former Franciscan **Bărăția Monastery** (14th century), where a tombstone reading: *Hic sepultus est comes Laurencius de Longo Campo* (1300) is preserved. It seems that Mayor Laurentius, the head of the Saxon community, who settled in Câmpulung during the first decades of the 13th century, is buried here. This inscription, the first documented attestation of the town, is the oldest written mediaeval document of Wallachia.

As an old customs point and princely capital, Câmpulung had always enjoyed a privileged position. Up until 1831 it was the only town in the Principalities to be established on the principle of self-administration, governed by a council headed by a judge, assisted by 12 annually elected councillors. The **Cross of the Pledge** on Negru Vodă Street, erected in 1674, during the reign of Gheorghe Ghica, testifies to the town's privileges of self-determination. Each newly elected mayor of the town had to swear before this cross to fight "to defend the unalienable rights of the Câmpulung people".

What better location for an **Ethnographic and Folk Art Museum** (✉ 5 Republicii Street ☎0248.811737 🕑 Tue-Sun: 9am-5pm) than a typical Câmpulung building – the Ștefănescu House (1735), the oldest civil structure in the town, where you can see a rustic kitchen, wooden furniture, old tools, pottery made at Costești, Băilești and Poienița, traditional costume, and more.

The beautiful **Golescu Villa** (✉ 3 Soldat Golescu Street), built in 1910 in the neo-Romanian style on a small hill overlooking the town, belonged to one of the oldest Wallachian families, whose history stretches back to the 15th century. The house is surrounded by a two-hectare terraced dendrological park, with rare and exotic trees acclimatised by engineer Vasile Golescu, the owner of the house. In 2004, Irina and Elena Golescu, the last descendants of the family, donated the house to the Pro Patrimonio Foundation, which has restored it and put it on the tourist map.

The Elie Mirea Villa (✉35 Matei Basarab Street) was designed by architect Ion Mincu.

Four kilometres south of the town, on the DN73 to Pitești, the remains of **Jidava Castrum** have been preserved. It used to be part of the *Limes Transalutanus* (a line of defences guarding the border of the Roman province of Dacia along the Olt River) and defended the road to the Bran Pass.

Just 8km from Câmpulung, **Nămăiești** village is famous for its cave hermitage, which dates back to the 16th century (1547). Traces of the original murals, in the naive style, can still be seen on the exterior walls. The hermitage preserves a miracle-working icon of the Mother of God, attributed to Luke the Evangelist; a cross from 1601, built near the spire by Radu Postelnicu; old books and manuscripts. Some historians believe that the monastery church was located on the site of a Christian catacomb from Roman times. There is an interesting legend about the name of Nămăiești Monastery. St Andrew the Apostle is said to have entered the cave to see whether

Photo: *The Church of Negru Vodă Monastery, Câmpulung Muscel*

there were any pagans inside whom he could bring back to "the right path"; not finding anyone, he left the icon of the Mother of God and Holy Infant as a sign of his passing. On emerging, he is supposed to have said to his companions, in Latin: *Nemo est* (*There is nobody inside*), whence the name Nămăiești. In Nămăiești you can also visit the George Topârceanu Museum, in the house where the poet wrote *Ballads Merry and Sad.*

The **Mateiaș Mausoleum**, 11km from the town, on the way to the Rucăr-Bran Pass, was erected to commemorate the fallen heroes of World War I.

The **Cetățuia Negru-Vodă Monastery** (or the Cetățuia Monastery) perches on top of an 881-metre-high rock on the left bank of the Dîmbovița, 22km southeast of Câmpulung. A quite steep path leads to the top, between huge, strangely shaped rocks that have tumbled down the river valley. The path forks, with one trail leading to the Chiliilor Valley, where several hermits settled, including Ioanichie, whose remains were discovered in a small cave halfway up a large cliff face, and the other to a cave church, 12m long, 4m wide and 3m high, said to have been built by voivode Negru Vodă, who founded it around the 13th century. It is worth noting a very unusual feature in the narthex: a Catholic altar, carved in the rock for Lady Clara, the wife of Nicolae Basarab, who was of the Catholic faith. The place is shrouded in legends, some with a basis in historical fact. In the period from from the feast of the Life Giving Spring to the Dormition of the Theotokos, water springs from the altar to form a tiny stream. Behind the main church there is a small cave carved into the cliff. It is called the Old Man's Cave or Zalmoxis' Cave. On the wall at the back you can see the figure of the Thracian Knight (worship of whom stretched from the Carpathians to the Mediterranean) and Negru Vodă's footprints embedded in the rock. South of the complex a new church has been built, which fails to blend into the surroundings, and a row of cells,

which seem to have dispensed with the simplicity of monastic life. Farther down, on top of a rock, a large cross has been preserved, said to have been erected by Negru Vodă himself; at its base there is a large rock that locals call the Table of Michael the Brave.

At the end of the DJ731, which branches off the Câmpulung–Curtea de Argeș road, you will find another impressive cave monument: the **Corbii de Piatră Monastery** in Jgheaburi village, dating from the 14th century. The church on the left bank of the Doamnei River is dug deep into a huge boulder, 30m high and 14m long. The interior murals, in the purest Byzantine style, have been preserved. Unusually, the nave has two altars.

THE RUCĂR-BRAN PASS

For 22.5 km between Bran and Rucăr there stretches a fairy tale realm, with rustic dwellings dotted along a mountain pass overshadowed on one side by the Piatra Craiului Mountains and on the other by the Bucegi Mountains. Hundreds of years ago, a famous commercial road used to pass through here, connecting the towns of Câmpulung (➤56) and Brașov (➤112). Today, this area of rolling hills, where flocks are still herded by shepherds well versed in the ancient art of making rounds of cheese in pine-bark collars, has become one of Romania's most popular tourist attractions.

Little villages such as **Cheia, Măgura, Drumul Carului, Peştera, Fundata, Fundăţica, Şirnea, Ciocanu, Podu Dîmboviţei** and **Dîmbovicioara** are now serious rivals to the renowned mountain resorts. What sets this place apart is the rural culture that has been preserved intact despite the tourism boom. Although they have opened their houses to outsiders and accepted the market forces of rural tourism, the villagers continue to herd their flocks, make delicious cheeses, and process wool. Every year, at the end of August, in Fundata – an old pastoral settlement – the Feast of the Mountain (*Nedeia munţilor*) is celebrated, bringing together the villagers from all over the area to chat and listen to folk music, take part in the *hora* (ring dance), admire traditional garb and sell their wares.

Bran, the village that attracts the most visitors in the region, is an ancient settlement of sheep breeders, which continues to be influenced by the transhumance. Every year, on the last Saturday of September, the *Scattering of the Sheep* festival is held (when the sheep return to lower plains and are redistributed to their owners) and the best livestock breeder is chosen. You can also take part in the *St. Panteleimon Fair* on 9 August, the *Sîmbra oilor Festival* (a sheep and wool festival) in September, the *Archangels Michael and Gabriel Fair* on 8 November, and the Days of Bran in August. If you want to learn more about local traditions, take the one-day *"At the Artisans'"* trip, where you will learn the secrets of the furrier's trade, weaving, knitting, needlework, and woodworking. You will learn how to paint Easter eggs in the Bran style, weave wicker basket, make traditional masks and dolls, and paint icons on glass and wood.

In the Porţii Valley, around four km from Bran, there is a small (800m) but modern ski slope with ski lifts. To get to the Zănoaga ski slope, take our advice and leave your car behind: take one of the horse-drawn sleighs from the centre of Bran or from outside your B&B.

Take a stroll through the villages of the Bran commune – Poarta, Predeluţ, Şimon, Sohodol – and admire the superb Transylvanian country houses dotted over the hills and valleys. The centre of each village is dominated by an old church, built by shepherds in the 18th century. Hikers will not be disappointed: three marked trails lead from Poarta village to Omu Peak (Bucegi Mountains). You can also make your way up into the Bucegi Mountains from Şimon village.

From Bran you can go to **Zărneşti** (20km away), whence you can reach the Piatra

Photo: *Rucăr-Bran Pass*

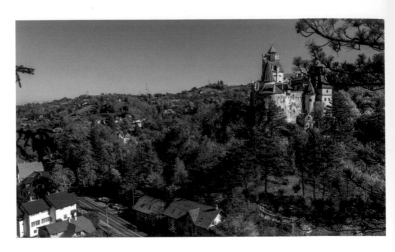

Craiului Mountains, the most spectacular massif in the Romanian Carpathians. A secluded limestone crest, the massif stretches for 25km, as far as Podu Dîmboviței. Consisting of limestone from the Jurassic, the massif is famous for its 160 caves (including Dîmbovicioarei, Urșilor, Dracilor, Stanciului) and 23 gorges (including Dîmboviței, Dîmbovicioarei, Peșterii, Brusturetului).

However, Bran's main attraction is **Bran Castle** (www.castelulbran.ro ✉ 24 General Traian Moșoiu Street, 📞 0268.237700 🕐 Mon: 12am-4pm, Tue-Sun: 9am-4pm (Oct-Mar), Mon: 12pm-6pm, Tue-Sun: 9am-6pm (Apr-Sept) 💰 30 Lei), built in 1212 on a 60-metre-high cliff by a Teutonic knight named Dietrich or Theodoric. Today, Bran Castle is synonymous with Vlad the Impaler, alias Dracula, although its history has very little to do with the historical figure. In 1377, the Saxons of the Bârsa Land, who had conquered the Teutonic knights' fortress at the end of the 13th century, built a stone citadel on the site. In the 15th century it became a stronghold during the Ottoman invasions. Later, Iancu of Hunedoara (1441-1456) repaired and consolidated Bran, then commissioned Vlad the Impaler, who had lost the throne of Wallachia, to defend southern Transylvania; it may well be that at this time the Impaler sojourned at Bran, which was an important border crossing, but there is no historical record of it. Prince Gabriel Bethlen (1613-1629) renovated the castle in the Renaissance style. Finally, in 1651, Prince Rákóczy II (1648-1660) sold it to the town of Brașov, which administered the castle for many years.

Although the initial purpose of the castle was solely military, in time its commercial role became more important, as it was a customs post on the border between Transylvania and Wallachia. After the customs office was moved from Bran to Giuvala, the castle lost its commercial clout.

On 1 December 1920, the City Council of Brașov donated Bran Castle to Queen Maria, in token of gratitude for her contribution to the Great Union of 1 December 1918. Between 1920 and 1927 the Queen converted it into her summer residence, with the help of the architect to the Royal Court, Karel Líman, who was in charge of restoration. The military appearance of the mediaeval castle was played down and the interiors underwent a radical transformation. The Gothic and the Renaissance styles blended with the rustic Transylvanian style.

In the castle grounds you will find the **Bran Village Museum** (🕐 Daily: 10am-6pm), which features a range of country houses and traditional 19th-century facilities (for wood and wool processing, for example).

In 1987, the **Customs Museum** (Daily: 9am-6pm, mid-April – mid-Oct) opened in the old mediaeval customs house in Bran. Merchandise headed to Flanders, Germany, Turkey, the Middle East and so on once had to pass through here. Documents on the type of goods shipped through the Bran Pass, maps, mediaeval coins, seals, measuring instruments, and means of transportation are all on display here.

THE MUD VOLCANOES

Along the Carpathian Arc, within the communes of Berca and Scorțoasa in Buzău, there are two plateaux (Pâclele Mici and Pâclele Mari) dotted with miniature volcanoes, whose domes reach up to 6m. Gas erupting from the ground squirts mud and water, which bubble away over the brim. This unique phenomenon has created a spectacular lunar landscape. Scorched by the sun, streams of slurry dry up in silver traces, excavating dry valleys with sulphur and salt-saturated soil, which allows only two salt-tolerant plant species to grow: *Nitraria schoberi* and *Obione verrucifera*. The Pâclele Mici Reserve covers 16.5ha, and the Pâclele Mari Reserve 22ha.

Leading from the Pâclele Mici car park, a footpath takes you 500m to heights covered with tirelessly roiling craters. Some ten metres from the Pâclele Mari there is a restaurant and guesthouse.

ȚARA LUANEI (THE CAVE HERMITAGES OF THE BUZĂU MOUNTAINS)

There are around 30 cave churches nestling in the Buzău Mountains, near the villages of Colți, Aluniș, Bozioru and Nucu. These enigmatic structures from the dawn of Christianity are Romania's Mount Athos.

The Cave of Dionysius the Spinner, reached by a rickety wooden ladder, the Fundul Peșterii cave, which preserves the marks of Akinakes daggers and 4th-century inscriptions, Iosif's Cave, Agatonul Vechi and Agatonul Nou, Ghereta, Fundătura and Piatra Îngăurită are all places where various pre-Christian rituals were performed and where hermits later used to pray.

Known as Țara Luanei (the Land of Luana), after a legendary king who is said to have lived here, the area preserves traces of 4,000-year-old settlements. Look closely and you will discover inscriptions, signs and symbols (such as the fish or the cross) carved here and there, and rocks of various shapes

Left: *The Mud Volcanoes*

Right: *Dionisie Torcătorul's cave*

The **Cozia Monastery**, on the right bank of Olt River, was built between 1387 and 1388 by master builders from Moravia. A tri-conch in plan, it is based on the Serbian church at Kruševac. It is the most beautiful achievement of voivode Mircea the Elder, whose tomb is in the narthex. In the nave, a fresco on the right wall depicts Mircea the Elder dressed in the garb of a Western mediaeval knight alongside his son, Mihail. The courtyard preserves a fountain, said to have been built by Neagoe Basarab.

Horezu Ceramics

Horezu is home to Romania's most important centre of traditional pottery. Horezu pottery became a genuine Oltenia brand in 2012, when it was included in the UNESCO list of Intangible Cultural Heritage. After the pots are shaped on the wheel, they are fired and painted with traditional motifs using a cattle horn tipped with a goose quill and natural pigments. Every year on the first Sunday of June, the municipality hosts the *Cocoşul de Hurezi Fair (Hurezu Cock)*.

(ancient altars, sundials, phalluses). Local guides (Diana Gavrilă ☎ 0749-911898) will tell you their stories and guide you along the winding paths of this place shrouded in legend and mystery, and which is also rich in stunning scenery.

And these are not the only attractions: in Colți there is an Amber Museum; at Bozioru there are odd-looking rocks; Țurțudui Peak offers glorious panoramic views; and the Salt Cave, which covers a few kilometres in area, can be found on the Meledic Plateau, in Mânzălești.

NORTHERN OLTENIA

Although not as well known, the land of Northern Oltenia is not short of surprises. Here you will discover numerous monasteries and hermitages, the unparalleled Hurezi Monastery (►63), which is a UNESCO site, resorts boasting waters that "work miracles", villages with old wooden churches, caves, and glorious gorges and river passes. Over 2,000 underground karst landforms have been identified in Oltenia.

The course of the ancient *Alutus River* (today's Olt) will lead you via ancient ruins – the remains of the *Limes Alutanus* chain of Roman castra – all the way to the Danube. The Drobeta, Romula and Arutela (Bivolari) Castra have survived in a better condition than elsewhere in the old Roman province.

Top: *Cozia Monastery*   Bottom: *Potter from Horezu shaping a clay pot*

Hurezi Monastery

In the village of Romanii de Jos, 3km from Horezu, you can visit the most important complex of Romanian mediaeval architecture, which defines the Brîncoveanu style: Hurezi Monastery (1690-1703), a UNESCO World Heritage site. Lying at the foot of the Căpăţânii Mountains, in the middle of a forest, the complex comprises the church of the *Ss Constantine and Helen* (1690-94), the chapel of the *Nativity of the Theotokos* (1697), the hospital church (founded in 1696-99 by Maria Brîncoveanu), the *Hermitage of Ss Peter and Paul the Apostles* (1698), the *Saint Stephen Hermitage* (1703), the Princely House, and Dionisie Bălăcescu's Belvedere (1752-1753). In the time of Constantine Brîncoveanu (1688-1714), Hurezi Monastery was a major centre of culture: it had a famous scriptorium, a school for scribes, secretaries and grammarians, a school for painters, which trained the master painters who decorated some of the most important churches of the 18th century, and a rich library (4,000 books), unique in South-Eastern Europe in the early 18th century.

The museum collection within the Hurezi Monastery contains old church items (books, icons painted on wood, precious textiles), some dating back to when the monastery was founded.

Behind the monumental **Bistriţa Monastery** complex, built by the Craioveşti boyar family in the 15th century, there is a steep path leading to the Cave of Bats, which conceals two tiny 18th-century churches (whose patron feasts are the Archangels and the Entry into the Temple of the Theotokos), which have been declared historical monuments. The cave is home to a colony of over 700 bats of seven different species. Traces of the prehistoric Coţofeni culture and cave bear fossils have also been found here.

On the road that follows the Bistriţa River towers the spectacular 1.5-km-long **Bistriţa Gorge**. One of the narrowest gorges in the country, the sheer limestone rocks are renowned for their rare plant and animal species and also for their 22 caves.

Just 4km from the Bistriţa Monastery, at the end of a road full of hairpin turns that climbs through the Căpăţânii Mountains, you will find the **Arnota Monastery**, built by Matei Basarab and Lady Elina in 1633-1634.

At Costeşti (Vâlcea County) you can survey the trovants or "growing rocks" as the local farmers call them. The **Concretions Museum** features odd-looking rock formations, some up to 10m high, mainly consisting of cemented sand dating back to Late Miocene.

Below the Polovragi Rock, in the middle of an orchard of chestnut trees, lies the **Polovragi Monastery**, built in 1505. To the right of the monastery, a forest road leads towards the two-kilometre-long **Olteţ Gorge**, which is pierced by 86 caves (most of them, unfortunately, inaccessible). The perimeter is home to a flower reserve with over 300 plant species typically found in limestone areas: the rustyback fern, wall-rue, clove pink, wild wallflower, clotbur, European Michaelmas daisy etc. Nearby stretches a centuries-old wood of chestnut trees, and 4km to the south, a meadow of daffodils. The most interesting example of

Photo: *Arnota Monastery*

karst geomorphology in the Olteț Valley is the **Polovragi Cave** (also known as the Cave of Pachomius), once an underground meander of the Olteț, cut into the left side of the gorge. On top of the cave, at an altitude of 1,000m, there are the ruins of a fortress (Argina) rumoured to have belonged to Zalmoxis. To get there, follow the trail marked by a red strip. It is worth it: the climb takes only 20 minutes. In the fortress, which dates back to the 2nd and 1st centuries B.C., iron tools and weapons, grey Dacian ceramics, coins, and a bronze plaque depicting the Knights of the Danube have been unearthed.

On the Stârmina peak in the Vâlcan Mountains near the Gurnia Waterfall stands the **Tismana Monastery**, built between 1375 and 1378 by monk Nicodim. Around it developed one of the most important mediaeval monastic schools. The Tismana chestnut wood and the Turkish hazel

reserve are part of an area under the influence of the Mediterranean climate.

In other secluded corners of Oltenia, monks withdrew into the wilderness, building hermitages: Turnu, Stânișoara, Ostrov, Bradu, Iezeru, Pahomie, Mamu, Dobrușa, Păpușa, Lainici, Pătrunsa, Cornetu.

To the north of Baia de Fier, at the mouth of the Galbenului Gorge, you will find the most visited speleological site in Romania after Bears Cave in Bihor: the **Women's Cave**. Evidence has been found to show that it was inhabited in the Middle Palaeolithic (bone skeletons), and *Ursus spelaeus* skeletons. The explanation for its name is that long ago, when the men went to war, the cave served as a refuge for women and children. The cave galleries are around 3,600m long and are on four levels. The lowest level is the Speleological Scientific Reserve and is not open to tourists, but you can visit the Small Dome (a sort of a Gothic dome), the Altar Chamber (with its Icon Screen, Great Chandelier, and Organ), the Bloody Rock, the Vault (echoing to the sounds of a colony of bats), the Great Basins, the Petrified Waterfall, the Turk's Chamber, the Chamber of Wonders, the Jellyfish Column, the Endless Column, the Silver Ceiling, the Bears Gallery, the Chamber of Pearls, and other wonders.

At Ponoare in Mehedinți County look out for **God's Bridge** – a huge vault left standing after the walls of a large cave collapsed. Also unique in Romania is the **Ponoare Lilac Wood**, a plant reserve located four kilometres from Baia de Aramă, a town where every year in the first half of May there is a Lilac Festival.

Oltenia still celebrates old pastoral festivals: the return of the sheep from higher pastures, at Baia de Fier, on the third Sunday of September; moving the sheep into the mountains, at Novaci, in May; and *Nedeia* (Feast of the Mountains) at Polovragi.

Peculiar to Oltenia are the *cule* (fortified boyar houses), also found in the lowlands of some Latin countries such as Italy, France and Spain.

Top: *Tismana Monastery*   **Bottom:** *God's Bridge*

The *Cule* of Oltenia

The *cule* (from the Turkish *kule*, "tower"), built by the old boyar families of Oltenia, combine elements of peasant, civil and military architecture. These fortified dwellings – miniature family citadels – were designed to defend against raids by Turkish marauders, who in the 18th century used to cross the Danube from the Ottoman camps in Bulgaria. The cule of Greceanu, Duca, Bujoreni, Poenaru, Izvoranu, Cernătescu, Cornoiu, Crăsnaru, Tudor Vladimirescu, Cuțui, Galița and Zătreni are now tourist attractions.

Oltenia`s health resorts – Călimănești-Căciulata, Olănești, Govora and Voineasa – have been rediscovered by tourists and regained their popularity. The mineral springs of Călimănești-Căciulata, a resort lying in the small Sub-Carpathian depression of Jiblea, 260m above sea level, was founded in 1827. From here you can set off hiking through the Cozia Mountains up to the Stânișoara Monastery, founded in the vicinity of the former sheepfold of the Cozia Monastery (▶62), the Nettle Waterfall, with a 30m drop, and the Cozia Cabin (1600m).

Olănești Baths, also called the "Golden Springs", are located in the Olănești Depression, in the foothills of the Căpățânii Mountains, 430-475m above sea level.

The peak of a mountain near the resort is home to a wooden church (Horea's Church) brought from Albac (1746). It has a 21-metre spire, another stunning example of religious architecture in the Romanian rustic style. You should also stop off at the St. Nicholas Church (1718), built by Drăghici Olănescu, which still has its original murals and a carved wooden door dating back to 1729, and make time to look at the old local houses built in the local traditional style, which are dotted around the resort (the Bădescu House – 1718, the Olănescu House – 19th century). The villages (Cheia, Pietrișu etc.) around the resort preserve many 18th-century churches, built and decorated in the post-Brîncoveanu style.

The **Govora Resort**, located where the Hința and Govora valleys meet, is surrounded by hills thickly wooded with beech, oak and pine. Here you can visit the Gheorghe Petre Archaeology and Feudal Art Collection, the Palace Hotel and the Bath Pavilion (late-19th century), designed by architect Ernest Doneaud. A road fringed with oak trees will take you 6km to the **Govora Monastery**, whose thick walls, tall tower and fortified gates lend it the appearance of a citadel. Matei Basarab set up a printing press within the monastery, which in 1640 printed the *Govora Code of Laws*, the oldest codex of ecclesiastical laws in Romanian to be printed in Wallachia.

Left: *The cula of Duca, Măldărești*

Right: *Govora Monastery*

Numerous trails lead from the **Voineasa** and **Vidra** resorts to nearby peaks: White Rocks, Mănăileasa Mare, Chica Lupului, Puru, Frătoşteanu Mare, Vânăta.

Travellers arriving in **Târgu Jiu** will be able to admire four masterpieces by Constantin Brâncuşi. He was born in Hobiţa and was one of the most important modern sculptors. His art was imbued with the spirit of tradition. He knew how to blend the simplicity of Oltenian folk art with the refined Parisian avant-garde, having a profound impact on the modern concept of shape in sculpture. *The Table of Silence, The Lane of Chairs, The Gate of the Kiss* and *The Endless Column* stand on a 1,275-metre-long east-west axis. The ensemble is a tribute to the fallen heroes of World War I. In the courtyard of court victualler Barbu Gănescu (18th century), where Constantin Brâncuşi lived between 1936 and 1938, there are 24 stone chairs, a round table, and two stone benches. The house of bread-maker Dimitrie Măldărescu (1710) is currently home to the School of Folk Art. The church of the Merchants (the Princely Cathedral) was built between 1748 and 1764, renovated in 1843, and painted between 1933 and 1940 by Mişu Popp and Iosif Keber in the Renaissance style. The iron bridge over the Jiu River was built between 1894 and 1895.

SOUTHERN OLTENIA

Craiova is at the heart of Oltenia and one of the most beautiful cities in Romania. Although attested in documents only since 1475, Craiova's history is much older; in the 4th century B.C. it was the site of the Dacian citadel of Pelendava. In the 15th century it became the administrative capital of Oltenia. The Princely Church was built between 1651 and 1652 by Matei Basarab. Destroyed in the 1838 earthquake, it was rebuilt by the French architect André Lecomte du Noüy between 1889 and 1893. Today, it is the Metropolitan See of Oltenia. The murals of the St. Elijah Church (1720) were painted by Gheorghe Tattarescu, one of the greatest Romanian painters of the 19th century. The Art Museum, housed in a palace built in 1896 and designed by French architect Paul Gottereau, has six sculptures by Constantin Brâncuşi. The House of the Great Ban, built in 1699 by Constantine Brîncoveanu, is now home to the Ethnographic and Folk Art Museum. Some of the civic buildings of Craiova may be considered genuine historical monuments: the Glogoveanu House, the Jianu House, the former Bank of Commerce (the present-day City Hall), the former Palace of Justice (the present-day University) and the Administrative Palace (the present-day County Hall and the

Photo: *Administrative Palace, Craiova*

County Council building of Dolj County). Romanescu Park, laid out between 1900 and 1903 and designed by French architect Emile Redont, stretches over 90 hectares and is one of the largest and most beautiful parks in the country. The Coșuna Monastery (formerly Bucovăț), located on the outskirts of Craiova, in the Mofleni district, dates back to 1483. Archaeologists have established that it was built on the site of the old Pelendava castrum, whence the stone was taken to build the foundations and bricks for the base and walls.

No Romanian would think of the town as a tourist destination, but **Slatina** has a number of surprises. Nestling between hills on the banks of the Olt River, it is home to a remarkable old quarter (Lipscani and Mihai Eminescu streets), which in its decay has preserved the atmosphere of times long passed. A visit to 25, Dinu Lipatti Street to buy *bragă* (beverage made from fermented grains) is a must. It is sold by the celebrated *Albanese Athlete* sweetshop, established three generations ago by the Memish family. Hashim Memish has tended the shop for more than fifty years and will be keen to tell you stories about old Slatina. The Clocociov Monastery (1645) is hidden away in a valley between two mountain slopes south of Slatina, and the Strehareț Hermitage (1668) is undisturbed in the middle of a forest, 1.5km north of the town. If you ever find yourselves in the area, give Slatina a chance! Did you know that this is where playwright Eugène Ionesco was born?

Twenty kilometres south-west of Slatina, look out for the **Brîncoveni Monastery**. It has a stone church built in 1699 by Constantine Brîncoveanu.

Despite the ironic smiles that the mere mention **Caracal** brings to many people's face (as the saying goes, it was at Caracal that the cart carrying fools overturned and spilled its load), the town is well worth a brief visit. Why? To admire the run-down but still splendid houses on the Iancu Jianu Street. To see a play at the superb

Theatre House, built between 1896 and 1901 and designed by Austrian architect Franz Bileck. To have a look at ruins of the Princely Court at 3, Mihai Viteazu Street, where the Matei Basarab, Constantine Brîncoveanu and Michael the Brave had their capital. To take a stroll through the romantic Constantin Poroineanu Park. And last, but not least, to visit the Romanați Museum, at 24, Iancu Jianu Street, which exhibits archaeological finds relating to the Vădastra culture.

Heading 25km north-east of Caracal, look out for the Neolithic village reconstructed within the premises of the Câmpia Boianului Museum at **Drăgănești-Olt**, founded by professor Traian Zorzoliu. The six huts (a fisherman's, farmer's, potter's, etc.) made of woven reed and earth, were built on a land enclosed by a defensive ditch and wattle fence, access being via a wooden bridge. As the Neolithic dwellings typical of the Gumelnița culture were erected on floodplains, a floating house was indispensable and served to store food supplies.

Photo: *Brîncoveni Monastery*

The Romanian tradition of the *Căluş* (the Horseman's Dance)

The *Căluş* (the Horseman's Dance), declared by UNESCO to be part of the World's Intangible Cultural Heritage, is a ritual performed in southern Romania, in summer, starting with Pentecost. Groups of young men (always an odd number and observing a strict hierarchical order, each with a separate role: the Mute, the Vătaf (the Master), the Master's apprentice, the Flag-bearer etc.) perform the *Căluş* dance – an ancient ritual with magical functions. In a clear state of euphoria, the *căluşari* dance until exhausted, to music played by gypsy musicians. The dance features clicking of the heels, stamping and leaping and is accompanied by chants. In the past, it was believed that this dance had healing powers, drove out evil spirits (and also witches), and restored soil fertility. It is the oldest Romanian folk dance. It is thought that it is a military dance passed down from the Dacians or the Romans, or that it is the heritage of a Roman or Egyptian drama representing the abduction of the Sabine women or the murder of the god Osiris by Seth.

A plain-looking and uninteresting lowland town, **Alexandria** comes alive each August thanks to the enthusiastic high-school students who take part in the Ideo Ideis National Youth Theatre Festival, launched in 2006. The Community Centre, a remnant of the communist past, hosts drama workshops, choreography, play-writing and visual education.

The almost 100 gypsy mansions flanking the road through the tiny community of **Buzescu**, 10km from Alexandria, have acquired worldwide fame after they featured in an issue of *National Geographic*. They have yet to be connected to the water supply and sanitation infrastructure, but they vie with each other to be the tallest and most kitschy, in an absurd abundance of pagoda-like towers, plaster lions and eagles, marble fences, golden statues, blaring colours and other decorations in dubious taste.

Corabia, a small and old port along the Danube, due to be revived with European funds, becomes the "Linden Town" for two months a year, in May and June, when its more than 4,000 old linden trees flood the town with their beautiful perfume. In the Celei district, at the southern end of the town, on the left bank of the Danube, the ruins of the Dacian citadel of Sucidava, the capital of the Gaeto-Dacian tribe of the Suci, have been preserved. Nearby, emperor Constantine the Great built the longest bridge over the Danube. There is a 26-metre-long corridor to a secret well, 18m deep, dug in the 6th century, so that in times of siege the locals would have access to a spring outside the walls, whose waters were tapped and brought up to the citadel.

On the remains of the former grain terminal dating from 1880, which came close to falling into disuse in the 1990s, poet Mircea Dinescu has founded an art colony (The Cetate Culture Port), currently famous for events that bring together sculptors, writers, painters and musicians, but also for lively parties accompanied by the Mambo Siria band of Roma musicians, wines from the estate's vineyards, and traditional fine foods showcased by poet Dinescu in his own unique style.

Photo: *Performing the* Căluş *dance*

THE DANUBE KAZAN GORGE

The show put on by the Danube River along the course of its wild gorge along the south-western border of Romania, between Drobeta-Turnu Severin and Baziaş is mind-blowing to say the least. The most spectacular section is the Kazan (or Kazan Gorge): for 9km, the Danube squeezes its way through the sheer sides of the Small (310m) and Great Ciucaru (318m) Mountains on the Romanian side and the Mali Štrbac (626m) and Veliki Štrbac (768m) on the Serbian bank. The width of the Small and Large Kazans upstream and downstream of Dubova does not exceed 150-350m. In the past, the waters used to boil and foam, as if in a fisherman's cauldron: whence the name Kazan (Cauldron).

The building of the Iron Gates I Dam near Gura Văii between 1964 and 1971 raised the water level by 33m. It thus solved the issue of navigating the Danube, previously a difficult and perilous endeavour due to rocks, sediment, whirlpools and all kinds of natural obstacles. Unfortunately, this human intervention on nature led to the sacrifice by drowning of part of ancient civilisation. Forever lost under the waters of the Danube, the Ada Kaleh Island was a typical Turkish settlement, right in the middle of the river! Many villages had to be relocated, with their inhabitants forced to leave the homes they grew up in.

The *Tabula Traiana* (Trajan's Plaque) has been preserved on one bank of the Danube, carved in stone by the Romans on their way to Dacia. The impressive effigy of king Decebalus (40m high and 25m wide), carved in 1998, looms where the Mraconia River meets the Danube.

The charm of the southern border of Romania partly lies in the scenic villages (Belobreşca, Pojejena, Coronini, Berzasca, Drencova, Dubova, Eşelniţa) along the Danube, as well as in the unmistakable atmosphere of the local ethnic communities of Romanians, Serbians, Czechs, Bulgarians and so on, who have been able to live in peace with each other.

The area surrounding the Kazans has been declared a nature reserve; it is home to the Oriental beech, the European yew, lilacs, Hungarian tulips, fig trees, and date trees. The Egyptian vulture and the horned viper can also be found in this habitat.

The city of **Drobeta-Turnu Severin**, on the bank of the Danube, is a genuine open-air museum. The Romans turned the ancient Dacian settlement of Drobeta into an important military centre. Close to the Danube, there are still remnants of the bridge built between 103 and 105 by Apollodorus of Damascus, the Roman castrum (2nd-5th century), Theodora's Tower (6th century), the Roman thermal baths, and the mediaeval citadel. On Şimian Island, downstream from Drobeta-Turnu Severin, can be found part of the 14th-century fortifications on the Ada Kaleh Island, which sank beneath the waters of the Danube after the Iron Gates I Dam was built.

Photo: *Danube Kazan Gorge*

Dobruja and the Danube Delta

Previous page: *Fisherman in the Danube Delta*

Dobruja and the Danube Delta

Mostly unknown, even to Romanians, Dobruja, located in south-eastern Romania between the Danube and the Black Sea, is probably the most original and mysterious of all the country's regions. It is the most visited by tourists, especially in summer, but, ironically, the least explored. Its access to the Black Sea and the stunning Danube Delta alone would have been enough to guarantee its complete success with the tourists. Beyond the barren appearance of these lands scorched by dry and hot winds you will be able to discover the magical endless expanses of the local steppe, fields carpeted with poppies and sunflowers, the mysterious tumuli of the nomadic Scythians, and landscapes that are an unspoiled wilderness.

The top natural attraction is the Danube Delta, described as amazing by all those who have delved into its maze of channels, marshes, lakes, sandbars and endless reed corridors. Wild and luxurious vegetation, harking back to the beginning of the world, blankets these expanses of land and water. A paradise for plants and wildlife, UNESCO has declared the Danube Delta one of the world's Biosphere Reserves.

Romania enjoys the rare privilege of having a long border along the Black Sea coast (around 240km). Along Romania's southern coast, stretching from Midia Cape to Vama Veche, there are both untamed rocky shores and exotic beaches of fine sand. The Mamaia, Năvodari, Northern Eforie, Southern Eforie, Olimp, Costineşti. Neptun, Jupiter, Venus, Saturn and Mangalia resorts are packed with thousands of tourists who come here to enjoy the summer sun and seawater.

However, there are tourists who want more than just to sunbathe, or rather, they want something extra. And Dobruja is home to dozens of alternatives to the standard "sea, sun and beach" package. Almost everywhere you turn, you find vestiges of ancient and Byzantine settlements (Orgame/Argamum, Troesmis, Capidava, Ibida, Halmyris, Heracleea etc). This is the area with the highest concentration of archaeological remains in Romania. The oldest settlements on the coast are the colonies established in the 7th and 6th centuries B.C. by Ionian Greeks (Tomis, present-day Constanța; Histria, present-day Istria) and Dorian Greeks (Callatis, present-day Mangalia).

Dobruja is by no means just another giant open-air archaeological reserve. Besides the fact that the dozens of sites bear witness to the historic waves of peoples who passed through these lands – Greeks, Romans, Genoese, Turks, Tartars, etc. – you will also find that they are surrounded by some of the most picturesque communities in Romania. Dobruja is home to many communities of Turks, Tartars, Lipovans, Aromanians, Armenians and Greeks who, thanks to their seclusion, have survived as particularly colourful small ethnic enclaves. There is still a long way before these villages become part of the tourist trail, but do not let that stop you.

After taking the Motorway of the Sun from Bucharest, which in summer is almost always packed with swarms of cars hurrying to reach the seaside resorts, and after crossing the bridge over the Danube at Cernavodă (a marvel of engineering, built by Anghel Saligny in 1885-90), you will begin your Dobruja adventure. Leaving the main road between Cernavodă and Constanța and taking a by-road will give you the opportunity to discover wild corners dotted with ancient ruins, where it is as if humans have not set foot in a very long time. You will follow in the footsteps of the early saints and martyrs, the founders of Christianity on Romanian soil. It is worth exploring this parched land that lies beneath the scorching sun, braving the lack of road signs and bumpy roads, in order to get some idea of these exotic places, which are perfect for archaeological, religious and ethnic tourism alike.

Dobruja Landforms

Even its landforms set Dobruja apart from other Romanian provinces: it has geologically the newest piece of land in the Danube Delta, as well as the oldest mountain range: the Măcin Mountains, a remnant of the Hercynian chain. From the rocky Dobruja Gorge to the Canaraua Fetii, Canaralele Hârşovei, Hagieni Forest and Fântâniţa-Murfatlar Forest nature reserves, from the fossil reserves at Cernavodă and Aliman and the Topalu Neojurassic Reef to the Agigea dunes and Techirghiol, Siutghiol and Taşaul lakes, the region seems to exhaust every possible landform. Beneath these limestone landscapes there are extensive networks caves, with their own particularities: Limanu (➤79), the only labyrinth cave in the country, Movile (➤78), and Adam's Cave in the Dobruja Gorge, featuring an altar dedicated to god Mithras. The subterranean churches in St. Andrew's Cave and Cassian Cave are the oldest places of worship in the region.

A Brief History of Dobruja

Once inhabited by Getae and Scythians, the land known in the ancient times as Scythia Minor (Lesser Scythia) was settled by Greeks in the 7th-6th centuries B.C. and was later part of Burebista's state, of the Roman and Byzantine Empires and then of Wallachia, in the time of Mircea the Elder. You can still sense the oriental flavour over Dobrujan lands, reminiscent of the times when the rulers of the land were Turkish (1417-1878). After the Russo-Turkish war in 1877-1878, Dobruja was returned to Romania.

CONSTANŢA

Constanţa is without a doubt the heart of Dobruja. The ancient Greek colony of Tomis, the most important seaport of the Black Sea basin, has a 12km beach. The current name of the city (Constantia) was adopted in the 4th century, after the Emperor Constantine built here a district called Constantiniana.

? DID YOU KNOW?

The name Tomis was said to be connected with the Legend of Jason, who passed through here with the Argonauts after stealing the Golden Fleece from the king of Colchis (modern-day Georgia), Aeëtes. His daughter, in love with Jason, loyally followed him. Absyrtus, her brother, was killed by the Greek hero and cut into pieces (the Greek verb tomein *means to cut) and thrown in her father's path to force him cease his pursuit. As a matter of fact, it is cannot be ruled out that the name of Cape Midia might refer to Medea. But this remains a legend, without any documented proof…*

Of ancient Tomis, founded by the Greeks and later ruled by the Romans, you can still see the ruins of the citadel and its outer wall in the **Archaeology Park** on Ferdinand Avenue, the Roman baths on Sailors Avenue, and the 4th-century tombstone featuring Christian symbols near the Mircea the Elder High school.

The main square is named after the poet Ovid, who spent the last nine years of his life (8-17 A.D.) in these barbarian lands at the edge of the Roman Empire, which he described in *Tristia* and *Epistulae ex Ponto*. A replica of Ovid's statue found

ere was made and installed at Sulmo, he poet's birthplace. The statue stands utside the former city hall and was lesigned in the neo-Romanian style y architect Ion Mincu; nowadays the building is home to the **History and Archaeology Museum** (www.minac.ro ⬛ 12 Ovid Square 📞 0241.618763 🕐 Wed-un: 8am-8pm (summer), 9am-5pm (winter) ⬛ 10 Lei), which has 24 rooms. The ground oor exhibits the most valuable items: the anagra-style figurine collection (from he early Hellenistic and Roman periods), nthropomorphic pottery, local sculptures iscovered in 1962 (the bust of goddess is, the aedicula representing Nemesis in er dual hypostasis, the statuary ensemble f Fortuna and Pontus, the statue of the nake Glykon (2nd century), representing god of Asian mythology, gold jewellery ollections (rings, earrings, bracelets, endants, little crosses), gems, cameos etc. he upper rooms hold copies of the *Thinker f Hamangia* and the *Sitting Woman statues* damangia culture – Neolithic period) and eramics belonging to the Gumelnița and oian cultures. Next to the Museum there is he **Mosaic Roman Edifice**, which you can sit – a 4th-century emporium, covering 000 square metres, where a room with a plendid 850-square-metre multi-coloured osaic decorated with geometric and oral motives has been preserved.

It is impossible not to be fascinated by the cosmopolitan atmosphere of Constanța. A simple walk through the city will reveal Moorish-style mosques, Armenian churches, Roman Catholic cathedrals, and Romanian, Bulgarian and Greek Orthodox churches.

The **Carol I Mosque** (✉ 5 Arhiepiscopiei Street) was built between 1910 and 1912 in the Arabic and Byzantine style for the Muslim community of Dobruja and is a copy of the Konia mosque in Anatolia. The beautiful carpet of Abdul Hamid II, 9x16m in size and weighing 490kg, is still preserved inside. It was donated by the Sultan to the mosque on Ada Kaleh Island (➤69). A spiral staircase of one hundred and forty steps leads up to the top of the 47-metre minaret, which provides views of the entire city centre.

The **Roman Catholic Church of St. Anthony of Padua** was built between 1935 and 1937, in imitation of 13th-century Roman basilicas in Northern Italy

In the 13th century the Genoese founded a settlement in Constanța, which was soon to thrive, and built the 8m-high **Genoese Lighthouse** (1860), which can still be seen today on the seashore. In the time of Carol I the seaport was modernised under the supervision of engineer Anghel Saligny; it was also the time when many hotels were built,

---

as well as an impressive Art Nouveau **Casino** (1909) which has become the symbol of Constanța. A coastal city could not possibly lack an **Aquarium** (📍20 Lei), with over 100 fish species and marine wildlife (sturgeons, stingrays, small red scorpion fish, starfish, piranhas, knifefish, flame angelfish, shovelnose guitarfish, catfish), and a **Dolphinarium** (www.delfinariu.ro ✉ 255 Mamaia Avenue 🕐 Tue-Sun: 10am-6pm. Dolphin training – Mon-Fri 11:30am; 1:30pm; 3:30pm, Sat-Sun: 11:30am; 1:30pm; 4pm. Planetarium demo – Mon-Fri: 10am; 12:30pm; 2:30pm, Sat-Sun: 10am; 12:30pm; 3pm 📍25 Lei).

The **Art Museum** holds valuable works signed by artists such as Nicolae Grigorescu, Ion Andreescu, Theodor Pallady, Theodor Aman, Dimitrie Paciurea, Ion Jalea, Frederick Storck and Corneliu Baba.

The Ion Jalea Sculpture Museum ✉ 26 Arhiepiscopiei Street ☎ 0241.617012 🕐 Wed-Sun: 10am-6pm, summer; 9am-5pm, winter), is housed in a neo-Romanian style building founded in 1919 and 1920 by Victor Stephanescu and has over one hundred sculptures donated by the Dobrujan artist Ion Jalea to the city of Constanța.

17km south-east of Constanța a series of galleries (churches and cells) carved into the chalkstone of Mount Tibisir has been unearthed, near the Danube-Black Sea Canal. This maze of rooms makes up the Basarabi Murfatlar Monastic Complex, which dates from 992; it is believed that here stood the first monastery on Romanian soil. The walls of the cave churches are covered in interesting inscriptions (in Gothic, Slavonic and Greek letters) and drawings (Christian symbols, geometric shapes), unfortunately deteriorating. For preservation reasons, the complex is not open to tourists.

Elderflower Cordial and *Bragă*

Give up bottled fizzy drinks and try elderflower cordial (*socată*) or, why not, *bragă*. Elderflower cordial is still made at home to this day, using macerated elderflowers; in just a few days it becomes an extremely refreshing fizzy drink. *Bragă* is on the brink of extinction, although in the past it was sold on every street corner. This Balkan beverage is 100% natural, made from fermented millet, and can still be found in places like Constanța, Mangalia, Galați, Slatina (➤67) and Drobeta-Turnu Severin (➤69).

Photo: *Constanța, aerial view of the Casino and Marina*

THE BLACK SEA SHORE

In Antiquity, the Black Sea was called *Pontus Euxinus*, meaning a sea "welcoming", "hospitable", "friendly to foreigners". Along the southern Romanian coast, stretching from the Midia Cape to Vama Veche, there are both untamed rocky shores and exotic beaches of fine sand. Many resorts have sprung up in the area: Mamaia, Năvodari, Northern Eforie, Southern Eforie, Olimp, Costineşti, Neptun, Jupiter, Venus, Saturn and Mangalia.

Mamaia Resort (3km north of Constanţa), located on a sandbar between the Black Sea and Siutghiol Lake, boasts 20% of the Romanian coast's accommodation capacity.

Northern Eforie (14km south of Constanţa) developed after 1894, when the Board of Civil Hospitals in Bucharest built a sanatorium. The two treatment units include hot water bathing facilities (with concentrated salt water from Techirghiol Lake or the sea).

Southern Eforie (18km south of Constanţa) has made its mark thanks to its amazing shoreline, with steps descending to a two-km-long beach. The first health resort in Dobruja was set up here in 1892. It was named Carmen Sylva until 1950 (the pen name of Queen Elizabeth, the wife of King Carol I of Romania).

Costineşti (28km south of Constanţa), located 2-4m above sea level, is a favourite resort for young people. The beach here, which faces south, has sunshine throughout the entire day, a "privilege" only a handful of European beaches enjoy.

Techirghiol (18km south of Constanţa) is a health resort on the shores of a lake known for the healing properties of its rich organic mud. The St. Mary Monastery in Techirghiol, with its beautiful 17th-century Transylvanian wooden church, has a modern treatment facility and provides accommodation. The Techirghiol Lake area is home to the red-breasted goose (*Branta ruficollis*) in winter, one of the rarest species in the world.

Mangalia (44km from Constanţa) developed on the site of the ancient colony of Callatis, founded by the Greeks in the 6th century B.C. and revived by the Genoese in the 13th and 14th centuries. It was called Pangalia, meaning the "most beautiful one" in Byzantine Greek. It is the only seaside resort with mineral spring waters (sulphur springs, mesothermal and radioactive). Mangalia has other attractions apart from the beach: the vestiges of a Roman-Byzantine basilica from the 5th-6th century, the Moorish-style Esmahan Sultan Mosque (1590), and the Archaeology Museum. Three kilometres from the resort you can visit the Mangalia Stud Farm, with a racetrack that offers carriage tours along the seashore.

Venus (3km north of Mangalia) is a beautiful natural amphitheatre on a promontory sloping down to the shore. At the northern end of the resort there is a pavilion for mud baths, using sapropelic mud, and sulphur water baths.

Jupiter (5km north of Mangalia) is a summer climatic health resort located between the Comorova Wood and the coastline. The beach, stretching over one kilometre along a golf course, is especially scenic.

Photo: *Mamaia seaside resort*

2 Mai (6km south of Mangalia), a small village founded by the Lipovans, is especially popular with young families and those seeking tranquillity in a place far from the tourist hotspots. It is actually one of the smallest resorts on the coast.

Vama Veche (10km south of Mangalia) is the epicentre of summer fun, and is mainly visited by students, hippies and party-lovers. The most colourful and lively resort on the Black Sea coast!

Many would rather give these resorts a miss in summer because of their crowded beaches and look for quieter, wilder places. Some head for the Vadu beaches (near Corbu village) or those of the Delta – **Gura Portiţei** (➤86) or **Sfântu Gheorghe** (➤87) (which in August is home to the prestigious annual *Anonymous* International Independent Film Festival).

The climate of the Romanian coast is temperate, influenced slightly by the sea. In summer, the average temperature is 22⁰C. Romanian beaches have the advantage of 10-12 hours of sunshine per day. On extremely hot days (when the temperature at beach level rises to 40⁰C), a sea breeze rich in aerosols cools down the air. With a low level of salinity, the Black Sea offers the best conditions for underwater and nautical sports. Swimming lovers have nothing to fear – neither from the tide, nor from the currents, nor from dangerous marine life. There are facilities for thalasso treatment in Mangalia and Neptun, or treatments using the famous Gerovital and Aslavital Romanian products, which prevent early aging and revitalise the body.

SOUTHERN DOBRUJA

The southern part of Dobruja is strewn with the ruins of ancient and Byzantine fortresses, with traces left by the first preachers of Christianity, scenic steep rocky valleys, such as Fetii Valley (Canaraua Fetii), and the remnants of once vast forests (Hagieni, Dumbrăveni, Esechioi, Cogea Cor, Tenghea). On the secluded roads you will no doubt come across the ubiquitous Dobruja turtle (*Testudo Graeca Ibera*), declared a natural monument. A considerable number of Turkish and Tartar villages have survived (Fântâna Mare, Dobromir, Lespezi), as if frozen in time for centuries.

Two kilometres from Mangalia the **Movile Cave** was discovered in 1986, maintaining a constant temperature of between 19 and 21°C. The main gallery, which is 200m long and 21m deep, leads to the 3m-high Lake Chamber, at the end of which there is a lake. Many new animal

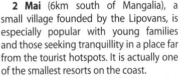

Left: *The busy resort of Eforie Nord*   Right: *Unspoiled beach at Corbu*

species have been found in this cave (two pseudo-scorpions, one millipede species, a new species of leech, four spider species and a water scorpion) living in a hydrogen sulphide-rich environment (similar to that on Mars), with low oxygen levels. It has formed a closed ecosystem, completely cut off from the outside world, whose survival relies on chemosynthesis. The entrance has been blocked with a rebar gate and the cave can only be visited by teams of two to three experts in sessions of up to two hours.

The hundred of galleries in the mysterious **Limanu Cave**, the only labyrinth cave in the country, are located 5km south-west of Mangalia and stretch for 4km. There are many legends linking this place to the worship of Zalmoxis. According to other stories, the cave is a gate to the Otherworld. The village elders say that the cave galleries stretch beneath the Danube to the Bulgarian city of Varna. Limanu is also called the Caracicola Cave or Icon Cave because of the carved faces at the entrance.

Fifteen kilometres west of Mangalia, the village of **Albești** is home to the ruins of a 4th-century B.C. Greek fortress, dotted along the brink of a ravine at the edge of a forest two kilometres from the centre of the village. The Greek stronghold had 1.2- to 1.6-metre-thick walls made up of large stone slabs without any mortar to bind them together.

Located in a valley flanked by exotic 30- to 40-metre-high sheer limestone walls pierced by caves, **Bașpînar** or **Fântâna Mare** village has been attested in documents since the 12th century. It is inhabited by a Turkish community of over 370 people. A genuine open-air museum, with archaic adobe houses and stone fences! On top of a hill four kilometres away, on the old village site, there is a cemetery, which in time has become an outright forest, after a tree was planted next to each grave, as tradition required. There are many old legends about this place, claiming for instance that it was here that Noah's flood took place or that an old arm of the Danube passed through here.

Dobruja's Turkish and Tartar Community

The Turks arrived in Dobruja in 1264, when an army of 12,000 soldiers led by Izeyddin Keykavuz and the missionary Sarî Saltuk, settled here, at the edge of the Byzantine Empire to serve as a defence against foreign invasions. Another group of Turks came here after the city of Varna was taken at the end of the 15th century. The army commander was believed to be Sarî Saltuk Dede, whose grave in Babadag (►82) became a pilgrimage site. Many Dobrujan settlements have Turkish names, such as Bașpînar (Great Well), Topalu (Limping Man), Techirghiol (Striped Lake) and Medgidia (after Abdul Medgid).

The 13th century was also the time when large groups of Tartars started to settle here; they were so many that, in the 16th century travellers were to call Dobruja "the Tartar Land"; now it is home to just 23,000 Tartars.

Of the more than 200 mosques large and small that once existed only 70 have survived, the most beautiful being the Carol I Mosque in Constanța (1910) combining the Egyptian, Byzantine and Romanian styles, the Esmahan Sultan Mosque in Mangalia (1525) – the oldest in the country, the Ali-Gaza-Pasha Mosque in Babadag (1610) and the Sultan Abdul Megid Mosque in Medgidia.

DID YOU KNOW?

One of the most important Muslim feasts is Hîdîrlez, on 6 May. This is when Turks and Tartars go to the cemetery to tend their forefathers' graves, before having a picnic, which culminates in Kureş traditional wrestling. According to tradition, this is the day when the two prophets Hîdîr and Ilias meet on earth to announce the arrival of spring to Muslims.

North-west of Adamclisi can be found the ruins of the **Tropaeum Traiani** citadel, and 1.5km away there is a triumphal monument, rebuilt in 1977 on the site of that erected in 109 by Apollodorus of Damascus to celebrate the Emperor Trajan's victory against the Dacians in 102. The citadel of the Getae, conquered by the Roman army, was settled by retired soldiers who had taken part in Trajan's Dacian wars and so in the 3th century it became a municipium (the second-highest rank of Roman city for non-Roman citizens). It is considered the largest Roman civilian settlement in Dobruja. A monument of triumph, cylindrical in shape, 38m in diameter and 39m high, it is clad in stone covered with bas-reliefs that depict scenes from the Dacian wars.

The beginnings of Christianity on Romanian soil

Dobruja is truly holy ground. It was here that St Andrew the Apostle, Christ's first disciple, came to preach Christianity in the 1st century A.D. It was here that the first Christian martyrs suffered martyrdom and it was also here that theologian John Cassian was born in 360, one of the doctors of the Western church and the author of 24 books of collations of the Desert Fathers (*Collationes*), in which he passed down the wisdom of the anchorites of Egypt and Antiochia.

Wherever you turn, you come across traces of the saints and early Christian places of worship. At Axiopolis (present-day Cernavodă) during the 4th century Saints Cyril, Chindeas and Tasius were martyred. Histria has five Christian basilicas. In the Independenţa and Dumbrăveni settlements (Canaraua Fetii) cave churches have been preserved and many more ruins of Dobrujan basilicas from the 4th-6th centuries can be seen in Capidava (present-day Topalu), Troesmis (present-day Turcoaia), Noviodunum (present-day Isaccea), Dinogetia (present-day Garvăn), Axiopolis (present-day Cernavodă), Ibida (present-day Slava Rusă), Ulmetum (present-day Pantelimon), Beroe (present-day Piatra Frecăţei) and Sucidava (present-day Izvoarele).

Close to **Saint Andrew's Cave**, near Ion Corvin village, in southern Dobruja, you can see the nine springs in which the Apostle baptised the first locals who converted to Christianity; once they made up the Cuzgun stream, whose name (Dove, in Turkish) might be a reference to that event. These places are regarded as the cradle of Romanian monastic life. The small cave was carved into the rock. The niche in the narthex was probably used as a bed by Saint Andrew. Today it is considered a healing place for the sick,

Photo: *Tropaeum Traiani*

who come to spend a few days here in the hope of seeing their health restored.

Forty kilometres away, next to the Bulgarian border there is another old monastic centre: **Dervent Monastery** was founded in the 20th century on the site where St. Andrew and his followers suffered martyrdom 2,000 years ago: it is said that afterwards four stone crosses emerged from the ground and began to work miracles.

The southernmost lateral lake, **Bugeac Lake**, accessible via the DN3, between Ostrov and Lipniţa villages, has steep banks that rise even as high as 30m. It is a place of wintering and passage for water birds, including the Dalmatian pelican (*Pelecanus crispus*), the ruddy shelduck (*Tadorna ferruginea*), the great egret (*Egretta alba*) and the great cormorant (*Phalacrocorax carbo*).

South of Bugeac Lake, in the commune of Ostrov there is a 27-hectare stretch of land, the **Esechioi Forest Nature, Wildlife and Flaura Reserve**.

Stretching along the green bank of the Danube, **Ostrov** (commune of Galiţa) is one of the most spectacular settlements in Dobruja. The village is famous for the wines made on the Ostrov Estate, which covers 1,600ha, incorporating large peach, cherry, apple, tart cherry, walnut and plum orchards. On a six-kilometre-long wild and uninhabited island in the middle of the Danube can be found the ruins of the powerful Byzantine citadel of **Păcuiul lui Soare** or **Vicina** (971), which used to be a port. To get there you need to ask for the help of locals who own boats.

At **Izvoarele** in the 1980s the remains of an ancient fortress were discovered, thought to be Sucidava, a political, military and religious centre mentioned in the time of Emperor Aurelius. An early Christian basilica was revealed, with numerous small crosses, a ceramic pitcher from the grave of Saint Mina in Egypt, and a liturgical set made up of 17 silver items from the 4th-6th centuries. Also at Izvoarele you can see a small wicker church without spires; another two such churches, also built during the Ottoman rule, may be seen nearby, at Satu Nou and Strunga.

NORTHERN DOBRUJA

The unique landscape (where else in the country is it possible to come across mountains, sea, delta, the Danube, gorges and woods?), old cave complexes (Niculiţel), ancient ruins, Lipovan villages (Slava Rusă, Slava Cercheză) and Turkish settlements (Babadag) are attractions that may convince you to spend a few days in the northern part of Dobruja. The fauna and plant life here are specific to the sea, Balkan steppe and sub-Mediterranean woods.

The **Hârşova Canarale** (steep rock formations), soaring from the banks of the Danube, consist of Jurassic limestone and contain the fossils of corals and soft-bodied organisms. On top once stood the Roman-Byzantine fortress of Carsium, of which only a few traces of the outer walls have survived.

The **Dobruja Gorges**, carved into the right side of the Casimcea Valley, between Târguşor and Cheia, were once coral reefs of the Thetis Sea and contain numerous unique Jurassic fossils. The DJ222 road is flanked by queer-looking steep slopes and

Photo: *Saint Andrew's Cave*

limestone walls, pierced by caves, such as the Adam and Bats caves.

The presence in the Dobrujan steppe of the low hills of the **Măcin Mountains** rock formation is breath taking. They are the oldest mountains in Romania, the remnants of the Hercynian range, from nearly 400 million years ago. Pricopanul Peak, in northern Dobruja, is known as the main migration corridor for over 180 bird species.

At **Niculiţel**, at the northernmost point of Dobruja, there is an early Christian monument: a basilica with a martyrion crypt (4th century), where the relics of saints Zoticos, Attalos, Kamasis and Filippos have been found. They suffered martyrdom at Noviodunum (present-day, Isaccea) in 303, during Diocletian's persecution. The caskets containing the relics of the four saints from Niculiţel, whose feast day is celebrated on 4 July, were moved to the Cocoş Monastery (1833), located 6 km away, at the foot of a hill covered in linden forests.

Another cave complex can be found in the Casimcea Valley, near Târguşor: **St. John Cassian's Cave** was used as a cell by monks from the 4th to 10th centuries. On the limestone plateau above the cave, a monastery was founded in 2003.

> **The Sprinkling of the Horses**
> The villages along the Danube, but also in northern Dobruja (Mihail Kogălniceanu, Luncaviţa), continue to preserve the custom of sprinkling the horses with Epiphany water (➤175) to protect them from the evil eye. The ceremony is followed by horse races, an occasion for the villagers to show off their horses and saddles.

The most important centre for the Turkish community is the town of **Babadag** (Father of the Mountains, in Turkish), which was the seat of the Pasha between 1677 and 1678. The Ali-Gazi Pasha Mosque was built from polished stone around 1610; its minaret soars to 21 metres. The Mausoleum of Sarî Saltuk Dede, the leader of the 10,000 Seljuk Turkish families that settled in Dobruja in two consecutive waves between 1263 and 1278 (➤79), is now a pilgrimage site. The Oriental-style Panaghia House (19th century) can be found nearby. It is now home to the **Oriental Art Museum** (Tue-Sun: 10am-6pm, May-Nov). Babadag Forest, north of the town, is made up of oak, linden, Southern European flowering ash, pedunculate

Photo: *Măcin Mountains*

oak, ash and Oriental Hornbeam. A swath of more 500 hectares was declared a nature reserve in 2004; within this perimeter can be found rare species of orchids (Orchis purpurea), irises, lesser celandine, monkey orchids and so on. We suggest you come in May, when the forest is bathed in the sweet scent of the linden trees.

When in **Enisala**, 11km from Babadag, it is worth making a stop at the **Museum of the Northern Dobruja Village** (🕙 Wed-Sun: 10am-6pm 🎫 4 Lei), which contains a traditional homestead preserved in situ, together with its annexes (barn, fodder sheds, summer kitchen and oven, corn granary). Observe the typical architecture of the houses (reed roof, blue window frames etc.) and the large range of items, from farming implements to household items (painted local carriages, saddles, spinning wheel, loom, fishing rods, fishing nets, cooper tools, blacksmith tools, pottery tools, ceramic pots and vessels used in the kitchen) and furniture.

The ruins of the spectacular Genoese citadel of **Heracleea** (13th century), with a six-sided tower and five rectangular towers, stand on a rocky hill overlooking Razelm Lake, 2 km from Enisala. In 1261 the Byzantine Empire granted the Genoese a commercial monopoly over the Black Sea.

They kept the control over the maritime trade until 1484. Licostomo (Two Wolf Mouths) is another Genoese port located in the Danube Delta between Vâlcov and Periprava.

Enisala Safari Village (www.safari.ro 📞 0722-300200), on the Razelm Lake, is a tourist complex made of stone, wood, and reeds, using traditional building techniques. It is the perfect spot to set out on eco-trips across Razelm Lake, into the Delta, or into the Măcin Mountains.

Dobruja's Lipovans

After the schism within the Russian Orthodox Church brought about by the reforms launched by Patriarch Nikon in 1654, the old-rite Christians (old believers), known to this day as Lipovans, found a home in Dobruja, during the 17th century. There are over 20,000 Lipovan Russians in the region. Traditional Lipovan villages are Slava Rusă, Jurilovca, Carcaliu and Sarichioi

---

Slava Rusă was founded on top of the ruins of the Roman fortress of **Ibida**, with 24 towers and three gates. Quite unusually, the basilica features three altars to the east. On the south-eastern edge of the village can be found the **Vovidenia Convent**, and 5km to the south-west the **Uspenia Monastery** nestles between two woody hills. These are the only old-rite monasteries in Dobruja, and the services are held in Slavonic to this day.

Along the Topologul Valley, 3 kilometres south-east of the Fântâna Mare village, in the commune of Ciucurova (Tulcea County), lies the **Fântâna Mare Lilac Reserve**, covering over 0.3 hectares.

A similar reserve (the **Sheep Valley**), covering 0.35 hectares, is found slightly to the north-east, between the towns of Ciucurova and Nicolae Bălcescu.

The **Peony Hill Nature Reserve** is located 4 kilometres north-east of Atmagea village in the commune of Ciucurova. Its 50 hectares are home to wild

Photo: *The citadel of Heracleea, perched on a limestone hill near Razelm Lake*

peonies (*Paeonia peregrina*), a protected species, declared a natural monument.

The **Carasan-Teke Nature Reserve**, located within the commune of Izvoarele, 10 kilometres north of Nicolae Bălcescu, is home to the fern leaf peony (*Paeonia tenuifolia*). A 340-metre-high volcanic cone has been preserved here, surrounded by limestone hills and plateaux.

The town of **Mihail Kogălniceanu** is home to a large community of Aromanian Farsherots, who arrived here as a result of a population exchange in 1940. The house of Gheorghe Celea was converted into the first museum in Romania dedicated to the Aromanians. The German community, which lived in the village (called Caramurat back then) between 1876 and 1946, left behind a neighbourhood of houses, a cemetery and a church built in 1897. The reason why the community flourishes today is the presence of an International Airport and NATO base nearby.

The commune of **Izvoarele**, located on the road between Tulcea and Măcin and overshadowed by the ridges of the Consul Mare hill, is the centre of the Greek community of Dobruja, which settled here 200 years ago. It preserves traditional Greek customs ("Dragoman", on the feast of St. John the Baptist, when an unmarried young man, mounted on his beautifully decorated horse, enters the courtyard of his beloved to offer her a round braided loaf as a token of love; "Lăzărel", celebrated on Palm Sunday, when girls younger than 16 sing and receive eggs, money, flour, and turn over their sieve at the end of the feast to ensure a bountiful summer; "Horhumbal", when lads wrestle with each other, start fires on top of the hill and roll cart wheels wrapped in straw down the hill; Elefterio, when women get together to spin wool and chat around a pit full of embers). From the Bulgarians they borrowed the custom of Soaking the Groom (newlyweds immerse their heads in the water trough) and the Old Women's Day – when the women party until the early hours without the company of men.

The German minority that arrived in Dobruja in the early 20th century left the area in 1942; only a church here and there remains to remind us of their presence, such as **Colilia Church**, a beautiful illustration of the Gothic style. After the village was abandoned, the church started to deteriorate; it was saved at the last minute when an Orthodox monastery was set up here, taking charge of its restoration.

The vestiges of ancient or Byzantine settlements are scattered all over northern Dobruja.

At Cape Doloşman, 6 kilometres from Jurilovca, near the Danube, the ruins of the Greek-Roman citadel of **Orgame/ Argamum** have been discovered. The citadel was mentioned as early as the 6th century B.C. by Hecataeus of Miletus. The archaeological site comprises four early Christian basilicas, an old Greek tomb, and curtain walls. Equally original are the Greek, Roman and Byzantine ruins of **Little Church (Bisericuţa) Island** on Razelm Lake, located just 3 kilometres to the south-east.

In north-eastern Dobruja, on the road between Murighiol and the Upper Dunavăţu look for the remnants of the **Halmyris Fortress**, built in the 2nd century by the Emperor Trajan. Initially a seaport on the Black Sea, Halmyris became a thriving trading hub.

Photo: *Wild peonies, a protected species, blooming in April-May*

Histria, named after the Danube (*Istros*, in Greek), was founded in the 7th century B.C. by Greek settlers from Miletus; it is the oldest city attested on Romanian soil. On the shores of the Sinoe Lake, previously a gulf on the Black Sea, have been preserved the ruins of fortifications, Greek temples, basilicas, dwellings, baths and roads.

Near the commune of Turcoaia, on the bank of the Danube, lie scattered the ruins of the Getic citadel of **Troesmis** (documented for the first time in Ovid's *Epistulae ex Ponto*), which was later to become an important Roman military centre, the headquarters of Legion V Macedonica. The area is one of the largest archaeological reserves: it consists of earthworks, aqueducts, a *myrtaeum*, etc. Thirty-three monuments unearthed by Engelhardt at Troesmis during the 1864-1865 excavations are exhibited at the Saint Germain-en-Laye Archeology Museum, nineteen kilometres from Paris.

Less than 20 kilometres from Troesmis, near Măcin, there are remnants of the Roman **Arrubium** castrum, attested in documents as early as 100. Some theories speculate that the name was of Celtic origin and that it was a place of worship of the god Jupiter Arrubianus.

Nineteen kilometres north of Măcin, opposite the Danube bend lies **Dinogetia**, a citadel erected by Romans on the site of an older Dacian settlement. Here survive the ruins of a 4th-century Roman basilica and of a 10th-century Byzantine small church. It is located 5 kilometres north-west of Gărvan village and can be reached via Măcin or Isaccea.

Right between Cernavodă and Hârşova, on a limestone cliff on the right bank of the Danube, lie scattered the mangificent ruins of **Capidava**, a Geto-Dacian citadel, soon to become Roman, which played an important military role in defending the Danube border.

Hopefully we have convinced you that Dobruja is not only about seaside resorts or the Danube Delta – the destinations for most tourists. The real Dobruja is hidden away beyond the side roads, within less travelled territory. The vestiges of Greek, Roman, Byzantine and Genoese citadels, the Turkish, Tartar and Lipovan settlements, the cave churches that were home to the saintly preachers of Christianity on Romanian soil – they all deserve to be included in the tourist maps of Dobruja.

THE DANUBE DELTA

As it flows into the Black Sea the Danube forms a delta, unanimously regarded as one of the most astounding sites in Europe. Covering 2.681 square kilometres, the Danube Delta is one of the largest wetland reserves and the largest expanse of reed beds in the world. Around 50% of its area is temporarily under water (especially in spring), 45% is permanently submerged and only 5% (alluvial plains) is the genuine "dry land" that never floods.

Navigation is possible along the main three branches of the delta: Chilia, Sulina and Sfântu Gheorghe (Saint George), almost entirely covered by the river transit network. There are centuries-old fishing villages on the sandbars, completely cut off from the rest of the world: Maliuc, Jurilovca, Sf. Gheorghe, Mila 23, Murighiol, Crişan.

Photo: *Danube Delta is a paradise for water birds*

For tourists who cannot do without modern amenities, there are luxury hotels, floating hotels and tourist complexes with all the comforts of the urban lifestyle. Those who are looking for something special may opt to lodge with the locals. You will wake up at the crack of dawn to see the head of the family go fishing and at lunch you will eat fish fresh out of the water, cooked in most ingenious ways. Every meal involves fish: you will be served fish borsch, skewed carp, fish meatballs, fish cabbage rolls, fish fingers made from sturgeon, fish brine and aspic, with the ubiquitous polenta and garlic sauce on the side, but also asp tarama, boiled crawfish and frog legs. To explore the sights, hire a boat and preferably a guide and wake up early in the morning to get acquainted with the real delta. It is best discovered by travelling the maze of narrow canals flanked with reeds, bulrushes and sedge. If you are lucky and your guide knows his way around, this "Noah's Ark" with over 1,200 plant and tree species, 320 bird species and 100 fish species will reveal some of its secrets. The place is full of life: the air vibrates with birds fluttering everywhere (pelicans, swans, cormorants, common shelducks, egrets, spoonbills, coots, white-tailed eagles), fish glide through the water (beluga, Russian sturgeon, starry sturgeon, sterlet, perch, asp, carp crucian carp, Prussian carp), and the reed beds teem with wildlife. The delta is home to turtles, snakes, vipers, nutria, foxes, otters, muskrats, boars, raccoon dogs etc. It is not easy to forget the carpet of white and yellow water lilies, with floating reed islets in between, nor the centuries-old trees or the climbing plants that make up the eerie landscapes of the Letea Forest or Caraorman, both nature reserves (you can only enter if you have a permit and are accompanied by a guide).

If you are a keen ornithologist, put your name down for one of the bird-watching sessions organised by the tourist agencies; the best time of the year for this is between April and September. In the Roşca-Buhaiova area lies Europe's largest pelican colony (the Dalmatian and great white pelican); another two Dalmatian pelicans colonies can be found on Sinoe-Ceaplace Island and Sinoe-Prundul cu Păsări island. Sacalin Island on the Sf. Gheorghe branch and the Isac and Uzlina lakes are nesting areas for rare species of birds.

At **Gura Portiţei**, between the Black Sea and Goloviţa Lake there is a narrow stretch of beach, very popular with those looking for alternatives to the overcrowded seaside resorts. The old Lipovan village is accessible

Photo: *Danube Delta is a maze of narrow canals bordered by reeds, bulrushes and sedge*

by boat or speedboat from Jurilovca (the trip takes around one hour). And if you arrive here, look for the seventeen houses behind the Lipovan church in Jurilovca, which make up the Old Women's Hermitage, where the poor local Lipovan women retire in their old age..

There is another impressively long beach 3 kilometres from Sfântu Gheorghe, where the Saint George channel empties into the sea. Every summer the Anonymous Film Festival takes place in this village, right at the heart of the delta. Around one and a half hour's away, at Sulina, there is an unspoiled beach, also at the river mouth.

Located where the Sulina channel flows into the Black Sea and accessible only by water, **Sulina** is Romania's easternmost town. It was ruled by pirates until the mid-20th century and it is also the final resting place of foreigners from the remotest corners of the earth, from Malta to Denmark, from Turkey to Germany, and from South Africa to Russia. Sailors, pirates, princes and princesses, simple clerks and travellers who just happened to end up here all rest in peace in the Sea Cemetery. Look for the tombstone of Ecaterina Moruzi, the niece of prince Ioan Sturdza, or that of feared Greek pirate Giorgios Kontoguris, marked by the emblem of his "trade" (a skull and crossbones), or that of Thomas Rutheford, the chief-engineer of the Kepler steamboat, or the twin monuments of the two English lovers, Anna Margaret Pringle and William Webster, who drowned here. Another monument commemorates for all eternity the love of a girl for her little sister, who jumped into a well trying to save her. The cemetery is divided in four sections, based on the religion of those buried there: old-rite Orthodox (Lipovan), Catholic, Muslim, and Jewish.

The newest beach on the Romanian coastline, half an hour from Sulina, is overshadowed by a 48-metre-high lighthouse, built by British and Austrians employees of the long-defunct Lower Danube River Commission, set up in 1870.

The Salt Lakes in Murighiol (87ha) developed around the lake of the same name, located between the municipalities of Murighiol and Plopu. The high content of salt and mineral-rich mud in the waters earned it the name of Murighiol, from the Turkish *moru*, "purple" and *ghiol*, "lake". It is the nesting place of many bird species: the Mediterranean gull (*Larus melanocephalus*), the common tern (*Sterna hirundo*), the red-crested pochard (*Netta rufina*), the Kentish plover (*Charadrius alexandrinus*), the black-winged stilt (*Himantopus himantopus*), the pied avocet (*Recurvirostra avosetta*), the black-necked grebe (*Podiceps nigricollis*), the white-winged tern (*Chlidonias leucopterus*), the whiskered tern (*Chlidonias hybridus*), the collared pratincole (*Glareola pratincola*), sooty tern, black-tailed godwit, snow goose and bean goose.

Founded by the Tartars from Crimeea, Murighiol village, 40km from Tulcea, was repopulated after the 1877-78 war with Russian Lipovans from neighbouring villages.

The main gateway to the Danube Delta is the city of **Tulcea**. Its harbour is the starting point for regular boat trips to the

Photo: *Old Lighthouse, Sulina*

most important destinations in the area. You can navigate along the three main branches of the delta: Chilia, Sulina and Sfântu Gheorghe (the last two are the distributaries of the Tulcea branch), which are entirely covered by the river transit network. Tulcea, founded on the site of the ancient city of Aegyssus, is home to a museum dedicated to the Danube Delta, which includes an aquarium. Also visit the Art Museum (the former mansion of the Turkish Governor of Tulcea, 1870), which displays important works by prominent inter-war avant-garde artists, such as the surrealist Victor Brauner, Frederic Storck, Oscan Han, Ion Jalea, and Gheorghe Petraşcu, and for something extra go to the Azizie Mosque (1876), a remarkable building with 32 windows.

Three of the most beautiful monasteries were established near the city of Tulcea: the Cocoş, Celic Dere and Saon Monasteries, each a short distance from the other. It is said that together with the Niculiţel basilica they are laid out in the form of a cross. The **Celic Dere Monastery** (1840) is where the bones of the first Dobruja martyrs, Epictetus and Astion, are interred, mentioned in the *Acta Sanctorum Iulii*; they were discovered in May 2001 at Halmyris (present-day Lower Dunavăţu). The **Saon Monastery** (1846) is another corner of paradise on the banks of the Danube. The nuns breed peacocks and ostriches, whose exotic presence has became familiar to all those pass by regularly.

Cruises provided by NAVROM (the River Navigation Company)

www.navromdelta.ro
SC Navrom SA offers regular trips to settlements in the Danube Delta:
- Tulcea – Periprava (Tulcea – Ceatalchioi – Plaur – Pardina – Chilia Veche – Periprava)
- Tulcea – Sulina (Tulcea – Partizani – Maliuc – Gorgova – Crişan – Sulina)
- Tulcea – Sfântu Gheorghe (Tulcea – Bălteni de Jos – Mahmudia – Sfântu Gheorghe)
- Crişan – Mila 23
- Crişan – Caraorman

ROUTES INTO THE DELTA

The Danube Delta Biosphere Reserve Administration (ARBDD, www.ddbra.ro), set up in 1990, has 24 routes into the reserves, fifteen of which are only by waterway services and nine by land, either on foot or by car.

Waterway Routes:

Route T1: Tulcea – Gârla Şontea – Mila 23 – Crişan – Tulcea; this route also has the following variant: Tulcea – Gorgova – Mila 23 – Crişan – Tulcea

Route T2: Tulcea – Litcov Canal – Crişan – Tulcea

Route T3: Tulcea – Stipoc Canal – Chilia Veche – Tulcea

Route T4: Tulcea (Câşla Lake) – Gârla Somova – Saon Monastery (Telincea Lake) – Tulcea

Route T5: Murighiol – Dranov Canal – Gura Portiţei – Dunavăţ Canal – Murighiol

Route T6: Murighiol – Dunavăţ Canal – Cocoş Canal – Mustaca Canal – Ring Canal – Dranov Canal – Murighiol (extends into the Ring Canal near the Lipoveni Canal and into the Mustaca Canal as far Razelm Lake, where you can proceed via Route 5 to Gura Portiţei).

Route T7: Murighiol – Uzlina – Uzlina Lake – Isac Lake – Gârla Perivolovca – Murighiol

Route T8: Murighiol – Uzlina – Litcov Canal – Crişan Canal – Puiu Lake – Erenciuc Lake – Murighiol

Route T9: Crişan – Roşu Lake – Sulina – Crişan

Route T10: Crişan – Mila 23 – Trei Iezere Lake – Crişan

Route T11: Crişan – Magearu Canal – Sulina – Crişan

Route T12: Chilia Veche – Sulimanca Canal – Matiţa Lake – Rădăcinoasele Canal – Chilia Veche

Route T13: Sulina – Cardon Canal – Periprava – Musura Bay – Sulina

Route T14: Sulina – Busurca Canal – Roşu Lake – Erenciuc Lake – Sf. Gheorghe – Cordon Litoral Canal – Sulina

Route T15: Sf. Gheorghe – Gârla Turcească, up to the entry into Meleaua Sf. Gheorghe – Sf. Gheorghe

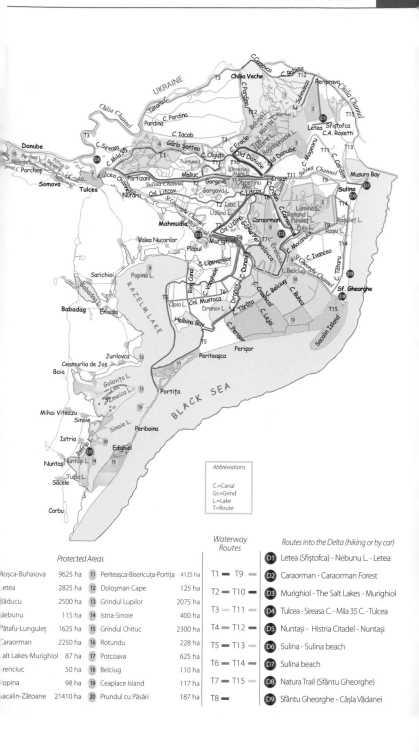

Abbreviations

C=Canal
Gr.=Grind
L=Lake
T=Route

Waterway
Routes

T1		T9	
T2		T10	
T3		T11	
T4		T12	
T5		T13	
T6		T14	
T7		T15	
T8			

Routes into the Delta (hiking or by car)

D1 Letea (Sfiştofca) - Nebunu L. - Letea
D2 Caraorman - Caraorman Forest
D3 Murighiol - The Salt Lakes - Murighiol
D4 Tulcea - Sireasa C. - Mila 35 C. - Tulcea
D5 Nuntaşi - Histria Citadel - Nuntaşi
D6 Sulina - Sulina beach
D7 Sulina beach
D8 Natura Trail (Sfântu Gheorghe)
D9 Sfântu Gheorghe - Câşla Vădanei

Protected Areas

Roşca-Buhaiova	9625 ha	11	Periteaşca-Bisericuţa-Portiţa	4125 ha
Letea	2825 ha	12	Doloşman Cape	125 ha
Răducu	2500 ha	13	Grindul Lupilor	2075 ha
Nebunu	115 ha	14	Istria-Sinoie	400 ha
Vătafu-Lunguleţ	1625 ha	15	Grindul Chituc	2300 ha
Caraorman	2250 ha	16	Rotundu	228 ha
Salt Lakes-Murighiol	87 ha	17	Potcoava	625 ha
Erenciuc	50 ha	18	Belciug	110 ha
Popina	98 ha	19	Ceaplace Island	117 ha
Sacalin-Zătoane	21410 ha	20	Prundul cu Păsări	187 ha

Moldavia

revious Page: *Dragomirna Monastery*

Moldavia

Nowhere in Romania are there more churches, monasteries and hermitage clustered in such a small space than in Moldavia. Most of them are centuries old.

Mainly erected by Moldavian voivodes of the Muşat Dynasty (Peter I Muşat, Iliaş Peter, Alexander the Good, Bogdan II, Stephen the Great, Peter Rareş), these splendid monasteries also served as princely tombs. According to chronicler Ion Neculce, Stephen the Great (1457-1504), "the Bastion of Christianity", had a church or monastery built after each battle he fought against the Turks, Hungarians or Poles during his 47-year reign. It is not clear how true this is, but what is certain is that the prince left behind dozens of places of worship. The reign of Peter Rareş carried on the tradition of the great ruler Stephen the Great; this was the period of the priceless exterior murals of the Voroneţ, Humor, Moldoviţa and Probota monasteries, which are UNESCO World Heritage sites. You have to see these "gems of Bukowina", unique illustrations of Moldavian feudal art in order to understand the fascination they have always exerted on visitors: Voroneţ (1488) – "the Sistine Chapel of Romania and even the East", with its famous fresco depicting the *Last Judgement*, painted on an inimitable blue background; Putna (1466-1469), which preserves collection of embroideries and church artefacts dating to the time of its founder, Stephen the Great; Humor (1530), with its admirable Byzantine exterior murals by Toma the Zographos; Suceviţa (1591), with its impressive *Ladder of Virtues* painted on the north side of the church; Moldoviţa (1532), dominated by the bright golden colours of its frescoes, the most famous of which is *The Siege of Constantinople* Arbore (1502), which has exterior murals by Dragoş Coman, regarded as "a Pisanello of Moldavia, the greatest artist of the 16th-century Orthodox East"; Bogdana (14th century), the oldest church in Moldavia; and Pătrăuţi (1487), Bălineşti (1494-1495) Probota (1530), and Dragomirna (1609), among others.

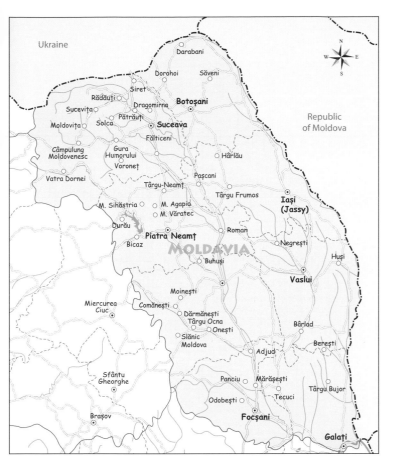

Photo: *Lucina stud farm*

JASSY (IAŞI)

Jassy, a city lying on seven hills like Rome, is the "heart" of Moldavia. It is home to an impressive number of churches, monasteries, museums and memorial houses, monuments, palaces and historic buildings. The city of Jassy began to develop in the 15th century, after Moldavia's rulers established their capital there. The period between 1564 and 1859, when it was the capital of the province of Moldavia, was when the most Jassy's most splendid buildings were constructed.

The **Palace of Culture** (www. palatulculturii.ro ✉ 17 Stephen the Great and Holy Square ✆ 0232.218383), is in the oldest part of the city. It was erected between 1906 and 1925 in the neo-Gothic Flamboyant style, on the site of the former Princely Court (attested in documents since 1434), to serve as the Palace of the Administration and Justice. Since 1955 it has been a vast museum complex, which consists of the Museum of Moldavia, the Moldavian Ethnographic Museum, the Museum of Art, and the Stefan Procopiu Science and Technology Museum. The building, with a total area of 36.000 square metres and 298 rooms, was designed by architect Ion D. Berindey, assisted by A. D. Xenopol and Grigore Cerchez. The Gothic Hall has a superb mosaic featuring griffons, double-headed eagles and lions. The medallions in the Chamber of Voivodes, on the first floor, depict Moldavian rulers and Romania's kings. The wood panels in the Henri Coandă Room are based on the scientist's own designs. The carillon with eight bells in the central bell tower plays the *Ring Dance of Unity* on the hour. At the time when this guide went to press, the palace was closed for restoration. In 2012, behind it the controversial Palas Jassy Business Centre was built (www.palasiasi. ro). It covers 270,000 square metres, and includes a shopping mall, office buildings, a four-star hotel, conference rooms and an Italian garden.

The **Saint Nicholas Princely Church** (✉ 65 Anastasie Panu Street), built by Stephen the Great between 1491 and 1492 and rebuilt between 1884 and 1904 by French architect André Lecomte du Noüy, used to be part of the old Princely Court, where the Palace of Culture was later built. Moldavia's rulers were anointed here from the 16th century until 1859. The earlier outer wall of the church has survived to this day, on the south-east side.

Within the perimeter of the church, Metropolitan Dosoftei set up a printing house, where in 1679 he published *The*

Photo: *Palace of Culture, Jassy*

Book of Prayer; between 1682 and 1686, he printed here the most important work of his life, in four volumes: *The Lives of the Holy Fathers*, a translation from Greek and Slavonic. The Dosoftei House (1677), also called the Arch House, currently houses the **Printing Museum** (🕘 Tue-Sun: 10am-5pm). The stone building, with a six-columned facade, has two floors with four rooms.

Stephen the Great and Holy Avenue, formerly Princely Street, starts from outside the Palace, along which the city's most important sights are to be found.

The **Church of the Three Hierarchs Monastery** (✉ 28 Stephen the Great and Holy Avenue 🕘 Daily: 9:30am-12pm, 3-5pm), built at the behest of Vasile Lupu between 1635 and 1639 to serve as the princely necropolis, is unique in Romania for its lush outer decorations carved entirely from stone. Thirty panels with traditional decorative motifs combined with Oriental and Western features cover the facade like embroidery, from the foundations to the base of the spires. A true architectural gem! The murals inside were painted from 1641 to 1642 by Russian masters Sidor Pospeyev, Yakov Gavrilov, Deiko Yakovlyev and Pronka Nikitin, from the Russian court, assisted by Moldovan artists Nicolae the Zographos and Ștefan the Zographos. In 1641 the Ecumenical Patriarchate of Constantinople donated to the monastery the relics of Saint Parascheva, the patron saint of Moldavia, rehoused in the Metropolitan See (▶96) in 1889. The remains of the founder's family are interred in two niches in the north wall, while the niches in the southern wall house the remains of scholar Dimitrie Cantemir and ruler Alexander John Cuza. The monastery had a printing press, which printed *Cazania românească* (Romanian Book of Sermons) and *Cartea românească de învățătură* (Romanian Book of Teachings) (1643) by Metropolitan Varlaam, the first book in Romanian to be printed in Moldavia, and a College, later to become Princely Academy. In 1711 Tsar Peter the Great dined in the refectory (the Gothic Room, currently the Mediaeval Art Museum) when

visiting Jassy; it was also here that in 1821, Alexander Ipsilanti started the movement to liberate Greece from the Ottoman yoke .

DID YOU KNOW?

According to tradition, the facade of the Three Hierarchs Church was initially completely gilded. This legend is probably the result of a mistranslation into Arabic and Turkish by Paul of Allepo and Evliya Çelebi, who gave a description of the church. It is therefore said that during a Turkish siege, they set fire to the church to melt the gold on the walls. Although it has been taken by many to be nothing more than a tale, traces of gold were once discovered around the northern windows and within the square bases of the spires. Whether they go back to the time of Vasile Lupu is still a mystery …

The church of the Three Hierarchs is next door to the **Catholic Cathedral** (✉ 26 Stephen the Great and Holy Avenue), an avant-garde building of cylindrical shape built between 1992 and 2005. The dome, 24m in diameter, has 24 lancet stained-glass windows.

The **Orthodox Metropolitan See** was consecrated in 1887, in the presence of King Carol I and Queen Elizabeth. Since 1889 it has housed the relics of Saint Parascheva, which thousands of pilgrims come to venerate, especially on 14 October, the saint's feast day. The interior paintings are by Gheorghe Tattarescu.

In 1891 the former **Roset-Roznovanu Palace** (✉ 11 Stephen the Great and Holy Avenue 🕿 0232.267582), built between 1832 and 1834 in the neoclassical style with baroque elements, became the **City Hall**. The sumptuous rooms inside are open to visitors free of charge on Saturdays, between 9 am and 12 pm with prior booking.

The superb **Vasile Alecsandri National Theatre** (✉ 18 Agatha Bârsescu Street 🕿 0232.255999), built between 1894 and 1896, based on the designs by Viennese architects Fellner and Helmer, on the site of the former City Hall, is the oldest theatre in Romania. The facade is executed in flawless neoclassical style and the Baroque and Rococo interior with perfect acoustics has superb curtains painted in 1896, depicting an allegory of the three ages of man.

Stephen the Great Avenue ends in the **Union Square**, where the *Hora* of Unity (a ring dance) was performed for the first time on 24 January 1859 when the principalities of Moldavia and Wallachia united to form Romania. To celebrate that moment every year on 24 January hundreds of locals gather here and dance the hora around the statue of Alexander John Cuza, the first ruler of the United Romanian Principalities. The mosaic pavements, fountains, and the flock of pigeons, which seem to have fallen in love with the place, transform Union Square into a pleasant area despite its dreary communist-period architecture which dates from the time of the Union Hotel (1969). The hotel held the title of the tallest building in Jassy (58m) until a few years ago. The Union Hotel clashes blatantly with its stylish neighbour, the Trajan Hotel (1882), designed by Gustave Eiffel. Also in Union Square, at no. 12, there is a tourist information centre (🕿 0232.261990).

The lively pedestrian-only **Alexandru Lăpuşneanu** Street, linking Union Square with Mihai Eminescu Square, lives up to its old names, Joy Street and Music Street. The Madame Alexandre bakery and the Italian Passini bakery may be long gone, much like the picturesque pubs visited by bohemian artists, the taverns alive with the music of fiddles and cobzas played by Roma bands, the shops filled with "charming contraptions" (music boxes, gramophones, phonographs etc.), where the Express building now stands, but something of the erstwhile atmosphere still lingers. At no. 4 you will find the Lăpuşneanu coffee shop, at no. 9-11 the Mignon Café, at no. 16 the Avant-Garde Bookshop, and at no. 24 the Antique Store opened by the famous antiquarian Dumitru I. Grumăzescu, who owns the largest collection of artefacts relating to Eminescu (around 10,000 items), as well as collections of miniature books, slide projectors, music boxes etc. On the site of the former Beer Hall, next to the Banu church (or the Paupers church), dating from 1802, can be found the Corso Garden. The superb mansion at no. 14, home to the Catargi, Paladi, Cantacuzino-Paşcanu and Ghica boyar families and where prince Alexander John Cuza (1806) lived from 1859 to 1862, now houses the **Union Museum** (☏ 0232.314614 🕓 Tue-Sun: 10am-5pm

Ⓖ12 Lei), displaying exhibits connected to the history of the Unification.

Mihai Eminescu Square is dominated by the **University Central Library**, located at the corner of the Carol I Avenue and Păcurari Street. The building was initially the headquarters of the Ferdinand University Foundation, but has been a university library since after World War II. On the outside it is decorated with neo-Doric and Ionic columns and medallions depicting major Romanian historical figures; both Carrara marble and Venetian mosaics were used in abundance in the interior.

The **Elizabeth Esplanade** or **Yellow Ravine** was developed in the late-20th century at the foot of the Copou Hill to connect the newly built train station (1870) with the city centre.

Carol I Avenue (formerly Green Bridge), which branches off from Mihai Eminescu Square, runs lengthwise over the legendary **Copou Hill**, where you can find the Al. I. Cuza University, Copou Park and the Botanical Garden.

The **Alexandru Ioan Cuza University**, founded in 1860, is the oldest in Romania. The building (1896) was constructed in the Classic and Baroques style by French architect Louis Blanc. The glorious Hall of the Lost Footsteps is adorned with 19 murals by Sabin Bălașa.

Copou Park, laid out as early as 1833, is the most celebrated and oldest park in Jassy. The Junimea lane is flanked by bronze busts portraying members of the famous late-19th-century Jassy literary society. The huge Eminescu linden tree, which is more than 100 years old, can also be found in Copou. There is a small museum dedicated to Eminescu nearby. The Obelisk of Lions (the Monument of the Constitutional Laws, 1834), one of the oldest monuments in Romania, is a 15-metre-high column, weighing 10 tonnes, resting on four lions. Every summer, the park hosts the Cucuteni pottery fair.

The **Botanical Garden** (105 hectares), a vast wooded area on Copou Hill, is home to Mediterranean, tropical and sub-tropical plant species, arranged in 12 sections.

The ponds reconstruct the Danube Delta habitat, the rose garden boasts 800 beautiful noble rose varieties, and the twelve greenhouses house exotic plants. There is a chrysanthemum exhibition every autumn, arranged in the shape of a waterfall, and in February you can admire an azalea exhibition.

Jassy, a hot spot of culture ever since its early days, has always been home to dozens of celebrities in various fields, whose houses have been turned into memorial museums: Ion Creangă, Vasile Alecsandri, Mihail Sadoveanu, Otilia Cazimir, George Topârceanu, Constantin Negruzzi, Mihail Kogălniceanu, Nicolae Gane, A. D. Xenopol, Emil Racoviță etc.

Raconteur Ion Creangă, author of *Childhood Memories* and many classic stories that have enchanted successive generations of children, lived in a cottage in the old Țicău neighbourhood during the last part of his life (1872-1889). It is a traditional two-roomed Romanian house, with a passage, porch, and shingle roof, surrounded by a flower garden.

The **Ciric Leisure Area**, 6km to the east of the city, is a string of lakes in the middle of woods. You can come here for a picnic or to go for a ride on the pedalos and boats. The complex includes an adventure park, a miniature golf course, cycle lanes and playgrounds for children.

Do not miss the **Golia Monastery**, dating from early-16th century, rebuilt by Vasile Lupu, the **Galata Monastery**, built from 1576 to 1578 by Peter the Lame, the **Cetățuia Monastery** (1668-1672), founded by Prince Gheorghe Duca, the **Frumoasa Monastery** (1583-1586) and the **Armenian Church** (1395). Few cities in Romania have such a dazzling array of churches as Jassy!

Travelling just outside the city, we suggest you visit **Cuza Hall at Ruginoasa** (🕐 Tue-Sun: 12pm-5pm) in the neo-Gothic style, built in 1804, and **Sturdza Castle from Miclăușeni** (🕐 Tue-Fri: 12-5pm, Sat-Sun: 12pm-6pm 📞 0232.713172), a superb complex in Late neo-Gothic style, located in the middle of the forest, 65km from Jassy. Owned by the Archdiocese of Moldavia and Bukowina, it has two guest houses run by the nuns from the Miclăușeni Monastery within the premises.

Guided tour of Jassy

Every Wednesday, between 9am and 11am o'clock, ICAR Tours organises a free sightseeing tour, from Union Square to the Palace of Culture. To join the tour, call 📞 0755-045330 or send an e-mail to ghid@icar.ro.

Photo: *Cetățuia Monastery*

SUCEAVA

Suceava became the capital of Moldavia in 1388, following a decision made by ruler Peter I Mușat. After that date, in the east side of the town, a Throne Citadel was constructed (the Fortress of the Mușatins), later extended by Stephen the Great.

The town of Suceava was the capital of Moldavia's most famous rulers: Peter I Mușat, Alexander the Good, Bogdan II, Stephen the Great, Peter Rareș, Vasile Lupu. After 1564, on Turkish orders, Alexander Lăpușneanu moved the capital of Moldavia from Suceava to Jassy, which was not fortified, and burned down all the citadels in the country, apart from Hotin.

Only ruins remain of the **Princely Court** (14th-17th centuries), within the perimeter of Ana Ipătescu Street, in the centre of Suceava.

The **Church of the Coconi (Crown Princes)**, also known as **St. John the Baptist Church,** is located at 3 Ștefăniță Vodă Street, in close proximity to the Princely Court of which it used to form a part. It was erected in 1643 by Vasile Lupu, as a chapel for the Princely Court. The church services here would be attended by the members of the ruling family, especially the crown princes or *coconi*. In the church courtyard, the Șipotul Mare Fountain has been preserved from the days of the court.

The **St. Demetrios Church**, at 1 Stephen the Great Street (formerly Princely Street), was built between 1534 and 1535 by Peter Rareș on the site of a 14th-century place of worship. Its layout is typical of churches from the epoch of Stephen the Great.

Many other monuments in Suceava transport us back to the town's heyday, when it stood at the crossroad of major trade routes.

The **Church of the Resurrection (Russian Church)**, at 14, Ana Ipătescu Street, was built in 1551 by Lady Elena, the wife of Peter Rareș.

The **Princely Inn** (late-16th century), the oldest and best preserved civic structure in Suceava, currently houses the **Ethnographic Museum** (✉ 5 Ciprian Porumbescu Street 🕐 Tue-Sun: 10am-6pm).

The construction of the St. George Church of **St. John the New Monastery** began during the reign of Bogdan III (1514) and was completed by Ştefăniţă Vodă (1522), both of whom were sons of Stephen the Great. Of the exterior paintings, dating to the time of Peter Rareş (1532-1534), only a few fragments have survived, on the south wall. In the church the relics of St. John the New are kept, brought to Suceava in 1402 by Alexander the Good and originally kept in the Mirăuţi Church. It has been listed as a UNESCO World Heritage site, along with six other churches in Bukowina. It is located at 2, Ion Vodă Viteazul Street, on the road to the Throne Citadel.

The oldest place of worship in the city, the **Mirăuţi Church**, founded between 1375 and 1391 by Peter I Muşat, was the see of the Moldovan Metropolitan from 1402. Up until 1522 all the Moldavian voivodes were crowned here. The church lies at the foot of Suceava's Throne Citadel.

Suceava's Throne Citadel, on the east side of the city, was for years synonymous with Moldavia's military might. It was the country's main bastion of resistance against Ottoman, Polish, Tartar or Hungarian threats. The original structure dates back to the time of Peter I Muşat (1374), who erected a rectangular fort (the Fortress of the Muşatins) with a chapel in the centre. The descendants of the Muşat dynasty, in particular Alexander the Good, followed by Stephen the Great, made improvements to the original bastion, endowing it with a moat and thick outer walls, according to the needs of the time, as well as with corner towers. Alexander Lăpuşneanu destroyed the Citadel on Turkish orders, burning it to the ground.

The **Museum of the Bukowina Village** (📞 0230.216439 🕐 Tue-Fri: 10am-6pm, Sat-Sun: 10am-8pm (in summer) Tue-Fri: 9am-3:30pm) covers more than six hectares of the plateau near Şipote Park, where Suceava's citadel stands. It is an open-air exhibition of 30 traditional wooden houses and annexes, including the Roşu House, the Şaru Dornei tavern, a potter's workshop from Marginea, a traditional oil press from Volovăţ, and a watermill from the Humor Monastery.

The **Şcheia Fortress** (or Western Fortress) formed part of the town's defensive system. It was built in the form of a 36-metre-thick quadrangle during the reign of Peter I Muşat (1375-1391) on Şeptilici Hill, in the north-west of the city, but was abandoned in the time of Alexander the Good (1400-1432).

Photo: *Suceava's Throne Citadel*

In the 17th century, there were more than 3,000 Armenians living in Suceava. **Armenian Street** still has many Armenian houses of special historical value, even though some of them have undergone major alterations over the years. Inside the **Zamca Citadel**, west of Suceava, there was a 16th-century Armenian monastery, enclosed by stone walls and a monumental gate. The monastery was fortified in 1691 by King Jan Sobieski of Poland, who used it to quarter his troops during an incursion into Moldavia. It is regarded as a site of great importance by the Armenian community of Romania.

CHURCHES WITH EXTERIOR MURALS IN NORTHERN MOLDAVIA (UNESCO SITES)

Bukowina's churches with exterior and interior murals are unique in Europe, which is why they have been listed as UNESCO World Heritage sites.

Built mostly by the Moldavian voivodes of the Muşat Dynasty, these superb monasteries served as princely tombs. According to chronicler Ion Neculce, Stephen the Great (1457-1504), "the bastion of Christianity", had a church or monastery built after each battle against the Turks, Hungarians or Poles during his 47-year

reign. The reign of Peter Rareş (1527-1538, 1541-1546) continued the tradition started by the great voivode Stephen. It followed the Byzantine style, but also showed openness to Renaissance humanism and art. Their most outstanding and original legacy is the murals that completely cover the outside walls of the churches.

The small **Pătrăuţi Church** (12km from Suceava) was built by Stephen the Great in 1487. A tri-conch in plan, with a spire above the nave, the building has preserved intact all its original murals. The votive painting is particularly impressive, displaying exceptional artistic mastery, along with the scene depicting the *Cavalcade of the Holy Cross*, an obvious anti-Ottoman allusion. In the courtyard of the church, near the south wall there is a round table made up of two stone slabs with a series of stones arranged all around, resembling chairs; it is said that this ensemble, dating to the time of Stephen the Great, inspired Brâncuşi when he created his Table of Silence.

The **Decollation of St. John the Baptist Church** (1503) in **Arbore** village (32km from Suceava) was part of the court of boyar Luca Arbore, the castellan of the Suceava Fortress under Stephen the Great. The exterior murals were painted in 1541 by Dragoş Coman from Jassy, regarded as a "true Pisanello of Moldavia", the greatest artist of the 16th-century Orthodox East". The founder's tomb is in the narthex, Moldavia's most impressive burial monument in the late-Gothic style.

The **Voroneţ Monastery** (5km from Gura Humorului, a town located 47km from Suceava) is reckoned to be a "Sistine Chapel of the East". The western facade of this remarkable building from 1488, founded by Stephen the Great, is entirely taken up by a *Last Judgment* scene. On the south wall the *Tree of Jesse* is depicted, next to which there are portraits of philosophers Plato and Aristotle. The upper side of the north wall depicts the scenes of the *Adam's sin, Adam ploughing, Eve spinning wool (the Creation of the World), Adam's Covenant* and the *Toll Houses*. The frescoes were painted after 1547, at the behest of Metropolitan Grigorie Roșca, using an inimitable and unique blue background, which has gained wide renown. The origins of "Voroneț blue" remain obscure to this day. It is certain that it contains azurite (copper carbonate), but exactly what has made it so formidably resilient throughout the centuries is yet to be discovered. It is also remarkable that the painters introduced folk and traditional motifs into the frescoes: Moldovan music instruments, such as the *bucium* (a type of alphorn) and the *cobza* (a string instrument), traditional embroidered fabrics, traditional costumes, local landscapes.

The **Humor Monastery** (6km from Gura Humorului) is one of the most important sites of Romanian mediaeval art. It was built in 1530 by the logothete Toader Bubuiog, the commander of Peter Rareș's artillery. It has preserved its amazing exterior frescoes, painted in Byzantine tradition in 1535 by Toma the Zographos from Suceava. The dominant colour is brick red, which makes it sets it apart from the other painted churches. *The Akathistos Hymn of the Annunciation*, *the Life of St. Hierarch Nicholas*, and *The Siege of Constantinople* are depicted on the south wall, the *Tree of Jesse* on the north wall, the *Last Judgement* on the west wall, while the lateral apses have a series of saints, angels, prophets, hierarchs, apostles, martyrs and holy fathers (*the Procession*). In the burial chamber (a crypt between the narthex and the nave) the *Flight into Egypt* is depicted. Around 300m away the ruins of an earlier church are still visible. It was constructed in 1415, during the time of Alexander the Good.

Moldovița (36km from Gura Humorului and 25km from Câmpulung Moldovenesc), built in 1532 by Peter Rareș, is among the most beautiful of Bukowina's churches with exterior murals. It stands out thanks to its frescoes, painted by Toma of Suceava in 1537, in shades of rusty-red. The best-known exterior mural is *the Siege of Constantinople*, on the south wall, an allusion to the anti-Ottoman wars of the time. The north wall displays scenes from the life of the Theotokos, the *Apostles' Sermon* and the *Toll Houses*, while the west wall is dedicated to the *Last Judgement*. The church has also made its mark thanks to its magnificent open porch with five broad arches and the priest's hole above the burial chamber (the crypt). It is enclosed by a wall more than six metres in height, which lends it the air of a fortress. Do not miss out on a trip on the steam train from the town of Moldovița, which runs for five kilometres from the monastery, as far as Argel, along an old narrow-gauge forest railway track.

The **Probota Monastery** (5km from Dolhasca and 27km from Fălticeni), built in 1530 by Peter Rareș, is one of the finest achievements of 16th-century Moldavian feudal architecture. The monastery church was painted both inside and out in 1532, in the style of the Peter Rareș epoch. Between 1522 and 1677 it served as a burial vault for Moldavia's princely family: here can be found the tombs of rulers Peter Rareș and Stephen Rareș and of Lady Elena Rareș. The interior murals are remarkable, particularly the *Pantocrator* on the spire pendentive, *The Last Supper* in the altar, *St. Nicholas and*

Photo: *Moldovița Monastery*

the *Crucifixion* in the nave, and the *Last Judgement* on the dome of the porch.

Surrounded by 3m thick walls much like a mediaeval fortress, the **Suceviţa Monastery**, 19km from Rădăuţi, was built by three of the Movilă brothers (Jeremiah, ruler of Moldavia, Simion, ruler of Wallachia, and Gheorghe, Metropolitan of Moldavia) around the year 1583. It is the last in the series of northern Moldavia's painted churches. Its most famous fresco is the *The Ladder of the Virtues* on the north wall. The southern facade features the *Akathistos Hymn of the Theotokos, The Tree of Jesse* and the *Protecting Veil of the Theotokos*. The murals were painted between 1595 and 1596 by brothers John and Sofronie.

Visiting the pottery workshops of **Marginea** and **Rădăuţi** is a must. The potters fiercely guard the secrets of their ancient black-burnished pottery techniques and their ceramic wares richly decorated with floral motifs. Observe, too, the staggering metamorphoses of wood: here, in Bukowina, where a culture of woodworking flourished, the beautiful open-porch houses and the churches with their finely carved wooden panels are architectural gems. The Museum of Woodworking in Câmpulung Moldovenesc, unique in the country, tells the story of woodworking in Bukowina.

THE LAND OF NEAMŢ

Neamţ has the highest density of monasteries and hermitages in the country; in effect, there is not one mountain (and it is a very mountainous area) without at least one hermitage or monastery tucked away somewhere. The region of the Neamţ, Secu, Sihăstria, Sihla, Agapia and Văratec monasteries is the spiritual heart of Neamţ.

Ideally, the best starting point to explore the region is the city of **Piatra Neamţ**, located on the banks of the Bistriţa and Cuejdi Rivers and surrounded by wooded mountain peaks: Cozla (650m), Pietricica (586m), Cernegura (852m) and Cârlomanu (704m). Four kilometres south-west of the city stands Bâtca Doamnei Hill (462m), dominating the reservoir of the same name. On these heights, the ruins of an ancient Geto-Dacian fortress have been discovered, identified as Petrodava, mentioned by Ptolemy in *Geography* (III, 8, 4). The fortress, with 3.5-metre-thick walls strengthened by ditches and earthworks, most likely dates to the 2nd century B.C. It was built on top of a Neolithic settlement (Cucuteni stage); two sanctuaries similar to those in Sarmizegetusa have been found within the same precincts. It must have been a important fortification, since it appears on several maps of Dacia made between the 16th and 18th centuries.

Photo: *Suceviţa Monastery*

There were a princely court and church in Piatra as early as 1446; from 1453, the settlement was a burg. In 1491, during the reign of Stephen the Great, a new princely court was built here, and between 1497 and 1499 both the Church of the Nativity of St. John the Baptist and the Bell Tower were constructed. All that survives of the Princely Court (⊠4 Stephen the Great Street), located on a plateau in the city centre, is the brick cellar (currently within the Peter Rareș High School), which now houses a museum, and fragments of the curtain wall. The St John Church is rectangular in plan, without a spire, with semi-cylindrical domes, a vault above the nave and two secondary domes above the narthex; there are two small niches in the thick lateral walls of the nave, reminiscent of the apses in tri-conch churches. The stone facades are decorated with ceramic discs and rows of glazed bricks. The 20m-high tower of Stephen the Great was turned into a fire lookout tower after an extra storey was added, and in 1861 a clock from Vienna was installed on top; there was once a school on the ground floor.

Next door you can find the **Museum of the Cucuteni Eneolithic Art** (⊠ 3 Stephen the Great Street ⏰Tue-Sun: 10am-6pm (Apr-Sept), 9am-5pm (Oct-Mar) Ⓢ 4 Lei), which has an archaeological collection unique in Europe. It was established in a superb building constructed between 1928 and 1930 by Carol Zane, with interior decorations by Vincenzo Puschiasis; between 1930 and 1948 it housed the Petrodava Bank, the first privately owned bank in Piatra Neamț. The rooms, on two floors, display around 300 ceramic exhibits from the Cucuteni culture. They were unearthed at more than 150 archaeological sites across the country: *The Frumușica and Drăgușeni Dance, The Târpești Thinker, The Gathering of Goddesses, The Four-legged Vase of Izvoare* and numerous other anthropomorphic and zoomorphic figurines. The International Cucuteni Culture Research Centre has been based in Piatra Neamț since 1995.

Cucuteni Culture

The Cucuteni-Trypillian culture, to give it its full name, covered an area of 350,000 square kilometres, stretching from south-eastern Transylvania and Moldavia to the Dnieper River in western Ukraine. Its name comes from the discoveries made here in 1884 and 1893, in the town of Cucuteni, Jassy County, and in Trypillia, near Kiev, Ukraine. It is thought to be the oldest Eneolithic culture in Europe (4th-3rd millennia B.C.) and one of the most spectacular and mysterious prehistoric cultures. It earned its fame thanks to its fine pottery, painted with swirling, circular, intricate patterns, using white, red and black. The culture mysteriously vanished, 90% of the discovered settlements having been completely burned down.

To the east of the Princely Court, near the Peter Rareș High School you can find a wooden **Synagogue**, bearing witness to the times when there used to be a large Jewish community in the city (at one point there were eight synagogues and a temple in Piatra). It was built after 1766, on the site of an older stone synagogue. In the early 18th century, the Jews were not allowed to build religious establishments from materials other than wood. It was assumed that the building dated back to the time of Stephen the Great, otherwise the failure to comply with the statutory

distance of 150 *stînjeni* (300m) from the nearest Christian church would remain unexplained.

At the base of the steps up to the plateau atop which stands the Princely Court you can find the **Youth Theatre** (✉ 1 Stephen the Great Square), where famous contemporary actors have performed.

The **Calistrat Hogaş Memorial Museum** (✉ 1 Calistrat Hogaş Street) was once the house where the author of the *On Mountain Trails*, a passionate lover of this region, lived. The stone structure, rebuilt in the 1880s, is one of the few in the city to have fully preserved the architecture typical of a late-nineteenth-century Moldavia burg.

Go for a walk along **Stephen the Great Street**, flanked by old and beautiful villas; it starts from the Princely Court area and leads to a small animal park located at the foot of Cozla Hill. The park was developed between 1900 and 1904, in the aftermath of the landslides of 1897, at the proposal of Mayor Nicu Albu. During the construction of the access roads, the excavations brought to light Dacian artefacts, most likely originating from a fortress that used to stand on the site. On two of the three terraced plateaux of the mountainside, you can find the Colibele Haiducilor and the Cercul Gospodinelor restaurants, which serve traditional Moldavian cuisine.

From the vantage points of Cozla you will enjoy sweeping panoramas of the city and have a view of the glittering waters of the Bistriţa River, Bâtca Doamnei Lake and Pietricica Mountain. Up on the peak there is a vast meadow, which in winter becomes a ski slope. This is also the final stop for the gondola lift, which runs from the train station.

On the Pietricica, Cozla and Cernegura peaks there are numerous fossil sites, covering a total area of 53 hectares. They are protected and have been declared natural monuments. Thirty-eight species of fossil fish have been identified here. In 1883, Leon Cosmovici, a professor at Jassy University, described a further 21 species new to science. A valuable collection of fossil fish is on display at the **Natural Science Museum** (✉ 26 Peter Rareş Street ☎ 0233.224211 🕐 Tue-Sun: 10am-6pm (Apr-Sept), 9am-5pm (Oct-Mar) ⑤ 3 Lei).

Setting out along the Bistriţa Valley you will be spoilt for choice in terms of possible routes: you can head for the holy sites of Neamţ (Bistriţa, Bisericani, and Pângăraţi monasteries); you can take your time and go around the Mountain Spring Lake, a 35-kilometre-long, unforgettable spectacle; you can make your way to the Durău resort, the main gateway to the heights of the legendary Ceahlău Mountain; you can travel to the astounding Bicaz Gorges and

Photo: *Museum of Cucuteni Eneolithic Art and the Tower of Stephen the Great, Piatra Neamţ*

Red Spring Lake; or you can move on to the highland villages of Galu, Farcaşa or Borca.

The DN15, which starts west of the city of Piatra Neamţ, on the way to Bicaz, follows the course of the Bistriţa River, reaching after approx. 8km the municipality of Alexander the Good (formerly Viişoara), at the foot of the Stânişoara Mountains. At the confluence of the Bistriţa and Viişoara, in Bistriţa village, there is a very old place of worship: the **Bistriţa Monastery**, built before 1407 by ruler Alexander the Good. In 1498, Stephen the Great built a bell tower chapel; he also donated to the church a bronze bell with Moldavia's coat of arms. In 1554, Alexander Lăpuşneanu rebuilt the monastery church. This place of worship, with its almost 12-metre-thick walls, is 41 metres long, 15 metres wide and 36 metres tall.

After Viişoara village (9km from Piatra Neamţ), a side road branches off the DN15 on the right, leading to Scăricica-Bisericani (4km). At an altitude of 650 metres, in the middle of the forest, on Pietrosu Mountain, you will find the **Bisericani Monastery**, built in 1498 by the monk Iosif on the site of a wooden small church dating to the time of Alexander the Good and completed in 1517 by Ştefăniţă Vodă, Stephen the Great's grandson.

Returning to the DN15, keep to the main road until you come to a side road leading 10km up to the Dimitrie Leonida Hydroelectric Power Station at Stejaru, built in 1960 on the middle course of the Bistriţa River. The power station is supplied by the Mountain Spring Lake (Bicaz) through a 5km long headrace tunnel excavated beneath Botoşanu Mountain. Here, on the left bank of Pângăraţi Stream, which flows through the Păru Mountain, lies another old monastic settlement: **Pângăraţi Monastery**, built in 1461, in the reign of Stephen the Great, by monk Simion from the Bistriţa Monastery. Burned down by the Ottomans during an invasion, the wooden church of the monastery of Saint Demetrius was rebuilt in stone between 1552 and 1558 by Alexander Lăpuşneanu. The novelty of the place is that there are in

fact two churches, one on top of the other. In 1806 the priest's hole in the basement built by Alexander Lăpuşneanu was turned into a separate church by Abbot Macarie. It is where services were held for the prisoners after the monastery was converted into a gaol. The underground church is connected with the one above by a semi-circular staircase.

The town of **Bicaz**, 28km west from Piatra Neamţ (on DN15), at the foot of the Ceahlău Mountain, at the confluence of the Bistriţa and the Bicaz, thrived during communism period after the dam and Mountain Spring reservoir (Bicaz) were built here, between 1950 and 1960, to the designs of engineer Dimitrie Leonida (1883-1965). The 35-km-long Mountain Spring Lake borders several settlements in Neamţ: Bicaz, Pângăraţi, Ceahlău, Hangu and Poiana Teiului.

Twenty-seven kilometres south-west of Bicaz stretch the **Bicaz Gorges**, a section of the Bicaz Valley where the waters rush for 8km through the Hăşmaş Massif in the Eastern Carpathians. The road from Bicazu Ardelean to Red Lake along the DN12C (which links Bicaz and Gheorgheni) is absolutely spectacular. The valley of the gorges formed by the erosion of the Mesozoic limestone of Hăşmaş is overshadowed by the Piatra Altarului Peak (1,121m), Piatra Pinteştilor Peak (847m), Piatra Arşiţei Peak (835m), Piatra Glodului Peak, Piatra Surducului Peak, Culmea Ucigaşului Peak and Poarta de Piatră Peak. Opposite Gâtul Iadului (the Neck of Hell), the narrowest section of the gorges, the rock walls of the Bardos Massif and the Piatra Surducului Massif, through which the Bicaz river flows, are so close to each other that they prevent the rays of the sun from ever touching the surface of the water.

Red Lake, covering more than 13 hectares and 10.5 metres deep, was formed in 1837, after large chunks of rocks on the north-western side of the Ghilcoş Mountain collapsed due to heavy rain fall, cutting off the Verescheu Valley (the Red Valley). Pine logs from the forest flooded at the time still float in the waters of the lake.

From the **Durău** climatic resort, located 800m above sea level, there are several trails leading to the top of the **Ceahlău Mountain** Peaks: Ocolaşul Mare (1,907m), Toaca (1,904m), Panaghia (1,900m) and Ocolaşul Mic (1,712m), which provide breathtaking views of Mountain Spring Lake, the Bistriţa River Valley, the Bistra River Valley, the Bicaz River Valley, and the Stânişoara, Bistriţa, Tarcău and Hăşmaş mountains. What set the Ceahlău Mountain apart, a mountain composed of limestone conglomerates, are its massive proportions and shattered landscape: steep slopes, pinnacles, rock slabs, ridges etc..

Another important tourist destination is **Târgu Neamţ**, located 44 km from the city of Piatra Neamţ, on the terrace of the Ozana River (Neamţ). Târgu Neamţ owes its development to the construction of a powerful fortress on a cliff, south of the Pleşu Peak, between 1374 and 1391, during the time of Peter I Muşat. Many times compared to an "eagle's nest", it has become a symbol of the town. The Humuleşti neighbourhood, once "an old and merry village of free peasants", preserves the house in which the unsurpassed raconteur Ion Creangă was born. Near the village of Vânători Neamţ can be found the Dragoş Vodă Auroch and Carpathian Wildlife Reserve. Do not miss out on the Folk Art Museum, created by

mask collector and designer Nicolae Popa from Târpeşti, 10km from Târgu Neamţ.

The **Agapia Monastery**, 9km from Târgu Neamţ, resembles an enclosure circumscribed by white-walled buildings whose porches come alive in summer with red geraniums. The main church, in the neoclassical style, was painted between 1858 and 1860 by Nicolae Grigorescu, when he was just 20 years old. The nuns lead both a coenobitic and idiorrhythmic life. In the monastic village, with its more than 100 houses designed in the local style, some of which are more than 200 years old, you can visit the Alexandru Vlahuţă Memorial Museum. It is the house where the writer spent many summers entertaining guests such as Nicolae Grigorescu, I.L. Caragiale, Mihail Sadoveanu and Barbu Delavrancea.

From Agapia you can reach the Văratec Monastery, either by following the forest road (4km), a real feast for the eyes, or by going back to the main road and taking the C road (DJ155E) towards Valea Seacă (7km). You will pass near the forest reserves of Pădurea de Argint (Silver Wood – a 2.4-hectare birch forest), on the lower terrace of the Topoliţa Stream, and Codri de Aramă (Bronze Wood – a 9.4-hectare forest of sessile oak), on Filiorul Hill.

Like Agapia, **Văratec** is an idiorrhythmic community; the nuns here live individually each in her own house in the monastic village. The monastery was founded in 1785 by Mother Olimpiada, the daughter of a priest from Jassy, a nun from the former Topoliţa hermitage, which once existed nearby.

From Agapia, a mountain road (7km), accessible to vehicles, leads to the Sihla Hermitage, and thence to the Sihăstria (3km) and Secu monasteries (3km).

Neamţ Monastery, one of the oldest monastic centres in Moldavia, was built in the 14th century by Peter I Muşat. It was later rebuilt by Alexander the Good; in 1497, Stephen the Great built the impressive Church of the Ascension here. The stone structure, a tri-conch in plan, 40 metres long, is a perfect illustration of the Moldavian style of the epoch.

Return to the 15B road, travel 2km towards Pipirig, and then follow the DC160 for another 4km to the **Secu Monastery** "fortress". The monastery church, built in 1602 by Vornic (minister of justice Nestor Ureche, the father of chronicler Grigore Ureche, combines Moldovan and Wallachian architectural features; strong curtain walls with towers at the four corners lend the monastery the appearance of a fortified citadel.

Sihăstria Monastery lies just 3km away, in the middle of the Atanasie Meadow. Step into the labyrinthine Sihăstria "fortress", through stone portal and along narrow "streets", where the monks' cells, small country houses, stand on platforms that can be reached by climbing up or down slate steps.

A 3-km-long forest road leads through the wood to the **Sihla Hermitage**. It was here, on top of the Sihla Mountain, almost 1,000m above sea level, in a cave nestling between massive boulders, which might collapse any minute, that Saint Theodora resided in the 17th century.

Roman, founded by Roman I Muşat, became an episcopal see under Alexander the Good. The episcopal cathedral, built between 1542-1550 by Peter Rareş, continues to bear witness to the glorious times of the distant past. It was in the house of Vornic Done that famous conductor Sergiu Celibidache was born in 1912.

The road to the "land of fairy tales" – the celebrated **Ancuţa's Inn** – is anything but boring. It will take you through villages which, although not very well known, are breathtaking for their old churches, the mysterious remains of former inns, and grand boyar mansions. Not counting the famous edifice of Stephen the Great at Războieni: the original monastery-mausoleum.

Photo: *Neamţ Monastery*

Transylvania

Previous page: *The church in Densuş*

Transylvania

Transylvania is a special place with historic, ethnic, cultural and ethnographic characteristics that set it clearly apart from the other Romanian provinces. A journey through Transylvania will take you into the heart of a different world, with citadels and fortresses from the Middle Ages, with Germanic burgs, fortified churches, numerous examples of Gothic, Renaissance and Baroque architecture, and old traditions.

The local population, organised into "lands" and voivodeships ruled by knyazes, was conquered by the Kingdom of Hungary between the 11th and 13th century. Hungarian settlers were brought into Transylvania after the establishment of feudal estates, and in order to reinforce their rule, the Hungarian kings invited Saxons and Szeklers to colonise the region. They were the architects of settlements typically German in structure, the traces of which are everywhere to be found in this region.

Romanians, Hungarians, Saxons and Szeklers – nations so different from each other – managed to create here a unique world, which has largely preserved its archaic atmosphere. Transylvanian towns and cities are different from anything you might see in the rest of the country: the mediaeval burgs acquired a distinctive baroque character after Transylvania came under Habsburg administration (1699). It was only after World War I that Transylvania, along with the other provinces inhabited by Romanians – Crișana, Maramureș, the Banat – united with Romania, on 1 December 1918, Romania's National Day.

It was in this region, located in the middle of the country and girdled by the Carpathian Mountain Range, that the heart of the Dacian kingdom (Sarmizegetusa in the Orăștiei Mountains) lay. The kingdom, conquered by the Emperor Trajan (in 106 A.D.), merged with the Roman Empire; the Romans ruled central and south-eastern Dacia for approximately 165 years. They built roads, castra and towns

(Colonia Ulpia Traiana Sarmizegetusa, Apulum, Napoca, Potaissa, Porolissum) and developed a mining industry.

Transylvania's villages, with their fortified churches, and towns, which were also once highly fortified, are now tourist attractions. You will be surprised to hear, in a remote village such as Viscri, to take just one example, more people speaking English, French and German than Romanian; and cities such as Sibiul and Braşov swarm with visitors from around the world almost all year round.

Lying within the Carpathian arc, Transylvania, "the land beyond the forest", is – surprisingly, given that it is one of the most visited areas in Romania – one of the regions with the most unspoiled scenery. Far from the madding crowd, deep in the forests, you will discover caves, karst and strange-looking natural landforms, most of which are listed as nature reserves.

The German and Hungarian community in Transylvania have kept the Fărşang and Lole traditions, which are rituals to banish winter and the evil spirits. They take the form of carnivals (*Fasching*) before the beginning of Lent.

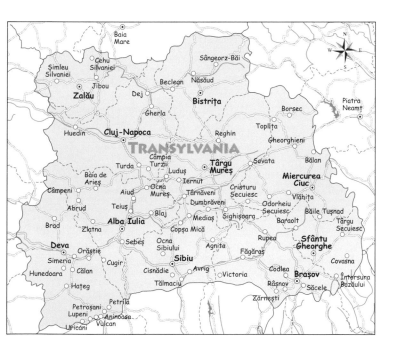

Siebenbürgen, "the land of the seven fortresses"

Once known as Siebenbürgen, "the land of the seven fortresses", Transylvania was defined by its seven legendary Saxon fortresses (German settlers were brought by King Géza II of Hungary to defend the mountain passes): Brașov, Bistrița, Cluj (replaced by Sebeș, after embracing Calvinism in the 15th century), Mediaș, Orăștie (replaced by Reghin in the 15th century), Sibiu and Sighișoara. The advent of the Saxons in this region gave birth to many legends, such as the *Pied Piper of Hamelin*, collected by the Brothers Grimm in 1816. According to the tale, the more than one hundred children from the German town of Hamelin, who disappeared into a cave after being lured away by the magic music played by a stranger on his magical pipe, mysteriously reappeared in Transylvania. In 1819, the Brothers Grimm pointed to the fact that a version of the legend had been passed down by Friedrich Müller, a priest of the Black Church in Brașov, who wrote: "We, the Germans of Transylvania, are the children lured from Hamelin by the magic pipe, who had long travelled underneath the ground before reappearing in the middle of Transylvania, emerging from the Merești cave, in the Vărghiș Valley, and who are scattered around our seven towns and many villages". What we have here is, of course, a mythical interpretation of a common historical truth: migration.

BRAȘOV

The tourist season in Brașov never seems to end. Come summer or winter, the old city of this mediaeval burg teems with tourists from all over the world. Statistics show that annually the city attracts more visitors than any other region in Romania. A walk down the lively Republic Street or around Town Hall Square, at any hour of the day, morning or evening, proves the figures right. People are equally enthralled by the typically Saxon layout of the houses and the architecture, with its Gothic, Renaissance and Baroque features. They also take advantage of the city's amazing location, at the foot of wooded hills and the Tâmpa Mountain, whose summit provides spectacular views. From there, 300m above the city, you can survey in a single glance the streets surrounding the large central square, the Black Church and the Town Hall Tower, important landmarks, soaring above the reddish shingle roofs.

First attested in documents more than 770 years ago, Brașov (Lat. *Corona*, Germ. *Kronstadt*) is the most important of the fortresses to have been established by the Teutonic Knights in Transylvania in the 13th century.

? DID YOU KNOW?

Designated in the 14th century as Civitas Coronensis, *meaning the "Fortress of the Crown", as it was a royal free city subordinate only to the King, Brașov's coat of arms features a crown with a tree that has 13 silver roots, symbolising the 13 municipalities of the Bârsa Land.*

Photo: *Brașov, at the foot of the Tâmpa Mountain*

The old city centre (Town Hall Square), flanked by Renaissance, Baroque and neoclassical buildings, is dominated by the famous **Black Church** (1384-1477), the largest Gothic structure in Romania, whose facades are adorned with sculptures. The Black Church got its name in the aftermath of a devastating fire in 1689, which blackened its walls. Inside, there are murals painted in the Renaissance style in the 15th century, more than one hundred Oriental rugs, and an organ with over 4,000 pipes, built between 1836 and 1839 by Carl August Buchholz. The main attractions in summer are organ concerts played on Tuesdays from 6 p.m. (in June and September) and on Tuesdays, Thursdays and Saturdays, also at 6 p.m. (July and August).

The **Town Hall House** (✉30 Town Hall Square), a building that originally belonged to the Furriers' Guild and later became the town hall, has Transylvanian Gothic, Renaissance and Baroque features, which testify to the successive changes it underwent from the 14th to 18th centuries. The 58m-high watchtower was where a trumpeter used to announce the time every hour on the hour and any immediate dangers, whence its name: the Trumpet Tower. The building was also used as a jail, with a gallows and pillory nearby.

It now houses the County History Museum and main Tourist Information Centre. It continues to display on its facade the old coat of arms of Braşov, the crown.

The **Merchants House** (✉14 Town Hall Square), an impressive 67-metre-long complex, made up of two wings separated by an interior courtyard, was built in the 16th century by Apollonia Hirscher, in the style of Western halls. It housed warehouses, workshops and traders' stalls (called "bridges" at the time), which sold various goods, particularly those made by the "beaters" (i.e. shoemakers) which goes to explain its other name, Beaters' Bridge. Today, it is home to the Corona Galleries, as well as the Carpathian Stag restaurant and wine cellar.

As Braşov developed into a powerful centre for merchants and artisans, it became necessary to fortify it, particularly after the devastating Tartar invasion of 1241 and the Turkish incursion of 1421. As early as the 14th century, defensive walls were built, 12m high, almost 2m thick and 3km long. The citadel was surrounded by a moat filled with water. In the 18th century most of the fortifications were pulled down as the town expanded, but what remains is more than enough to prove that Braşov was in the Middle Ages one of the most powerful citadels in Transylvania.

Photo: *Town Hall Square, Braşov*

Take a stroll along the **Alley Beyond the Walls**, a pleasant pedestrian street between the old northern walls and the Graft Stream (diverted into the old citadel moat), which flows gently past the foot of the Warthe Hill (Straja). On top of the hill above stand the Black and White Towers (15th century), two sites that provide a panoramic view of the entire mediaeval burg. Another path starts from behind the Black Tower and leads in the direction opposite to the White Tower, across the hill up to the road to Poiana Braşov. A deck and a drawbridge would previously have made the connection between the White Tower and the Graft Bastion opposite, but lying at the foot of the hill. At the north-western end of the alley stands the Blacksmiths' Bastion, which currently houses archives. There is a moat on the south side as well, drained in the 19th century and turned into a path.

The **Alley beneath Tâmpa** is today flanked by the Drapers' Bastion, Spinners' Bastion and Weavers' Bastion, the last of these being the best-preserved monument of its kind in Transylvania. Six-sided, with two square towers and two- to three-metre-thick walls, it currently houses the Museum of Braşov Citadel and Bârsa Land Fortifications. If while walking through the streets of Braşov you have ever wondered what they looked like in mediaeval times, this is where you will find the answer: the weapons chamber displays a scale model of the burg in the 15th century. The interior courtyard, the best vantage point to survey the four layers of defences, featuring impressive galleries with oak beams, often hosts classical music concerts.

Almost opposite the Spinners' Tower is the cable car station to the **Tâmpa Peak**, 967m above sea level and 300m above the city. The trip from the Casa Pădurarului chalet-restaurant to the station and Panoramic Restaurant at the top lasts less than three minutes. An alternative would be to go on foot. The effort is worthwhile, as most of the mountain has been declared a nature reserve (180ha). It is home to species such as the iris, *Anemone transsilvanica*, purple morning glory, viper's bugloss, snake's head fritillary, and others. There are five trails (each takes around one hour) and six stopping places. You can chose the Knights Road, a path with 25 bends, or the Gabony Steps, which start from Dobrujanu Gherea Street and lead to the peak of the Tâmpa Mountain (the trail is marked with yellow triangles). The panoramic view takes in the entire city of Braşov, and even the Bârsa Land beyond, when the sky is clear

---

Left: *Alley Beyond the Walls*   **Right:** *Alley Beneath Tâmpa*

Between the Tâmpa Peak and Saddle lie the ruins of the Braşovia fortress, probably built by the Teutonic knights in the 13th century.

As you head back into the city, on the west side of the old burg stands the **Tower of Katherine's Gate** (1540), one of Braşov's landmarks. It has four little towers on each corner, symbolising the *ius gladii*, the right to apply the capital punishment

Westward, beyond Katherine's Gate, stretches the Romanian district of **Scheii Braşovului**. Originally, Romanians were not allowed to live within the walls of the Saxon citadel or to build Orthodox churches there. Unlike the old city, Scheii has a more rural feel to it, with overgrown courtyards and meandering streets zigzagging up the hill. At the exit from the district (around 2km from Union Square) can be found the Solomon Rocks, a gorge in a spectacular rocky valley, which has inspired many legends; locals come here for picnics at weekends. Many houses in Schei have icons painted on their front wall and wooden gates, and here and there you will to see wayside shrines guarding the crossroads. The oldest is the Cutun shrine (1292), in the St. Trinity Church cemetery. Others, some carved in stone and built as chapel-shrines covered in frescoes, are also strikingly beautiful: the Young Men Shrine on Coasta Prundului, Ilie Birt's Shrine/the Captain's Cross (on Tocile), the Ştim/ Gruiu Shrine (where Coasta Street and Curcanilor Street intersect), the wayside shrine on Cloşca Street, the Pajiştea Mare Shrine, the Crucea Dreptăţii Shrine, the Furnică shrine. The spires of the beautiful St. Nicholas Church, built of stone on the site of an earlier wooden place of worship that dated from 1292, dominate Union Square. It was extended between 1583 and 1595 by Petru Cercel, the ruler of Wallachia, and by Aron Vodă, the ruler of Moldavia. Nearby, the first Romanian school in Braşov was established, the church thus became an important centre of Romanian Orthodoxy, thanks particularly to the work of deacon Coresi, who printed here the first book in Romanian, a Christian catechism (*Întrebare creştinească*, 1559).

Junii of Braşov (The Young Men of Braşov)

Seven groups of "young men" set out from outside St. Nicholas Church on the Sunday of St. Thomas (the first Sunday after Easter), in accordance with an old Braşov tradition. It is a folk feast whose meaning is now lost in the mists of time. It may be that it was originally a rite of passage for young men or a celebration of the rebirth of nature, or that it marked the only day in the year when Romanians were allowed free entry into the Saxon city. To this day the *Junii Tineri* (young bachelors), *Bătrâni* (older married men), *Dorobanţi* (infantrymen), *Braşovecheni* (men from the old city), *Curcani* (soldiers wearing feathers in their hat bands), *Roşiori* (horsemen) and *Albiori* (men with white fur caps), all dressed in traditional costume, ride their horses through Union Square towards the old city of Braşov, and thence to the Solomon Rocks, where an outdoor feast is held, with dancing and feats of strength, such as mace throwing. In the evening they descend into the city again. The occasion is a grand parade: locals and tourists gather along the route taken by the *Juni*, who ride to the accompaniment of a brass band.

Photo: *Junii* of Braşov (*The Young Men of Braşov*)

As well as the Saxon and Romanian communities, there were many Szekelys in Braşov, who settled to the east of the citadel in the Blumăna district. The area is dominated by University hill and the Fortress (Cetăţuia), a sixteenth- to seventeenth-century fortification, with bastions at its corners, which stands on top of a wooded hill. Today, it houses a Romanian restaurant.

The oldest building in the city is not within the old city, but some distance away, at the end of Long Street, which does not belie its name. This area, known as Braşovechi (old Braşov), is dominated by the Romanesque St. Bartholomew Church, built of stone in 1223 by Cistercian monks, and by the St. Martin Church, a former chapel from the 14th century. It is the oldest site in Braşov. The facade shows the outline of an earlier solar dial.

The area around Braşov is one of the most popular tourism regions in Romania; from here you can set out on excursions to the fortified churches in the villages of Făgăraş, Rupea, Râşnov and Prejmer, and the mediaeval castles of Bran, Racoş and Hoghiz.

Just 12km away can be found the mountain resort of **Poiana Braşov**, above which soars the Postăvaru Massif. Winter sports enthusiasts will find there numerous ski slopes of varying degrees of difficulty.

THE FORTIFIED CHURCHES AND RURAL FORTRESSES AROUND BRAŞOV

The rural fortress of **Hărman** (*Honigberg* in German, or *Mons Mellis* in Latin, meaning the Mountain of Honey), 10km east of Braşov, has at its centre a Romanesque basilica attested in documents since 1240. It is protected by a 12-metre-high wall with seven defensive towers.

The **Prejmer church** (*Tartlau*), 15km from Braşov, was built between 1241 and 1250 in the early Gothic style. Originally a Cistercian monastery, it underwent changes between 1512 and 1515. It was fortified in the 15th-16th centuries, becoming the strongest rural fortress in Transylvania. The walls are 6m thick and 12m high. There are 275 rooms on three or four storeys connected by wooden staircases. The church preserves a valuable 15th-century polyptych altar and an organ from 1803.

Although not a UNESCO World Heritage site, the fortified church of St. Peter in **Ghimbav** (*Weidenbach*), 9km west of Braşov, is worth a visit. The floral motifs painted on its ceiling are rather unusual. The village made the headlines in 2009 when, on the road to Cristian, an Orthodox church with a gilded roof was constructed, costing one million Euros.

Left: *Cetăţuia, Braşov*
Right: *Prejmer Church*

Next page: *Saxon feast at Biertan*

FORTIFIED CHURCHES OF TRANSYLVANIA

In the centre of each rural settlement founded by the Saxons in the Romanian province of Transylvania in the 12th century stands a church fortified with defensive walls, which also used to serve as a refuge in times of danger. Most of these fortified churches (13th-16th centuries) resemble small fortresses and were built after the great Tartar invasion of 1241, when the land was plundered. Dominating their surroundings, some of them had two or three enceints, towers, sentries' walkways on top of the walls, barbicans, and secret passageways. Inside, the walls were lined with storerooms, where the villagers kept their food supplies and where they took shelter when their villages were attacked.

Transylvania's fortress churches are not unique in the world, but they are significant for the originality of their rural-type defensive system and for their number. Since they were long secluded, far from foreign influences, they have kept many archaic elements that have long since disappeared in other parts. It is impressive how many of them can be found within a rather limited area. There used to be 300 fortified churches in Transylvania, but today only 150 villages still preserve such structures. Having said that, the number is still very high!

Although by and large built on the same pattern, the fortified churches are distinct from each other, which makes seeing them worthwhile. No matter how many churches you visit, there are no two alike. Some have unusual features, Cistercian (Prejmer) or Baroque (Ighişul Nou) influences, or other architectural novelties (such as the massive tower above the church and Roman chapel adjoined to the south wall at Axente Sever), while others combine Roman, Gothic and Neoclassic elements (Cristian, Braşov County). Their walls have revealed murals beneath layers of plaster applied after the Reformation (which strictly banned figurative religious images). Many churches have preserved items fashioned by the goldsmiths and the silversmiths of the old mediaeval burgs, stone and wood carvings, furniture decorated with Saxon motifs, very old and valuable organs, and clocks dating from the 16th century (such as the one at Hărman).

Unfortunately, many of the fortified churches have badly deteriorated and in some cases are near to collapse. The heritage of the Saxons, who left their villages during communism and after 1990 to emigrate to Germany, is in danger of extinction. Seven of the churches – Biertan, Câlnic, Dârjiu, Prejmer, Saschiz, Valea Viilor and Viscri – have been listed as UNESCO World Heritage sites. However, many are at risk of decay due to poor maintenance; others (Archita, Ighiş) have fallen into oblivion, since they are in very remote areas. Restoration work on some of the churches have been started by both the Romanian and foreign authorities. A unique case is the Axente Sever complex (*Frauendorf*), which has a guesthouse (☎0735-569996, muzeulcetate@yahoo.com).

Charles, Prince of Wales, bought a Saxon house in Viscri and has supported the Mihai Eminescu Trust's projects to restore the property and breathe new life into the area, in order to encourage tourism. The trust under Prince Charles's patronage has begun restoration work on the churches of Meşendorf, Cloaşterf, Roadeş, Floreşti, Buneşti, Mălâncrav, Axente Sever and Apold.

Transylvania's Saxon villages, with their unitary architecture, and the fortress churches in their midst have become tourist destinations almost overnight, drawing thousands of tourists from Germany, Britain, Belgium and France.

The **Cristian** Church, 13km west of Braşov, is defined by the way in which Romanesque architectural elements (the west portal) and Gothic features (the rosette, three keystones), dating from the 14th century, merged within a neoclassical structure, the result of rebuilding work in the 19th century. Near the village lies an oak forest with trees more than four centuries old.

Perched on top of a 500-metre-high hill, 17km south-west of Braşov, the **Râşnov Citadel** (Germ. *Rosenau*, Lat. *Villa Rosarum*, The Rose Meadow), originally built by the Teutonic knights, provides unforgettable views of the Bârsa Land. The well in the courtyard, which is almost 150 metres deep, took seventeen years to dig, according to legend, work carried out by two Turkish prisoners, who were promised their freedom after they finished. Also in Râşnov traces of a Roman castrum and the Cumidava fortress have been found, reckoned by geographer Ptolemy to have defended the road across the Carpathians, today's Bran Pass. Râşnov is also home to the oldest building in Transylvania, built by the Basarab Dynasty: the Saint Nicholas Church (1384), restored by Michael the Brave in 1600.

The **Hălchiu** Church (*Heldsdorf*), 15km north of Braşov, built in the 13th century and rebuilt in the 15th century, has preserved its polyptych altarpiece from 1522-26, in the late-Gothic style, considered to be the largest mediaeval altarpiece in Transylvania.

The **Feldioara** Fortress (*Marienburg*), located 20km north of Braşov, on the way to Sighişoara, is regarded as the most significant fortification built by the Teutonic knights in Transylvania, and was attested as early as 1225. The complex is perched on top of a hill bordered on three sides by the Homorod River. It was restored as part of a project launched in 2013.

THE ŞINCA VECHE CAVE CHURCH

Known as the Temple of Wishes, the cave complex at Dealul Pleşu, 2km from Şinca Veche village, 50km north-west of Braşov, continues to stir lively debate. Officially, the site dates back to 1742, when the local monks were forced to convert to Catholicism at the orders of Empress Maria Theresa, but many claim that it dates back to Dacian times or even earlier. The presence of two shrines and the lack of a cross mean that many argue that the church is not Christian in origin.

The complex carved in the rock is made up of five chambers connected by tunnels. The church has a ten-metre-high spiral chimney, hollowed from the inside, rather like an inside-out dome. It allows a glimpse of the sky and lets in the rays of the sun. On the wall of the room with the altar are inscribed a Star of David and Yin-Yang sign.

Left: *Râşnov Citadel*   Right: *Şinca Veche Cave Church*

Associated with various unexplained phenomena and mysteries, Şinca Veche has become a place of pilgrimage. It is said that the wishes made in the vaulted room come true if they are made with a pure heart. According to tradition, the girls in the village must come to Dealul Pleşu three times a year – on Saint George's Day, Meatfare Sunday, and the Feast of the Transfiguration – and set fire to a wheel of straw and send it rolling down the hill if they are to find a husband.

FĂGĂRAŞ FORTRESS

The remarkable feudal complex at the heart of the town of Făgăraş, 67km north-west of Braşov, dates from the 14th to 17th centuries. In the 17th century it made its mark as the capital of the first rulers of Transylvania and as the political and administrative centre of the Făgăraş region. It later became a much-feared prison, its warehouses and cellars being used as cells for rebellious peasants.

The fortress has 85 chambers, and is girded by a moat filled with water. It currently houses the Valer Literat Museum of the Făgăraş Land, the municipal library, and a wine cellar.

The year 2012 saw the revival of the changing the guard, bringing back the mediaeval atmosphere in order to attract tourists. At 3 o'clock in the afternoon, outside the gate the guards in mediaeval attire put on quite an original show.

The **Dumbrava Vadului Daffodil Meadow** stretches over 400 hectares at the bottom of Vad village, 20km from Făgăraş and 80km from Braşov. In May, when the jonquils, as the locals call them, are in bloom, the place becomes magical. It is here that on the Feast of Ss. Constantine and Helen the Daffodil Festival is held.

SIGHIŞOARA

The amazing Sighişoara, which has rightly gained renown as the "Transylvanian Nuremberg", sits on Citadel Hill (425m), on the left bank of the Târnava Mare River. It is surrounded by other hills: Gării, Stejăriş, Brădet, Lunca Poştei and Hula Daneşului.

The fortress of Sighişoara was founded by Saxon settlers brought by King Géza II of Hungary, either in 1191, according to chronicler Georgius Krauss, or in 1198, as others claim. The only inhabited citadel in south-eastern Europe, declared in 1999 a World Heritage site by UNESCO, Sighişoara has preserved all the elements of the mediaeval world. Its urban planning follows the traditional pattern of mediaeval citadels: there is a longitudinal axis (north-south) – School Street, running from Citadel Square to the School on the Hill – intersected by a transversal axis (east-west), which connects the two main portals into the city: the Clock Tower and the Tailors' Tower. The junction used to be the civic and commercial centre of the community: Citadel Square (*Burgplatz*). The other streets of the town (Citadel Wall Street, Joiners Street, Tinsmiths Street, Monastery Street and Bastion Street) run parallel to the longitudinal axis.

Without a doubt, a symbol of Sighişoara, the **Clock Tower**, once named the Town Hall Tower (as the first floor long served as the town hall), has guarded the main gateway into the town for centuries. Built in the 13th to 14th centuries, the tower was originally simple and austere, probably similar to the Tailors' Tower that guards the second gateway into the city, on the west side. It was not until the 16th century that the structure began to assume its current form, when two extra storeys were added and it was fitted with a belvedere. After its destruction in the devastating fire of 1676, the tower was rebuilt by architects Veit Gruber of Tirol and Filip Bonge of Salzburg and carpenter Valentinus Ausländer. The impressive Baroque-style roof is the work of these three itinerant craftsmen. The last repairs were done in 1894 by the company owned by the Leonhardt brothers, which was when the roof was adorned with beautiful multi-coloured enamel tiles,

in shades of red, yellow, blue, green and white, glinting dazzlingly in the sun. Since the 17th century, the fifth storey of the tower has housed a famous clock with figurines. At first the clock told only the hour; in 1648, master Johann Kirchel from Königsberg, made improvements, so that it would chime the quarter hours. He also installed a minute hand and a mechanism to tell the days, consisting of seven carved linden-wood figurines, each 80cm high, representing the days of the week. Housed in a niche on the facade facing the Lower Town, the mechanism to which the seven figurines are fitted rotates once every 24 hours, at midnight to be precise, when in the fretwork window the figurine representing the new day appears. From the belvedere of the sixth floor of the tower there is a superb view of the mediaeval citadel of Sighişoara and its surroundings.

The Clock Tower houses a large part of the citadel's archival treasures of the citadel: it was here that local doctor Josef Bacon (1857-1941) created the town's **Museum of History** in 1899.

In the shadow of the Clock Tower lies the citadel's main square, around which revolved the entire daily life of the town. It was here that trials were held, executions took place and the pillory stood, to which

Photo: *Sighişoara*

criminals were bound with a six-kilogram stone hanging from their necks.

The houses around Citadel Square and Museum Square (in front of the Clock Tower) were inhabited by nobles and wealthy patricians, who had the highest status within the city; it was from their ranks that the mayor and the City Council members were elected. The grand appearance of these edifices (the Venetian House, the Vlad Dracul House, the Duldner House, the Wagner House, the Stag House), contrasting with that of the humble houses of craftsmen, makes one think of palazzo-style residences. Damaged by the fire of 1676, most of them were later rebuilt, undergoing changes in the 18th century.

Also on the lower plateau of the citadel, in the shadow of the Clock Tower, stands the **church of the Dominican Monastery**, attested in documents as early as the year 1298. After 1550, when the monastic estates were secularised, the Dominicans were forced to leave Sighişoara, and the church was taken over by the City Council. Since then the Monastery Church has been the main place of worship for the Evangelical community of Sighişoara. In the polygonal apse of the rectangular choir can be found an altar in the Baroque style, built in 1680 by two itinerant masters: sculptor Johann West and painter Jeremias Stranovius. In 1680 the two masters constructed and painted the organ, on the west side of the naves.

After the destruction wreaked by the Tartar invasion of 1241, King Béla IV took measures and recommended that the Saxons fortify with strong walls the towns in the territory they had settled, which was divided into Seats. By the end of the 14th century, the fortification system of Sighişoara, inhabited mainly by wealthy craftsmen and traders, had been largely completed. The ample construction work of that time stands as testimony to the prosperity of the town, thanks mostly to its guilds. The document whereby the statutes of the guilds were renewed in 1376

mentions that in the citadel of Sighişoara there were 25 trades organised into 19 guilds. At that time Sighişoara's level of development was comparable with that of the burgs of the German lands. The guilds had to support the church financially, as well as the citadel's defences. Each guild had a patron saint, whose statue was made on commission, and their own seats and pews within the church; the wealthiest guilds were responsible for the defence and maintenance of a tower and section of the curtain wall. Consequently, each tower was named after the guild that took care of it: the Tanners' Tower, the Tinsmiths' Tower, the Ropers' Tower, the Butchers' Tower, the Furriers' Tower, the Tailors' Tower, the Cobblers' Tower and the Blacksmiths' Tower. Time has made the defensive role of these fortifications redundant. Today, they are picturesque attractions for thousands of tourists.

Whether you set out along the main axis of the city (School Street) or follow the line of the fortifications, proceeding to the left or the right of the Clock Tower, your steps will lead you to the same place: the base of the steep wooden "tunnel" of the original **Scholars Stair**, a curiosity of Sighişoara, built in 1654 by Mayor Johann Both to make it easier for students to reach the School on the upper plateau of Citadel Hill during harsh winters. Initially, the wooden stair, covered by a shingle roof, had 300 steps; today, it has 175, interspersed with broad platforms.

Photo: *Vlad Dracul House*

After climbing this picturesque tunnel-like stair, through whose wooden slats glint the rays of the sun, if you are lucky to catch fine weather, you reach the top of the hill where the old Gothic church and Evangelical gymnasium school stand. On your return, you can descend the slope of Stair Lane, which will take you right back where started: School Street.

The massive form of the Church on the Hill (the 14th-15th centuries), which stands atop the highest point of the citadel, draws the eye from afar, whether you are inside or outside the citadel. The church is famous for its old crypt (the only one of its kind in Transylvania), which is below the choir stalls. It is in fact the earlier Romanesque basilica, dating from the first half of the 13th century, on top of which the Church on the Hill was built. Following painstaking restoration, carried out over eleven years, between 1992 and 2003, the Church on the Hill now houses the Museum of Saxon Art and a Romanian Saxon Cultural Centre. Near the church can be found the town's Evangelical Cemetery and its chapel. From here we can descend along the old walls, which girdle Citadel Hill for a length of more than 920m. It used to be reinforced with strong bastions and fourteen defence towers, of which only nine remain.

THE FORTIFIED CHURCHES AND RURAL FORTRESSES AROUND SIGHIȘOARA

The fortified church at the centre of **Saschiz** village, 20km south-east of Sighișoara, was built between 1493 and 1496. It has one nave and an elongated choir and rests on 22 buttresses. It has a sentry's walkway above the arches. In the enceint there is a Clock Tower similar to that at Sighișoara. On a hill near the village, in the middle of a forest, the ruins of an old fortified church dating from 1347 have been preserved. It used to have six towers.

The fortress church at **Cloaşterf**, 28km from Sighișoara, was built between 1521 and 1524, under the supervision of Master Ştefan Ungar of Sighișoara, according to an inscription behind the altar. Above the nave and the choir there is a fortified level, fitted with arrow slits and murder holes. Inside you can still see the wooded balconies painted in the 16th and 17th centuries and the Baroque altarpiece, painted in 1716 by Andreas Hermann of Sibiu.

Meşendorf, an old Saxon village 37km from Sighișoara, whose name has remained almost unaltered, preserves a fortified complex, built in the 14th century in the Romanesque style, and later altered in the early-Gothic mode. The triptych altar dates from 1653, the galleries from

Left: *The original Scholars' Stair, Sighișoara*   Right: *Biertan*

1701, and the organ (built by Johannes Hahn of Sibiu), from 1765.

At the heart of **Viscri**, there is a fortified Gothic church built between the 15th and 17th centuries, with two enceints and five defence towers. It was built on the site of a Romanesque chapel from the 12th-13th centuries. You can find it 42km south of Sighişoara, on the road to Braşov.

The spectacular **Rupea Citadel** stands on the summit of a basalt cliff, 52km south of Sighişoara, on the road to Braşov. After painstaking restoration work, carried out from 2009 to 2013, the curtain walls and the four towers have been rebuilt and a modern access road constructed. The citadel on the Cohalm Hill was built and extended between the 14th and 17th centuries and served as a refuge for the villages in the area.

The fortified church of **Mălâncrav**, 25km south-east of Sighişoara, has preserved a valuable ensemble of murals painted in the Gothic style in the 14th century, which depict 53 Old and New Testament scenes.

Within the walls of the stronghold in **Biertan** village, 30km south-west of Sighişoara, a fortified church was erected between 1492 and 1516. The complex consists of three enceints reinforced with towers and bastions. The hall-like church, constructed in the late-Gothic style, with Renaissance touches, holds a beautiful polyptych altarpiece (15th-16th centuries), pews with intarsia inlays (16th century) and a stone pulpit (16th century).

On a hill above **Alma Vii** village, 45km south-west of Sighişoara, on the way to Sibiu, can be found a church from the first half of the 15th century. The fortified enceint with its 1.5-metre-thick walls is guarded by four towers at each of the cardinal points.

In **Dârjiu** village (Harghita County), 36km east of Sighişoara, a Romanesque church was built in the 13th-14th centuries, later altered in the Gothic style and then fortified (the polygonal enceint has high walls and a gate tower). Inside, Gothic style murals have been preserved.

SIBIU

The old city of Sibiu makes up a single unified whole that combines the architectural influences of a typical mediaeval German burg and the Viennese Baroque. In Sibiu you can find steep narrow streets flanked by old Saxon merchant houses, large squares whose magnificence is a reminder of the times when they used to play a central role in the community, curtain walls, bastions and towers that once were part of a formidable defensive system, passageways, flights of steps and bridges that take you right back to the Middle Ages, and also sumptuous Baroque buildings, constructed after Transylvania came under Habsburg rule in 1699.

The city on the bank of the Cibin River developed on the site of the ancient Dacian-Roman *Cedonia* settlement, traces of which have been unearthed in the present-day Guşteriţa district. Its foundation is linked to the Saxon colonisation of Transylvania, on the orders of King Géza II in the 12th century. It was attested in documents for the first time in 1191 (as Cibinum), and later as Hermannstadt. After the Tartar invasion of 1241, Sibiu was fortified in four stages (from the 13th to the 16th centuries) with massive redbrick walls, whence the name Red Citadel. The walls, equipped with 39 defensive towers and five bastions stretched for around 4km. Of the old Saxon citadel there still remain

Photo: *Rupea Citadel*

the Soldisch and Haller bastions and the Stairs Tower, Town Hall Tower, Carpenters' Tower, Harquebusiers' Tower, Potters' Tower, Great Tower, Tanners' Tower and Gunpowder Tower.

Open to pedestrians, the Upper City is made up of three squares bordered by baroque buildings. The most imposing is **Large Square**, which is 142m long and 93m wide. The main landmark in Large Square is the **Brukenthal Palace**, built between 1781 and 1785 by Baron Samuel von Brukenthal, Governor of Transylvania between 1777 and 1787, who was a tireless collector of European art. In 1790 he opened his collection to the public; in 1817, in accordance with his will, the first museum in what is now Romania opened in Sibiu. Rectangular in plan, the three-storey building has two interior courtyards, the last being flanked by two imposing stone telamons. The baroque interiors, which have preserved their original furniture and decorative elements (Rococo and Empire stoves, Murano glass chandeliers, wall coverings of jacquard crimson silk damask, flowery floss fabric and paper painted with Oriental motifs, medallions with reliefs cut in gilt linden wood depicting mythological scenes, stucco, original locks and hardware items), house the collections of the **Brukenthal Museum** (www.brukenthalmuseum.ro

Photo: *Sibiu, view from the Council Tower*

✉ 4-5 Great Square 🕐 Tue-Sun: 10am-6pm (21 Mar-21 Oct), Wed-Sun: 10am-6pm (21 Oct - 21 Mar) 💲 European Art Gallery: 20 Lei, Romanian Art Gallery: 12 Lei). The Art Gallery consists of the Brukenthal Picture Gallery, the Romanian Art Gallery, the Prints and Drawings Cabinet, and the Decorative Art Collection. The Picture Gallery has a total of 1,200 paintings from the Flemish and Dutch school (including Peter Paul Rubens), German and Austrian school (including Lucas Cranach the Elder), the Italian School (including Tiziano Vecellio da Cadore).

The **Roman-Catholic Church of the Holy Trinity** (🏛 3 Large Square) was built by Jesuit monks between 1726 and 1733. Both the exterior and the interior of the edifice are a glorious illustration of the Baroque style. Inside you can find beautiful stained glass windows manufactured in 1901 in Budapest.

On the west side, next to the Brukenthal Palace stands the **Blue House** (🏛 5 Large Square), probably dating from the 17th century, but subsequently altered to include Baroque and Classical touches. Above the entrance is emblazoned Sibiu's old coat of arms. The building, named after the colour of its facade, was owned by apothecary Georg Vette, originally from Gdansk.

Through the arches of the Town Hall Tower (13th century), which formed part of the second layer of fortifications, you enter **Little Square** (called in the Middle Ages Circulus Parvus), which was once a commercial centre. Most of the buildings with entrance porticoes around the square used to belong to the goldsmiths' guild, one of the wealthiest and most powerful in Sibiu (at the time, the city was a major centre for processing the gold extracted from the Apuseni Mountains). The House of Art (21, Little Square) was originally the Butchers' Guild Hall. It was taken over by the Furriers' Guild, but was later given over to highly various uses, including a grain warehouse and concert hall. Today, it houses the **ASTRA Museum of Transylvanian Civilisation**. The vast structure, mentioned in documents dating back to 1370, has a series of eight

arches. At the end of the 18th century, during renovations, the coat of arms of Sibiu was painted on its upper-storey facade. Under the tower of the house at no. 24, you enter the picturesque Goldsmiths' Passageway, which is still redolent of the old mediaeval atmosphere; it leads to Goldsmiths' Square. One room of the five-century-old Goldsmiths' Guild House (25, Little Square) is decorated with a multi-coloured stucco guild emblem, done in 1745. On the ground floor can be found a typical loggia with semi-circular arches; each of the four arches differs in span and height.

The **Pharmacy Museum** is at no. 26 (📞 0269-218191 🕐 Wed-Sun: 10am-6pm (21 Mar-21 Oct), Thu-Sun: 10am-6pm (21 Oct-21 Mar) 🎫 10 Lei), one of the few of its kind in the country. It was created in 1972, in a building dating from 1568, featuring Gothic and Renaissance touches, which was the *At the Black Bear* apothecary shop at the beginning of the 17th century. The Citadel of Sibiu boasts the first apothecary shop ever attested (1494) in Romania. The 6,600 museum exhibits are arranged according to the layout of a classic apothecary's shop: the sales room and laboratory, along with a homeopathy section and storerooms for medical instruments. The homeopathy collection includes instruments and items from the *At the Angel's* apothecary's shop. It appears that Samuel Hahnemann, the father of homeopathy, worked in Sibiu for a year and a half.

The **Luxemburg House** (✉ 16 Little Square), restored between 1999 and 2003 by the National Sites and Monuments Service of Luxembourg, as part of a UNESCO project, serves as a cultural and tourist, information and documentation centre. The goal of the restoration was to bring out the beauty of a Saxon historic monument, founded on the wall of the first enceint of fortifications.

In the Hermes House (11, Little Square), once the headquarters of the Small Craft Enterprises Society – a Neo-gothic edifice built between 1865 and 1867 – the **Franz Binder Universal Ethnography Museum** opened in 1993 (🕐 Tue-Sun:10am-6pm (May-Sept), 9am-5pm (Oct-Apr) 🎫 20 Lei), the only one of its kind in Romania. The permanent display (*Culture and Art of the Peoples of the World*) brings together exotic items from Africa, China, Japan, Oceania, Middle East, Brazil, Lapland and Australia. In the basement there is a projection room, where those interested in the culture and art of peoples outside Europe can watch documentaries on the topic.

The charm of Little Square lies in the **Bridge of Lies** (*Lügenbrücke*), the first bridge made of cast iron in Romania (1859). Be careful when you cross it: legend has it that if you tell a lie the bridge will collapse instantly. There are other "stories" about it: it was here that they used to execute the witches whose predictions had not come to pass, or here merchants in the habit of

---

Photos: *Sibiu Town Hall and Brukenthal Palace*

cheating their customers used to sell their goods, or here cheating lovers used to stroll, or here women selling goods at the farmers' market used to stop for a chat…

The bridge leads to **Huet Square**, the first fortified enceint of Sibiu. The square is dominated by the **Evangelical Church** (Daily: 9am-7pm in summer, 10am-4pm in winter) – one of the most imposing Transylvanian Gothic structures (14th century); its tower soars to 73.34m in height. The church choir houses a bronze baptismal font impressive for its size, cast in 1438 by Master Leonhardus from cannons seized from the Turks in 1437. It is decorated with 228 panels in relief, showing religious and secular scenes, accompanied by Gothic inscriptions. The north wall of the choir is covered by a huge fresco, representing the *Crucifixion of Christ*, the work of Johannes von Rosenau in 1445. The painting reveals the influence of the Austrian, Italian and Dutch schools of painting. The biblical scene reveals secular elements: shields and the coat of arms of Austria, Bohemia, Hungary and Silesia. The balcony on the southern side of the church houses the beautiful organ built in 1672 by Slovak Master Johann West and decorated in the Baroque style in 1674. In the transept an old polyptych altarpiece from the Evangelical Church is on display (15th-16th centuries); the paintings on its side panels were inspired by Albrecht Dürer's Passion. In the atrium, a

chapel made up of three naves, consisting of a massive tower, built after 1448, you can admire an impressive gallery with 67 tombstones, the oldest dating to the 15th century. The atrium is also home to a stone pulpit carved in 1520 by Andreas Lapicida, a group of wood carvings: *Jesus between two angels* (16th century), an altarpiece from Dobârca, and a marble baptismal font, both from the 17th century.

Descend to the vault of the nearby Stairs Tower (13th century) in order to follow the **Stairs Passageway** (13th century), which has become one of the best-known images of the mediaeval Sibiu, and then go down into the Lower City, whose streets are watched over by the "city's eyes": the characteristic eye-shaped skylights found on the roofs of Saxon houses.

We recommend a visit to the Ursuline Church (34-36 General Magheru Street), the Franciscan Church (12-14 Şelari Street), the Altemberger-Pempflinger House, which served as a City Hall between 1549-1948 and which currently houses the **History Museum** (2 Mitropoliei Street) and the Orthodox Cathedral of the Holy Trinity (35 Mitropoliei Street), which is neo-Byzantine in influence, built at the behest of Metropolitan Andrei Şaguna, between 1902 and 1906, and designed by architects Virgil Nagy and Iosif Kamner from Budapest, who took the Hagia Sophia Church in Istanbul as their inspiration.

Photo: *Bridge of Lies, Sibiu*

THE DUMBRAVA FOREST

Four kilometres south-east of Sibiu lies the Dumbrava Forest (980ha), a sightseeing must if you are visiting the city. It was here that the Zoological Garden was founded in 1928 (www.zoo.sibiu.ro ✉ 142 Calea Dumbrăvii ⌨ Daily: 10am-4pm (Ian, Nov, Dec), 9:30am-5pm (Febr), 9:30am-5:30pm (Mar, Oct), 9:30am-6:30pm (Apr, Sept), 9:30am-7:30pm (May, Aug), 9:30am-8pm (Jun, Jul) ⓢ 3 RON), the first of its kind in Romania.

It is here too that you will find the **ASTRA Museum of Traditional Folk Civilisation** which covers an area of 96ha (www.muzeulastra.ro ✉ Calea Răşinari ☎ 0269.242419 ⌨ Mon-Fri: 10am-6pm (on Monday the historic sites are closed), Sat-Sun: 10am-8pm ⓢ 17 RON). The exhibits of this impressive open-air museum are dotted around a six-hectare lake. A walk around the museum's five sections, for which you should set aside a whole day, will provide you with the opportunity to discover the most representative structures of the Romanian village. In the "food production and animal husbandry" division you can find mills of every kind (post mills, tower mills, stump mills, smock mills, manual mills, floating mills, horizontal-wheeled mills), as well as more ordinary structures: an ice house, fish-sorting shed, sheep pen, wine cellars, fruit crushers and presses, traditional oilseed presses, huts, chandler's workshops, fisherman's houses from the Danube Delta. We suggest that from here you proceed to the "public buildings" section, where you can find a traditional tavern from Bătrâni (Prahova County), which is open for business and always full of customers looking to get a sense of the atmosphere of the Romanian village; a wooden playing area for *popice* (skittles) from Răşinari, where you can test your skill at the game; a traditional inn from Tulgheş (Harghita County), where you can sample Romanian cuisine; a dance hall/barn from Botiza (Maramureş); a monumental gate from Şugatag (Maramureş); and a wooden swing from Bicaz-Chei (Neamţ County), which will introduce you to the world of village fairs and festivals.

On the other side of the lake, dedicated to "means of transport", you will be able to see a cable ferry from Turnu Roşu and a floating bridge from Constanţa.

The folk crafts division, dedicated to the production of wood and raw mineral materials, features the homesteads and workshops of blacksmiths, coopers, carpenters, bucket-makers, potters, woodcutters and stonemasons. It also includes a section of traditional wooden architecture: homesteads from Gorj and Maramureş and a church from Bezded village (Sălaj County), dating from the 18th century, with beautiful interior murals that were restored in 2001.

The final section ("Manufacturing household objects") brings together homesteads where hemp, silk and goatskin were processed, the workshops of furriers, cobblers and *suman* makers (a *suman* is an overcoat of felted wool), and various annexes.

The monumental sculpture exhibition may be regarded as an open-air art gallery. At the edge of the museum, along and beyond the Riders' Path, there is a three-hectare area with around twenty modern wood sculptures by Romanian and foreign artists, who have taken their inspiration from the world of Romanian folklore (the titles include: *The Knight, The Gate, Noah's Ark, The Dialogue, The Holy Place, The Return of the Prodigal Son*).

Photo: *ASTRA Museum of Traditional Folk Civilisation*

Apart from the standard display area (10km of walkways with numerous bench seats), the ASTRA Museum also provides other means of entertainment: trips in canoes across the lake, carriage or sleigh rides, night visits (for which purpose spotlights and special effects lighting have been installed), and even the chance to extend your visit here for a few days, while staying at the two Diana hotels within the grounds. They have an accommodation capacity of 70 beds (☎ 0269.202451).

You can reach the ASTRA Museum by public transport: trolleybuses T1 and T4 or the tramway to Rășinari.

MĂRGINIMEA SIBIULUI

The ethnographic area called Mărginimea Sibiului is made up of 18 villages scattered over the foothills of the mountains of south-western Sibiu County: Boița, Sadu, Râu Sadului, Tălmaciu, Tălmăcel, Rășinari, Poplaca, Gura Râului, Orlat, Fântânele, Sibiel, Vale, Săliște, Galeș, Tilișca, Rod, Poiana Sibiului and Jina. It is bordered by the Sad Valley to the south, the valley of the Săliște River to the north, the valley of the Olt River to the east, and the valley of the Sebeș River to the west.

These old Romanian settlements, covering an area of 200 square kilometres, are emblematic of the pastoral transhumant culture. The conservative villages in the area present a series of archaic characteristics, long since vanished in other corners of the country. The typical architecture, of Saxon influence (houses and courtyards laid out in a straight line, connected by massive gates), but incorporating many Romanian elements, the folk garb (with its unmistakable black and white combinations), the winter customs (carolling bands of unmarried young men), and the ancient traditions (icons painted on glass), the dances (*Călușarii* or the Horseman Dance, the stick dance, *brâul* or men's chain dance, and *sârba lui Ghiboi*, a three-measure dance) all lend the area the distinctive feel of a living museum of traditional rural life.

There is barely a village in Mărginimea Sibiului that does not have its own ethnographic museum, which says a lot about the respect and care the inhabitants take in preserving the characteristics of the land intact. The Romanian Orthodox churches with exterior murals are another must-see.

Rural tourism has thrived in these parts lately, as the villages are all easily accessible from the city of Sibiu.

Rășinari (12km south-west of Sibiu), the oldest village in the region, was attested as early as 1204. You can get there by taking the Sibiu–Păltiniș road or by a means of transport not very common for a village: there is a tram line between Sibiu and Rășinari, which runs daily, taking you past the Dumbrava Forest (➤127). The village has enough tourist attractions to fill half a day: the house where philosopher Emil Cioran lived, now a museum (1092, Emil Cioran Street), the house where poet Octavian Goga lived, also a museum (880, Popa Bratu Street), the Church of Saint Parascheva (1383, Emil Cioran Street), with its exterior murals dating from 1760, the Bishop's Palace (1486, Episcopiei Street), the first episcopal see in Transylvania, the Church of the Holy Trinity (Andrei Șaguna Street), and the Andrei Șaguna Mausoleum and the Ethnographic Museum. In the Ștezii Valley, around 3-4km from the village, on the way to Păltiniș, can be found the Alpin, La Lungu and Curmătura Ștezii chalets; many mountain trails set out from here. Nearby you can still find the remains of earthworks from a feudal citadel (13th-14th centuries).

The Orthodox Church of the Annunciation (1790) in **Cristian** (11km from Sibiu) has preserved its exterior murals painted by Stan from Rășinari and Ioan the Zographos.

Further away, 17km west of Sibiu, **Orlat** stretches along the Cibin River; near the village (around 3km away) can be found remnants of the Low Citadel (11th-12th centuries), located where the Cernavodă Stream flows into the Cibin River, and the Wall Citadel (13th-15th centuries), identified with the royal castrum of Salgo, located near the train station at Sibiel. Orlat was where the command of the I Border Regiment, founded by Empress Maria Theresa, had its headquarters; unfortunately, the building, built in 1763, underwent major alterations in the 20th century. The church of Saint Nicholas (1796) was painted by Simion the Zographos.

A secondary road leads from Orlat to **Gura Râului** (Mouth of the River) (6km), thus named because it lies where the Cibin River leaves the Cindrel Mountains. It is actually one of the most scenic settlements of Mărginimea Sibiului, as it is fortunate enough to lie next to the Cibin reservoir and gorges. Other local attractions are the Village Museum, the Church of Saint Parascheva (18th century) and the traditional hydraulic devices still up and running (including an oilseed press).

The main road takes you from Orlat to the **Fântânele** village (3km), with its Orthodox church (1771-1774) featuring exterior murals; not far away, passionate mountain hikers will discover another cabin: Fântânele.

Just 3km away can be found **Sibiel**, a marvellous touristic village dotted with guesthouses. The Icons Museum in Sibiel holds one of Europe's largest collections of icons painted on glass. It is worth visiting the Orthodox Church of the Holy Trinity (1765-1767), as well as the village's three triptychs, dating from the early 19th century, executed using the fresco technique. On a hill 2km south-east of the village fragments of earthworks and a stone citadel have been preserved (12th-13th centuries).

Four kilometres separate Sibiel from **Vale** village, a secluded and quiet settlement nestling among orchard-covered hills. The Church of the Holy Trinity (1763) is captivating for the beauty of its recently restored frescoes.

From here, the road runs for 2km into **Săliște** (21km from Sibiu), one of the largest settlements of Mărginimea Sibiului. The Museum of Famous Săliște People is a tribute to the village's most illustrious sons. The Orthodox churches of the Ascension (1761-1785) and Saint John the Baptist in Grui (1742) preserve fragments of exterior

paintings, which date from 1788. In what the locals call Şanta Crucii are exhibited in the open air impressive wooden sculptures made by artists who took part in the seven Săliște Woodcarvers Camps. The works have been gathered together in Woodcarvers Park in Poiana Soarelui.

Next to Săliște there are two other villages: **Galeş** (2km to the west), with its village museum and Orthodox church from the 18th century, and **Tilişca** (4km to the west), which has a number of significant historic sites: the Dacian citadel (2nd century BC - 1st century AD) at Dealul Cătănaş, which used to form the second layer of fortifications in the Orăştie Mountains; the ruins (barely visible) of a fortress from the 13th century; the Church of the Archangels Michael and Gabriel (18th century).

Further down, **Poiana Sibiului** (12km west) has an ethnographic museum describing the pastoral customs of the area, and a church with paintings dating from the 1790.

In **Jina** (20km to the west), another gateway to the Cindrel Mountains, you can visit two Orthodox churches, with murals from 1810; do not miss the old village cemetery with its impressive two-metre-high crosses. Within the perimeter of the village, outside the Sebeş Valley, rise three cliffs that have been declared natural monuments: Masa Jidovului, La Grumazi (south-west of Jina) and Pintenii din Coasta Jinei (the Spurs in Jina's side) (north-west of Jina).

Photo: *Jina, one of the most picturesque villages in Mărginimea Sibiului*

PĂLTINIŞ

An upgraded road links Sibiu and the Păltiniş climatic resort (32km south-west), passing through Răşinari (➤128). The resort, the highest in Romania (1,442m) was founded at the end of the 19th century by the Transylvanian Carpathia Society and lies in the heart of the pine forests of the Cindrel Mountains, below Onceşti Peak (1,717m), both of which are connected by a chairlift service. Păltiniş has two ski slopes, fitted with ski lifts and baby-lifts, plus several cross-country skiing trails.

The resort is the starting point of many of the trails that lead into the Cindrel Mountains (the Cibin Gorges, the Sadul Valley) and Lotrul Mountains.

It was here that famous philosopher Constantin Noica lived in seclusion during the communist regime. His grave is in the cemetery of the Hermitage of the Transfiguration. Villa 23, where Noica, like a modern day Socrates, entertained friends and disciples throughout his years of seclusion (1975-1987), has been renovated by the Humanitas Foundation, which has restored it to its erstwhile purpose by turning it into a School of Philosophy.

Bus 22, from the Sibiu bus terminal, runs several daily services to Păltiniş.

AVRIG

Located in the Olt Valley, in the foothills of the Făgăraş Mountains 25km south-east of Sibiu, Avrig's main attraction is the Brukenthal Palace, a monumental Baroque complex dating from 1771, made up of three wings in a U-shaped layout. The structure is surrounded by a beautiful terraced garden, with an orangery on the north side. The former summerhouse of baron Samuel von Brukenthal, the governor of Transylvania, has been converted into a restaurant and hotel (www.palatulbrukenthalavrig.ro).

Avrig's Evangelical Church was built on top of an earlier Romanesque basilica from the 13th century. In the graveyard of the Palm Sunday Orthodox church (18th century) can be found the tomb of Gheorghe Lazăr, the celebrated pedagogue responsible for establishing the school system in Romania, who was born in Avrig.

The area is the starting point for many mountain trails leading into the Făgăraş Mountains (Avrig Lake, Negoiu Peak). Nearby you can find the Poiana Neamţului (14km to the south) and Bărcaciu (20km) chalets and the Fântâniţa Haiducului motel (8km vest).

It is 20km from Avrig to **Cârţişoara**, the starting point of the 91.5-kilometre-long Transfăgărăşanul high-alpine road (➤55), which runs across the ridge of the Făgăraş Mountains to Curtea de Argeş, passing the Bâlea waterfall and glacial lake and the Vidraru Dam. The most important site in Cârţişoara is the Badea Cârţan Ethnographic Museum and Memorial House.

A road leading off the E 68 will take you north, along the other side of the Olt River, to Cârţa (24km from Avrig, 47km from Sibiu), where the ruins of a Cistercian abbey from 1202 have been preserved. It is one of the most significant examples of the early Gothic style in Transylvania.

THE FORTIFIED CHURCHES AND RURAL FORTRESSES AROUND SIBIU

Cisnădie, a scenic Saxon settlement, is as old as Sibiu, just 10km to the north (12th century). Cisnădie has preserved its mediaeval urban layout from the 12th-14th centuries, with cobbled streets bordered by rows of Saxon houses. Over time, it became an important craft centre, specialised in sickle making; the drapers' guild created a whole tradition here, as the Museum of the Textile Industry, unique in Romania, bear witness. However, the major local sight is the fortified Evangelical Church of Saint Walpurga, a Romanesque three-nave basilica from the 13th century, subsequently altered in the Gothic style. The massive seven-storey bell tower is particularly striking. In 1797 the first lightning rod in Transylvania was mounted atop the tower. The church was extended with three layers of walls fitted with numerous towers (some remain to this day, including the Guard Tower, the School Tower, the Sickle Makers Tower, the Lard Tower), bastions, defence corridors and ditches, turning it into a true citadel.

On the narrow plateau at the top of the wooded hill of Saint Michael in **Cisnădioara**, located just 4km to the west, a fortified stone basilica (13th century) has been preserved. It is deemed to be one the most significant examples of the Romanesque style in Transylvania. The complex was mentioned in 1223, in an act whereby it was donated to the Cistercian monastery in Cârța. The church, with its three naves, square choir and semi-circular apses, has a beautiful Romanesque portal on the west side, consisting of four arches supported by columns with capitals and flanked by blind arches. Inside the church, since 1940, can be found the tombstones of German and Austrian soldiers who died in the battles of Sibiu during the First World War. Cisnădioara boasts another Baroque Evangelical church (1764), with a tower from an earlier Gothic structure, with painted pews dating from the 17th to 18th centuries, and an ethnographic museum that has valuable Saxon ceramics and painted pieces of furniture. The Cretaceous limestone formations (Piatra Broaștei, or Rock of the Frog), 500m to the south-west of Cisnădioara, are part of a protected geological reserve covering an area of 9ha.

Slimnic (*Stolzenburg*), 17km north of Sibiu, on the way to Mediaș, is dominated by a picturesque fortification atop Burgbasch Hill. The Gothic chapel on the northern side, on the ground floor of the three-storey bell tower, can be traced back to the beginnings of the fortified church, in the 14th century.

The 14th-century fortified church in **Axente Sever**, 40km north of Sibiu, is impressive for its tower, which stands between the aisles and the polygonal choir. Access to the bell tower is from above the choir, something equally uncommon.

The fortified church in **Valea Viilor**, a village formerly named Vorumloc, was built in the 13th century; at the end of the 15th century it was enclosed with strong eight-metre-high defensive walls, fitted with towers. You can admire here a Gothic aedicule and pews in the Early Renaissance style (1528). It is 50km from Sibiu, on the way to Mediaș.

In **Câlnic** village, 60km west of Sibiu, can be found one of the oldest citadels in Transylvania, which was built around 1200. The oval-shaped enceint is consists of of a chapel, a three-storey keep – Siegfried Tower (1270-1272) – and two watch towers. In the 15th-16th centuries it was converted into a fortified structure to protect the village by surrounding it with outer walls.

The *Lole* of Agnita (parade of masked characters)

Lole is an old custom observed by the Saxons from the villages along the Hârtibaciu Valley (Sibiu). Groups of people dressed in colourful rag costumes and wearing scary masks dance through the village, making a hellish racket (cracking whips, ringing huge cowbells and jingling the bells tied around their ankles). The origin of Lole is linked to the devastating Turkish invasions of the Middle Ages. During one such an attack, the inhabitants of Agnita, under siege inside their fortified church, were about to surrender, when a very brave woman persuaded them against it. Dressed in very large man's clothes, on which she had stitched colourful patches and rags, with small bells and cowbells of every size around her waist, so as to make the loudest noise possible, and cracking a whip, she rushed at the besieging enemy, who fled. Thus Agnita was saved…

The Alba Carolina fortress, a star-shaped fort, reinforced with seven bastions, was built in the Vauban style between 1715 and 1738, and was designed by Giovanni Morando Visconti. There had been another fortress on the same site as early as the 10th century. The Alba Carolina originally had six gates, decorated in the Baroque style with bas-reliefs by Johann König depicting mythological scenes. The Roman-Catholic Cathedral of Saint Michael (13th century), within the walls, is where Iancu of Hunedoara is interred.

ALBA IULIA

Alba Iulia is chiefly known as the city where on 1 December 1918 the act of Unification between Transylvania, the Banat, Maramureș, Crișana and Romania was signed. It was also here, some centuries before, on 1 November 1599, that Michael the Brave proclaimed himself ruler of Wallachia and Transylvania, fulfilling the first stage of bringing the Romanian provinces under the same flag. In the Orthodox Cathedral of the Holy Trinity Ferdinand I was crowned King of Greater Romania in 1922.

We suggest you follow the route of the three lines of fortification in the Cetate (*Citadel*) district: the Roman castrum (106), the mediaeval fortress (16th-17th centuries) and the 18th-century Vauban-style citadel, which encompasses the other two.

The ancient city of *Apulum* developed around the most powerful Roman stone castrum in Dacia: the base of the famous 13th Twin Legion (Legio XIII Gemina). You can still see the ruins of the Southern Gate (*Principalis Dextra*) and the up to two-metre-thick south wall. The castrum, which was quadrilateral in shape, covered 37ha.

The mediaeval fortress (16th century) was built on top of the walls of the Roman castrum and it was fortified in 1625, during the reign of Prince Gabriel Bethlem, whence the name of the south-eastern bastion: the Bethlem Bastion.

ȚARA MOȚILOR (MUNȚII APUSENI) – HIGHLANDERS' COUNTRY (THE APUSENI MOUNTAINS)

Țara Moților is also known as the "Stone Country" of the Apuseni Mountains, a realm of highlands and freedom. The Romanian natives, whose villages are perched high on the mountain peaks, at altitudes of over 1,400m, have always known how to fight for their rights. Nothing could dampen their resolve to preserve their freedom. There is no *moț* (as the inhabitants of the Apuseni Mountains are called) who does not take great pride in saying the names of Horia, Cloșca, Crișan and Avram Iancu, all sons of the Apuseni.

These villages perched high in the mountain have preserved their woodworking culture unchanged. The local houses and churches are as beautiful in their simplicity as those in Maramureș. Visit the craftsmen's workshops at Pătrăhăițești to watch the coopers making wooden buckets and churns. In some of the villages of the Apuseni (including Chișcău), the locals display in their courtyards miniature folk art collections, which tell the story, in their own way, of the "history of wood". The Ethnographic and Folk Art Museum in Lupșa attempts, on a different scale, to showcase traditional values.

The traditions and customs of the *moți* have a unique charm. The Maindens' Fair on Găina Mountain, a centuries-old traditional festival, has already won the hearts of Romanians everywhere; year after year, on the Sunday prior to the Feast of Prophet Elijah, thousands of people from all over the country repeat the sacred ritual of climbing up to the clearing at the top of a 1,467-metre-high mountain. Whoever has come to the fair at least once will never be able to forget the sounds of the *tulnic* (traditional alphorn), which greets the rising sun, the alternately quick and slow rhythms of the *tropotita* (a stomping ring dance) and *țarina* (a dance in pairs), and the legends about the hen that laid the golden eggs.

The Apuseni Mountains, most of which have been declared a nature reserve, have many tourist trails to offer. It is the land of the river of gold, the Arieș, the towering Turda Gorge, Cetățile Ponorului (the Fortresses of Ponor), with the Burning Fire Glacier, the Ruginoasa Hole, and the Yellow and Warm Someș (Someșul Cald) Gorges.

The Fortresses of Ponor, a spectacular karst complex, consists of a 70-metre-high gateway and three large limestone cirques (dolines), situated in a forested depression, 300m deep and 1km wide. From the so-called Balconies you get a breath-taking view of the entire complex.

The Yellow Gorges, a canyon whose sides soar more than 200m, sprawl across 6km, along which numerous waterfalls, pulsing springs and an underground tunnel have formed. Although stunning in their beauty, they are extremely difficult to explore.

The Someșul Cald Gorges, whose sides are more than 100m high, is also home to many caves; upstream, the Rădeasa Stream has formed the Fortress of Rădeasa, a cave made up of a 230-metre-long tunnel, accessible through a lancet stone gate 15m high and 7m wide. Here, we are in the very heart of the karst: countless gorges (Râmeți, Aiud, Întregalde, Ampoița, Galda, Vălișoara) lend the Apuseni Mountains their unique appearance. The Padiș Plateau, with its 13 sinkholes, is the destination of every hiker. Do not miss the odd-looking natural landforms, such as the Snail Hill, once a seabed where millions of calcified seashells have been preserved, or the Detunata Goală, a rock formed from solidified lava. Nor should you ignore the marvellous hidden side of Apuseni; we are referring of course to the 400 caves beneath the mountains: the Scărișoara Glacier, the Bears Cave, the Fortress of Rădeasa, the Meziad Cave, Huda lui Papară, and many more.

The **Bears Cave**, located next to the Chișcău village, 482m above sea level, is perfectly lit to reveal its famed stalactites and stalagmites, all with suggestive names: the Enchanted Palaces, Water-Lily Lake, the House of the Gnomes, the Pagodas, the Bear on the Ceiling, the Witch, the Conclave of Elders. Fossils of *Ursus spelaeus* have been discovered in the cave, hence its name.

THE DACIAN FORTRESSES IN THE ORĂȘTIE MOUNTAINS

The Orăștie Mountains in south-west Transylvania were once the nucleus of the Dacian kingdom. Between the 1st century BC and 1st century AD, the Romanians' ancestors – the "immortal" Getae (Dacians), who worshipped Zalmoxis – built within the mountains several fortresses, strategic structures and watch towers over an area of 200 square kilometres. The fortresses, surrounded by

Photo: *Sarmizegetusa Regia*

the walls of perfectly interlocking limestone blocks (*murus dacicus*), were a defensive system unique in the history of European architecture. The numerous shrines around them bear witness to the profoundly religious spirit of the Dacians. The original combination of religious and military architectural elements is the main feature of these fortresses, which date from the classical stage of the Dacian civilisation.

The Dacian strongholds, conquered by the Romans at the beginning of the 2nd century A.D., are the only vestiges left from the legendary forefathers of the Romanians.

The military, political, economic and religious centre of the Dacians was **Sarmizegetusa Regia** (Grădiştea de Munte Village, commune of Orăştioara, Hunedoara County). It is located 1,200m above sea level, at the highest point of Grădiştea Hill. It stretches over several man-made terraces. The upper plateau connects with the sacred shrines area, covering two terraces by a *via sacra*, a monumental paved road of limestone slabs. Before being conquered and destroyed by the Romans, Sarmizegetusa Regia was a major centre of metal working in Europe.

The access roads to the capital were protected by a string of fortresses, strategically placed: Costeşti-Cetăţuie (commune of Orăştioara, Hunedoara County); Costeşti-Blidaru (commune of Orăştioara, Hunedoara County); Luncani-Piatra Roşie (commune of Boşorod, Hunedoara County); Băniţa (Hunedoara County); Căpâlna (commune of Săsciori, Alba County). All these fortifications have been included on the UNESCO World Heritage list.

Ulpia Traiana Sarmizegetusa (commune of Sarmizegetusa, Hunedoara County), 40km to the east of the former capital of the Dacian kingdom, Sarmizegetusa Regia (destroyed by the Romans), was founded between 108 and 110 by Terentius Scaurianus, the first governor of the province, on the site of the Legio V Macedonica camp. The city, which

covers over 20 hectares, populated with military personnel who took part in the Dacian wars, became the political, economic, military, administrative and religious centre of the Roman province of Dacia. Within the perimeter of the archaeological site can be found a forum, amphitheatre, spas, shrines, sanctuaries and other edifices.

THE ROMAN CASTRA OF SĂLAJ COUNTY

The northern border of the Roman Empire (*limes*) ran across the ridges of the Meseş Mountains, where 80 towers and castra were built. The most important military settlement was the castrum of **Porolissum**, quadrilateral in shape, 250 by 300m in area, located at Măgura Pomăt on the territory of today's Moigrad village (8km from Zalău). Two hundred hectares of land still preserve the ruins of an amphitheatre (dating from the time of Emperor Hadrian and rebuilt in 157 A.D.), a shrine dedicated to god Liber Pater (2nd century), subsequently converted into an early Christian basilica, defensive walls and towers, and traces of the Roman road linking the capital city of the Dacia Porolissensis province and Napoca. The most prominent vestige, however, is the Praetoria Gate on the north-eastern side, which has been reconstructed.

Photo: *Ulpia Traiana Sarmizegetusa*

Since 2005, usually at the end of July, Zalău has held a *Roman Heritage Festival*, which focuses on the area's rich past; there are parades of people dressed in the costumes of the time, artisans' fairs (potters, stonemasons, blacksmiths, weavers, tanners etc.), concerts, Roman wrestling, and dance performances.

Also part of the north-western limes of Roman Dacia were the castrum in the commune of Buciumi (114), the headquarters of the Cohors II Augusta Brittonum garrison, the Certinae castrum at Romita, and the castrum at Tihău.

HUNEDOARA

The city is situated in the Cerna Valley, in the foothills of the Poiana Ruscă Mountains, and is now synonymous with the **Hunyadi Castle** or **Corvin Castle** (14th century), considered to be the most important example of secular Gothic architecture in Transylvania. The castle was altered in the Gothic style and later in the Renaissance style by Iancu of Hunedoara and his son Matthias Corvinus. The rooms that most appeal to tourists are the Knights Room, the Council Room and the Treasury Room; the "Do not Be Afraid" Tower is equally famous.

Hunedoara is also home to a beautiful Orthodox church whose plan is in the form of a Greek cross, dating from 1458, built on the site of an earlier Romanian church.

ȚARA HAȚEGULUI (HAȚEG LAND)

Regarded as the south-western bastion of Transylvania, the Hațeg Land, girded by mountains on every side, was in the Middle Ages one of the most powerful centres of the free Romanians, organised into Knezates. In this "land", attested as early as the 1247, which overlapped with the nucleus of the Dacian state and Roman Dacia, can be found some of the most important Romanian sites of religious, military and civilian architecture. In many cases, the materials used when building the mediaeval structures came from Roman edifices. The villages preserve Orthodox churches, most dating from the 12th to 14th centuries, as well as many other historic buildings: knyaz fortresses (Răchitova, Mălăiești, Colț) and the manor houses and castles of the gentry (Nălaț-Vad, General Berthelot, Săcel, Râu de Mori). Although merged into the Kingdom of Hungary during the 13th and 14th centuries, Hațeg was the only place where Romanians managed to preserve a certain degree of autonomy and political rights, as a reward for the courage they had showed during battles against the Ottomans. From amongst them rose families such as Cânde (Kendeffy) and Cândreș (Kenderessy), who succeeded in ascending the social hierarchy of Hungary and Transylvania.

Photo: *Hunyadi Castle or Corvin Castle*

The area, covering over 1,000 square kilometres, crossed by the Streiul, Râul Mare and Galbena rivers, has a remarkable tourist potential. Close by can be found the **Retezat National Park**, with its many hiking trails, and farther north, Ţinutul Pădurenilor (the Land of the Foresters) and Cinciş Lake, one of the most stunning lakes in the country. It is here that we can find the best-known auroch reserve, as well as a Dinosaur Geopark, created after the discovery of dwarf dinosaur fossils in the area.

The knyaz churches of Haţeg are remarkable for their eclectic architecture. They were built using materials from Roman sites and combine the Romanesque and Gothic architectural styles. Their murals draw on the Byzantine tradition. In most cases the bell tower, pyramidal in shape, stands on the west side.

The church at **Streisângiorgiu** (12th century), today a district of Călan, is one of the oldest places of worship in Romania. Built in the Romanesque style, it still preserves murals from 1313-14, painted by Teofil the Zographos.

The church at **Densuş**, a highly unusual structure, was erected in the 13th century on the site of a pre-Christian building (possibly a Roman mausoleum or shrine) from the 4th century, using the building materials (inscribed stones, tombstones, water troughs) from Ulpia Traiana Sarmizegetusa. The valuable interior murals, painted by Stephen the Zographos, date from the first half of the 15th century.

At **Sântămăria-Orlea**, another 13th-century church (originally Orthodox, but now Reformed), in the late Romanesque style, preserves beautiful interior murals, painted in three successive stages, the earliest layer dating from 1311. It is assumed that it was built by the ruling Cândea family. It falls into the category of churches with a rectangular altar and a bell tower on the west side.

The **Cândeşti Family/Kendeffy Castle** (14th century), located on the bank of the Râului Mare River in Sântămăria-Orlea, was rebuilt in the Baroque style of the 18th century.

In **Strei** (1km from Călan) there is another stone church, dating from the late-13th century and early-14th century. It has a short nave, a rectangular altar and a bell tower on the west side. It was erected on the ruins of a Roman-style villa rustica. The interior paintings (14th century), the work of Master Grozie, combine Byzantine, Romanesque and Gothic elements. It seems that originally the facade was also covered by paintings, traces of which are still visible on the south and east walls.

The ruins of the **Colţ-Suseni** fortress (3km from Râu de Mori), built in the 14th century by Knyaz Cândea, tower above Râuşor Valley from on top of a cliff. It appears to have been the inspiration for Jules Verne's novel *The Castle of the Carpathians*. At its foot you can find the church of the Colţ Hermitage, also from the 14th century, built as a court church for the Cândeşti family. The stone church, whose pyramidal tower rises – unlike in the other stone churches of Haţeg – above the altar, has preserved a series of interior murals, painted after 1377.

Preserved on the west wall of the church at **Ostrov** (14th century), commune of Râu de Mori, there is an icon of the church's patron saint, the *Theotokos with the Infant*, painted in a semi-circular niche above the entrance into the nave. The church is surrounded by a stone wall made of materials taken from Roman buildings.

At **Ribiţa**, also built by the knyazes, the Church of St. Nicholas, dating from the 14th century, is impressive for its Gothic architectural features and its murals, which observe Byzantine tradition. According to the dedicatory inscription, the painting dates back to 1417. Also remarkable is the votive painting of the founders, Lord Vladislav, Lady Stana and their son.

The narthex of the **Crişcior** church (15th century), founded by Knyaze Bâlea, preserves its original murals. Of particular artistic and historical significance is the votive painting in which voivode Bâlea is depicted alongside his wife Vişe and their son Iuca. Also worth noting are the pointed archways, an element typical of the Gothic style.

The Hungarian Community of Transylvania

There are approximately 1,500,000 Hungarians living in Transylvania (6.6% of Romania's population and 20% of Transylvania's population). The Hungarian community of Cluj numbers 60,000, and that of Târgu Mureş 70,000, accounting for 47% of the population. In Cluj there is a Hungarian State Opera House, a Hungarian State Theatre, and the Babeş-Bolyai University, many of whose departments teach in Hungarian.

ŢINUTUL SECUIESC (SZEKLER LAND)

The Szeklers (*székely*) – an ethnic group of uncertain origins (possibly Turkic), absorbed by the Hungarians, represent the majority population in south-eastern Transylvania. They are mentioned in documents as early as the 10th century as a people related to Hungarians, although regarded as separate, as the *Unio Trium Nationum (Union of the Three Nations)* of 1437 bears witness. The *Union* laid out the rights of the three privileged ethnic groups, the Hungarians, Saxons and Szeklers, over the Romanians, the majority local population of Transylvania.

The most important Szekely settlements are in the counties of Covasna and Harghita and in a large part of Mureş county, which overlap the three Seats, the Szekely administrative units of the Middle Ages. Today, the region is home to over 600,000 Szeklers and Hungarians (accounting for 57% of the population); in Harghita County, Szeklers and Hungarians represent 84% of the inhabitants, and in Covasna, 73%.

Odorheiu Secuiesc, the city with the largest ethnic group, is 95% inhabited by Szeklers and Hungarians. In the centre of the city, the ruins of a 15th-century citadel have been preserved.

Sfântu Gheorghe, a town located on the bank of the Olt River, between the Baraolt and Bodoc Mountains, is reckoned to be one of the oldest Szekler settlements. The Szeklers who settled here in the 12th and 13th centuries were organised into Seats (Three Seats is the former name of the Covasna County). Those wishing to find out more about the Szeklers' history and traditions can visit the National Szekely Museum in Sfântu Gheorghe.

Miercurea Ciuc, a town located in the Ciuc Depression, is ranked as one of Romania's coldest places, with the lowest annual average temperature. The Mikó Citadel, built in the 17th century in the neo-Renaissance style, is now the Ciuc Szekely Museum. The Franciscan Monastery at Şumuleu, 3km from the centre of the town, is regarded as the spiritual capital of the Szeklers; every year, at Pentecost, thousands of Roman-Catholic pilgrims make the journey here. The monastery church was built by Iancu of Hunedoara in the 15th century. Şumuleu is also home to the Day of the One Thousand Szekler Girls Festival.

Târgu Mureş was in the 15th century a thriving craft centre. From those times have remained the ruins of the mediaeval citadel and the Tailors', Potters', Butchers', Cobblers' and Furriers' bastions. The charm of the city lies in its main square – the Square of Roses – which is bordered by the Secession-style structures of the County Council Hall and the Palace of Culture, the Baroque Toldalagi Palace (now the Ethnographic and Folk Art Museum), the Neo-Byzantine Orthodox Cathedral, the Jesuit Monastery and the Apollo Palace. It was once a major Szekler centre, hence the name *Novum Forum Siculorum/Székelyvásárhely*, meaning the Szeklers' Burg.

In other counties, traces of the Szeklers' presence have likewise been preserved. Rimetea (*Torockó*) village, in the former Arieş Seat, Alba County, spreads over the foothills of the 1,171-metre Pietrei Secuiului (Szekler Rock). Of its more than 600 inhabitants, 500 are Hungarian. It is a beautiful village, with classical white houses (built after the devastating fire of 1870), many of which are listed buildings. Just 5km south-west of the village, atop a pointed rock, lie the ruins of the Colţeşti citadel (1296).

CLUJ-NAPOCA

The former Dacian citadel of Napoca became a *municipium* under Roman rule and later a *colonia* (*Aurelia Napoca*). After the Aurelian retreat, it was not until 1213 that the citadel was mentioned in documents, as *Castrum Clus*, whence the name Cluj. In 1316, Cluj was elevated to the rank of civitas by Charles Robert of Anjou, King of Hungary, and in 1405 it was granted the status of a free city by Sigismund of Luxemburg, as well as the right to build a second fortified enceint. King Matthias Corvinus, who was born here, granted it a series of privileges, which helped the city flourish.

The tourist attractions include the Church of the Benedictine Monastery (1222), the Reformed Church (1486-1494), with an equestrian statue of Saint George killing the dragon outside, made in 1373 by sculptors Martin and Gheorghe, the Jesuit Church (Piarist Church), the Orthodox Cathedral, whose dome was inspired by the Hagia Sophia, the Baroque palace of Count Bánffy (1773-1785), which is now the Art Museum, the Teleki Palace, built in neo-classic style between 1790 and 1795, the National Theatre and Romanian Opera House, which opened in 1919, the City Hall Palace, the Matthias Corvinus House (15th century), the house where Franz Liszt stayed in 1846, the Babeş-Bolyai University, the Botanical Garden, and the open-air Ethnographic Museum on Hoia Hill.

Fărşang: The Carnival of Transylvania

In the last days of February, on Meatfare Sunday or at the beginning of spring, the Hungarians and Szeklers celebrate Fărşang. Six weeks before Easter, on the first Sunday, when the doll Nichita is born (or Johann, in German tradition), the young men from the villages dress up in comical costumes and masks and go from door to door, collecting money or food for him. The doll, symbolising the evil that has accumulated throughout the year, falls sick the following day and once again the young me set out through the village. The parades end on the third day, with the young men dressed as priests and holding candles. At midnight Nichita is set on fire, and then buried in the hope that all the evil from the village and within people's hearts will thereby be destroyed. The participants doff their masks, and the celebrations end with a grand ball.

Photo: *Cluj-Napoca*

ȚARA NĂSĂUDULUI (NĂSĂUD LAND)

Most of the Năsăud Land, also known as the Rodna Valley, lies within Bistrița-Năsăud County. This area of central and northern Romania, along the upper course of the Someșul Mare River, where the Transylvanian Plateau meets the Rodna, Țibleș, Călimani and Bârgău Mountains, is one the most scenic destinations in Romania, but has yet to open up to tourism. Here, in the middle of forests, lies the "land" of the fast-flowing Bistrița River, one of the most stunning ethnographic areas in Romania. Nearby extends the "land" of Bârgău, whose settlements – Prundu Bârgăului, Tiha Bârgăului, Bistrița Bârgăului, Rusu Bârgăului, Josenii Bârgăului – have preserved their ancient customs. In the Bârgău Valley and Sălăuța Valley there are villages which continue to celebrate old traditions, where old craftsmen are still appreciated for the items they fashion, and where traditional costume is worn on special occasions.

The most picturesque local traditions include the Wreath of Maieru, during the wheat harvest, and *Înstruțatul boului* (when a bull is decked with flower wreaths), at Pentecost. Midsummer is celebrated at the summer solstice (24 June), and seems to be a remnant of ancient sun worship; it is a time to pick flowers, which are woven into wreathes employed in magic rituals.

The southbound route starts from Bistrița and leads to the salt massif at SărăȚel, the Castle of Count Bethlen Balazs of Arcalia, surrounded by some of the most glorious parks in the country (16 hectares), the Lechința vineyards and the Romanesque basilica at Herina (13th century).

On the right bank of the Someș River lies the city of Năsăud, overshadowed by a line of hills. It was here that the Năsăud Border District at the Habsburg Empire border was located in the 18th century.

Sângeorz-Băi (50km from Bistrița), a climatic health resort south of the Rodna Mountains, in the valley of the Someșul Mare River, is famed for its Hebe mineral springs, which have the highest concentration of calcium anywhere in South-Eastern Europe. Here you can find one of the most ingenious museums in the country: the Museum of Comparative Art.

Rodna, located in an area dotted with "nature reserves", has all the makings of a remarkable tourist destination. In addition, it is a gateway to the Rodna Mountains National Park. It has preserved the ruins of a 10th-century fortress. Nearby, there is a climatic health resort, Valea Vinului, with two mineral springs. From the commune of Șanț, which has embraced rural tourism without sacrificing its rustic feel, we can reach Valea Mare, with has a modern tourist complex in the middle of a forest.

Traces of the last Quaternary Ice Ages are common in the Rodna Mountains: the glacial cirques on Pietrosu, Buhăescu and Negoescu, the Schneider's Lake and Zalion's Gully caves. Other destinations in these spectacular mountains of the Eastern Carpathians include the Lala Mare Lake, the Izvorul Cailor and Puzdre waterfalls, the Beneș Gate (Corongiș Gate), and the Iza Cave and the Blue Spring. The area, with a high density of nature reserves, has been declared a National Park. The peaks here often soar to higher than 2,000m, and so hiking should only be undertaken by the properly equipped.

Photo: *Traditional costumes from Năsăud Land*

The Banat and Crișana

The Banat and Crişana

The Banat is a province truly privileged in its geographical location; this land in south-western Romania is bordered by the Southern Carpathians, the Danube River and the Tisza and Mureş rivers. The weather here is much milder than in the rest of the country, thanks to Mediterranean influences. In the lowland region, in the southern Banat, lilac is almost ubiquitous. The Cerna Valley is home to the oldest climatic health resort in the country: Băile Herculane, historically attested since 153 A.D.

Those looking to enjoy the mountain should visit the climatic resort of Semenic, located 1,400m above sea level, on the plateau of the Semenic Mountains, which has several upgraded ski slopes.

The ethnic diversity so characteristic of the Banat is a natural consequence of its frontier location; these picturesque communities, a mixture of Romanians, Hungarians, Swabians, Serbians, Czechs, Slovaks, Bulgarians and Ukrainians, will offer visitors a valuable lesson in tolerance.

Locals boast that Timişoara is the "the leading light" in everything. In 1884 it became the first European city to have electric street lighting. In 1857 the city was connected to the European railway network. It was here in December 1989 that the spark of revolution was struck, leading to the downfall of the communist regime.

Crişana begins north of the Mureş River. It is also Romania's gateway to Western Europe.

In Oradea, a city located just 12km from the border, the Black Eagle, Apollo and Ullmann Palaces are fine examples of Art Nouveau architecture.

THE BANAT

SEMENIC NATIONAL PARK – CARAŞ GORGES

Points of access

From the north: the DJ582 county road (Reşiţa – Slatina-Timiş)

From the east: the DN58 national road (Anina – Reşiţa)

From the south, from Anina and the Nera Gorges: the DN57B national road

Sprawling over 36,214 hectares, the Semenic National Park and Caraş Gorges in the Banat Mountains comprise ten protected nature reserves. The highest summits in Semenic, thus named after a rare plant that grows here (*Antennaria dioica*), are Gozna Rock (1,447m), Semenic (1,446m) and Nedeia Rock (1,437m), from where you can get a spectacular view of the surrounding valleys and the Godeanu and Ţarcu Peaks.

At the foot of the mountains lie several small mountain resorts: Văliug-Crivaia, Secu, Gârâna and Trei Ape, and at an altitude of 1,410m you can find the **Semenic resort**, which has the longest ski season in the country; there are six ski slopes and a chairlift service. They are all situated around 40 to 50km from Reşiţa (an old industrial centre on the Iron Road in the Banat) or Caransebeş, the main cities in the region.

The Semenic resort is a good starting point from which to reach Pădurea de la Izvoarele Nerei (the Forest of the Nera Springs) (5,000 hectares), reckoned to be one of the largest unspoiled forests in Europe. The beech trees here are more than 350 years old. From here you can set out towards the splendid **Caraş Gorges**, among the longest and wildest in the country, which stretch for more than 19km between Caraşova and Valea Comarnicului; the moss covered river stones make a wonderful sight and in May the blooming lilac bushes along the stone ledges make the area look like something from a fairy tale. There are around 50 caves and sinkholes, of which the most impressive is the **Comarnic Cave** (Sat-Sun: 10:30am-12:30pm, 1-3pm, 3:30-5:30pm), on three levels. Equally spectacular is the Popovăţ Cave, which has been declared a natural monument. The outline of the entrance into the Cave of the Bat is rather like the outline of Africa. Also within the gorge, on the right bank, 200m above the river, atop a steep cliff can be found the ruins of the Caraşova Fortress.

DID YOU KNOW?

Legend has it that the Caraş River owes its name to a Turkish aga who passed through here during a war and, as he was gazing from the fortress over the river, he called it Kara Su (black water in Turkish.)

The **Trei Ape** resort is located at an altitude of 850m, near the reservoir of the same name, which is fed by the waters of the Semenic, Grădişte and Brebu rivers out of the Semenic Mountains and empties into the Timiş River.

Gârâna (originally *Wolfsberg*), located at an altitude of 935m, on a hillside near the Trei Ape reservoir, was founded by German settlers brought from Bohemia to supply the steel plants of Reșița with charcoal. Since 1996 an International Jazz Festival has been held here every August. Also in 1996, a Sculpture Park was opened, on the road into town from the direction of Văliug.

The **Văliug-Crivaia** resort is located 650m above sea level, on Gozan Lake, and is ideal for water sports. There are also two ski slopes: the 800-metre-long Casa Baraj and the 5,800-metre-long Semenic-Văliug, which takes you from Semenic all the way to Văliug.

The **Secu** resort is 12km from Reșița, on Secu Lake.

In the foothills of the mountain, in **Gârliște** village, look out for the windmills, which have been declared historic monuments. The wild Gârliștea Gorges lie in the same area: they are 9km long, including 4km of sheer cliffs pierced by 100 caves, including the 258-metre-long Galați Cave and 397-metre-long Water Cave. The most pristine section is that between Cleanțul Gherii and the northern slope of the Moghila Hill. The gorges are crossed halfway by the spectacular **Anina–Oravița railway line**. It is part of the Anina–Baziaș line, the oldest mountain railway track in Romania, built between 1847 and 1854, during the Austro-Hungarian period, to carry the coal from the Anina coal mine to Baziaș harbour. The line, which has been likened to the Austrian Semmering, is 34-km-long, has a difference in altitude of 337m and passes through 14 tunnels (the longest being 660m) and over ten viaducts, including the Jitin, the country's highest, at 37m). The trip takes two hours. The trains depart from Oravița at 7am, 2:45pm and 7:28pm, and from Anina at 9:09am, 4:40pm and 9:42pm (the 7:28pm and 9:42pm trains are not in service on Saturdays and Sundays).

Located in a karst depression, at an altitude of 650-770m, **Anina** (originally *Steierdorf*) was founded on 24 June 1773, when families of Austrian colonists settled here (from Stiria, Austria). They made the manganese used in the Oravița steel plant. The steel plants at Anina, built between 1858 and 1927, have been declared historic monuments. From the Sommerfrische resort (or the Aurora of Banat) only remnants of the sanatorium and the mine survived, dating from the 1893-1895 period and located 5km south-west of Steierdorf-Anina, in the middle of a pine and beech forest; famous guests once included Italian tenor Enrico Caruso and American dancer Josephine Baker.

Oravița is most famous for the Old Theatre or Mihai Eminescu Theatre (1817), the first theatre in Romania, on whose stage poet Mihai Eminescu once performed with his troupe. It was built in the Baroque style, in imitation of the Burgtheater in Vienna, but on a smaller scale. The Roman-Catholic chapel, the first miners' church in Oravița, dates from 1707. The *La Vulturul Negru* (At The Black Eagle's) apothecary shop, founded in 1763 by Edward Winter and subsequently bought by the Knoblauch family, currently houses the Mountain Pharmacy Museum (🏛 Mon-Fri: 8am-12pm). It preserves original furniture and instruments from the late 17th century and a library of old books. In 1859 Oravița hosted the largest industrial, commercial and manufacturing exhibition in whole of the Austrian Empire.

Both resorts lie around 35 to 50km from **Reșița**, the main city in the area. The first foundries of the Reșița Steel Plant were commissioned (now TMK-Reșița) on 3 July 1771, making the town the oldest steel industry centre in Europe. In 1872 it was here that the first train locomotive was manufactured (the Reșița 2, with a 948 mm gauge), on display at the Steam Engines Museum, along with other models produced between 1872 and 1959. The centre of the city is crossed by a 700-metre funicular built in 1964 to carry limestone from the mountain up to the steel plant; unfortunately, the installation, with a total length of 3.5km, has been left in a state of disrepair and is completely unusable, although it could have become a tourist attraction. Made of stainless steel manufactured at the Reșița Machinery

Plant, the robotic water fountain in the centre of town, inaugurated in 1984, is the work of sculptor Constantin Lucaci; the central parts depict a furnace and a Kaplan turbine head. The Museum of the Banat Mountains (🕒 Tue-Sat: 9am-5pm), at 10, Boulevard Republicii opened in 1959. The welded bridge over Bârzava (or the Bridge in the Stavila district, between the Castanilor Street and the Zimbrului Street), commissioned in 1931, was the first all-welded bridge in Romania.

THE NERA GORGES NATIONAL PARK – BEUȘNIȚA

This park, which covers 36,758 hectares, located in the southern part of the Anina Mountains, in Caraș-Severin County, is famed for its undisturbed wilderness area, which looks like a realm from a fairy tale. Through the park runs the Nera River, which forms spectacular gorges, the longest in the country, stretching for more than 22km between Șopotul Nou and Sasca Română villages and bounded by the Anina and Locva Mountains. There are karst lakes all along the gorge, shrouded in legend (the Eye of the Bey and Devil's Lake), caves and sinkholes (Plopa, Ponor, Dubova, Peștera Boilor), islets, and old disused windmills. In spring and early summer, the foaming waters of the Nera are perfect for rafting. The courses of the Bei spring and its tributary, the Beușnița,

with its many ledges and waterfalls formed from travertine deposits, are equally beautiful.

The **Beușnița Waterfall,** located on the Beu River, upstream of the Eye of the Bey Lake in the Nera Gorges National Park, is made up of a series of waterfalls, the largest cascading down a moss-covered wall from 15m. Access is via the road between Anina and Orșova, from Șipotul Nou village. It is 6km from the park entrance to the waterfall, and on the way you will pass the Văioaga Waterfall and Eye of the Bey Lake.

Photos: *Nera Gorges*

The **Devil's Lake**, the largest karst lake in the country, can be reached from Sasca Montană. It is 20m in diameter and 9 to 12m deep (although according to local legends it is bottomless). The waters of the lake are of an absolutely fascinating bluish-green hue.

Leaving the park, you should travel towards **Eftimie Murgu village** (originally Rudăria) in the Almăj Valley. There are twenty-two watermills with horizontal wheels still in operation along the Rudărica River, stretching for 3km, both inside and outside the village. In this enchanted place it is as if time has stood still.

In **Mehadica** there is a series of windmills, which have been declared historic monuments.

BĂILE HERCULANE

Developed by the Romans after the year 102 to exploit the mineral waters of the Cerna Valley, where they erected temples, baths, monuments and statues to the gods Hercules, Asclepius and Hygieia, Herculane (*Ad aquas Herculis sacras ad Mediam*) is the oldest resort in Romania. Unfortunately, what was once the "pearl of Europe" is now something of a ghost town, with rundown and decaying buildings.

The symbol of the resort is the statue of Hercules, cast from cannon iron and given to the town by Duke Karl. All around there used to be pavilions built in the first half of the 19th century. The complex consisting of the Casino, the Carol and Franz Joseph Hotels and the Imperial Austrian Baths was the centre of the resort during the time of the Austrian-Hungarian Empire.

The sixteen hot springs are situated one after another over an area almost 4km wide. The region enjoys a temperate continental climate with sub-Mediterranean influences. The average annual temperature is 14°C (22°C in July and 1°C in January).

Among the most prominent guests of the resort were Emperor Joseph II, Emperor Francis I and Empress Carolina, Emperor Franz Joseph and Empress Elizabeth, King

? DID YOU KNOW?

According to legend, the white waters of the Beuşniţa Waterfall were the bridal veil of a shepherdess from nearby Potoc village, with whom a Muslim bey had fallen in love. Enraged, the bey's father sent his servants to stab the girl. The young man found his beloved murdered on top of the cliff over whose lip the waterfall tumbles. He took revenge and fought against his father's men, until he lost an eye and plunged his dagger into his own heart. On the spot where his eye fell appeared the lake that is now called the Eye of the Bey, fed by a spring created by the bey's tears. The waters of the waterfall and the spring merge near the lake, as if the two lovers were finally united, even in death.

The waters of **Bey's Eye Lake** – whose vivid, magical shades of opal and seem almost unreal – never freeze.

In 2013, the **Bigăr Waterfall**, along the course of the Miniş river, 12km from Bozovici, was nominated by the most beautiful waterfall in the world by the World Geography website. The 45th parallel passes near this stunning cataract.

Photo: *Beuşniţa Waterfall*

Carol I of Romania, King Alexander of Serbia, King Michael, and Queen Maria.

Herculane is the ideal starting place for hikers wishing to visit the Domogled Gorges, Outlaws' Cave, the Cerna Waterfall, Steamy Cave, etc.

TIMIȘOARA

In 1307, King Carol I Robert of Anjou of Hungary, decided to build a stronghold in this place, named as *Castrum Timisiensis* in documents dating back to 1212. It was rebuilt in the 15th century by Iancu of Hunedoara, appointed Governor of Timiș in 1440. The Hunyadi Castle, now the Museum of the Banat, is one of the major attractions of Timișoara.

From 1552, for two hundred years Timișoara was under Ottoman rule and became the seat of the *pashalik* (Ottoman province). In 1716 it was conquered by the army of Eugene of Savoy, and came under Austro-Hungarian rule, during which time the Bega River was embanked and Timișoara's finest Baroque buildings were constructed. By the end of the 19th century, Timișoara was a modern city, with electricity, a telephone network, and public transport.

The locals usually boast that "Banat is the leading light" of the country. Timișoara, the most important city of the Banat, is the place with the highest number of "firsts" in Romania: it was here that the first horse-drawn tram was introduced, followed by the first electric tram, electric street lighting and telephone service.

The city on the Bega is home to the most interesting 18th-century Baroque architecture in Romania. A shining example is the old Hauptplatz, now called **Union Square**, dominated by the **Roman-Catholic Cathedral**, the Baroque Palace, and the Serbian Diocese complex: the Orthodox Church of the Serbian Diocese and the seat of the Diocese, which is also the Serbian Community Palace. The Roman-Catholic Cathedral (1774) was designed by architect Joseph Emanuel Fischer von Erlach, one of the leading representatives of the Viennese Baroque. The Baroque Palace (1733), originally the County Council, is now home of the **Art Museum** (☎ 0256.491592 🕐 Tue-Sun: 10am-6pm 🅂 10 RON), where you can admire 15th- to 17th-century art by Italian artists, including Donato Veneziano and I. Bassano etc., European engravings, eighty paintings by Corneliu Baba, icons

Photo: *Union Square, Timișoara*

on wood, and decorative art. The 350-room Palace of Justice (now the County Court) was built between 1850 and 1854 in the Renaissance style, in imitation of the Palazzo Medici in Florence. At 9, Mercy Street, on the corner of Union Square, you will find the impressive **Brück House**, built in 1910 in the Art Nouveau style; its facade is decorated with ceramic tiles with Hungarian folk motifs. Other outstanding buildings are the Lion House at no. 6, the At the Elephant House at no. 3, the Three Hussars House at no. 2, and the Canons Houses at no. 8, 9, 10 and 11. Right in the centre of the square can be found the Holy Trinity Monument or **Plague Column** (*Pestsäule*), in the Baroque style, which was made in Vienna in the 1740s to commemorate the victims of the plague of 1738-39, which devastated the Banat, and which was brought to Timișoara by water down the Danube and the Tisza rivers and then via the Bega canal; at the base of the column you can see the statue of Saint John of Nepomuk, the patron saint of the Banat, at whose feet lies the new province, represented in the form

of a maiden. Between the Dome and the column stands a mineral well more than 400m deep. In summer, the huge square is the venue for various cultural events.

The current centre is **Victory Square** (originally Opera Square), where demonstrations in December 1989 led to the fall of the communist regime in Romania. It is bordered to the north by the Opera House, and to the south by the Metropolitan Cathedral. Within the square there are a number of other significant buildings: the National Theatre, the State Hungarian Theatre, the State German Theatre, the City Hall, the Concert Hall, the Museum of the Banat (Hunyadi Castle), the Timiș, Capitol and Studio cinemas, as well as striking 19th-to 20th-century palaces. The promenade on the right, starting from the Opera House and leading to the Cathedral, is called the Corso, and the one on the left the Surrogate. The former was the promenade used by the nobility, whereas the latter was reserved for workers and the young. The Corso is flanked with works by architect László Székely: the Dauerbach Palace, the Szécheny Palace, the Chamber of Commerce Palace, the Piarist High School, the Weiss Sándor Palace and the Neptune Municipal Bath.

Between the two main squares lies the **Liberty Square**, with a statue of St. John of Nepomuk (1722) at its centre, the oldest Baroque sculpture in Timișoara.

Placed in the niche of a house at the corner of Francesco Griselini Street and Proclamația de la Timișoara Street, you can find a replica of the **Guilds Tree**, a Timișoara oddity; this iron-clad trunk, dating back to 1828, is covered in nails and screws of all shapes and sizes, hammered, according to the legend, by the apprentices returning home after long years as apprentices to one of the master locksmiths of the Austro-Hungarian Empire. The original is kept in the Museum of the Banat.

In the early 20th century, the old city of Timișoara gained a number of stunning Art Nouveau buildings: you can find outstanding examples in Victory Square

Photo: *Metropolitan Cathedral, Victory Square, Timișoara*

(the Dauerbach Palace) and Union Square (the Brück House, the Discount Bank).

Just a stone's throw away from Victory Square stretch the green banks of the Bega Canal, with parks on each side. Timişoara is rightly known as the City of Flowers or the City of Parks. In the past you could travel across the city from one end to the other without leaving a park. Central Park, one of the largest in Timişoara, is accessible from Victory Square, on the side with the Orthodox Cathedral. The Park of Roses (🏛 Tue-Sun: 8am-10pm) was developed in 1891 by florist Wilhelm Mühle, who planted over 300 varieties of roses for the Industrial Exhibition at which Emperor Franz Joseph took part; destroyed several times, the garden was rebuilt after 2011, and today it boasts around 900 varieties of roses. Every year, on the last Thursday of May, Timişoara celebrates the Day of the Rose. Alpinet Park (or the Arboretum), with its various alpine and sub-alpine species, was created by Mihai Demetrovici in 1924; it is bounded by the Bega Canal, the Traian and Episcopiei bridges and the Tudor Vladimirescu Embankment.

The old Fabric and Josefin districts are very picturesque. They developed around 2km from the city centre, outside the Citadel walls, as required by the rules imposed by the Austrian administration. Here you can find craftsmen's houses from times long passed, which once belonged to German, Hungarian, Serbian and Swabian inhabitants.

Fabric, to the east of the Citadel, was, after industrialisation began in the 18th century, a centre of manufacturing and factories, making felt, brick, wire, and silk, as well as paper mills, of guilds and craftsmen: cobblers, slipper makers, saddle makers, furriers, coopers, fishermen, bakers, butchers, wigmakers, tailors. Its look today is, however, the result of the 1880-1910 architectural projects, when so many buildings in the Secession style were constructed that you will see one every step of the way. Its heart is Trajan Square, bordered by the Serbian Church of St. George and the Mercury Palace (1909), thus named after the statue in the corner, representing the Roman god of trade. Notice within the square the obelisk with a cross and an ammonite (fossilised shell) almost half a metre long and the inscription in Serbian. Situated in a small square at the end of the People's Park (or Queen Maria Park), the Fabric Synagogue, built between 1897 and 1899 in the Secession style with Moorish, neo-romantic and neo-gothic details, is currently used as a concert hall by the National Theatre. A lamp posted above the Colterm offices, housed in a Secession-style building from 1900 at 11, Romans Square, reminds us that Timişoara was the first city in Europe to have electric street lighting. In the heart of the district, at 28, Stephen the Great Street, there is a brewery established in 1718.

16 December 1989 Avenue separates the Fabric district from the Josefin district (originally called Maiere), the historic neighbourhood that developed south of the Citadel, beyond the Bega, on the site of some leased gardens (maiere, in German). It received its current name in 1773, in honour Joseph II, Maria Theresa's son, who visited Timişoara several times. Plevna Square is a treasure trove of 1900s architecture: at no. 2 you can admire the House with a Beautiful

Photo: *Opera House, Timişoara*

Gate, the most remarkable example of Art Nouveau ironwork in the city, at no. 4, the Peacock House (the Nicolin House), at no. 5, the Jakob Klein Palace, with its glorious Secession bas-reliefs between the first and second floors, and at no. 7 the Peacock and Owl House (the Johann Hartlauer House). In the centre of Saint Mary Square there is a monument carved in Carrara marble and sited where, according to a city legend, the Virgin is supposed to have appeared to those taking part in the savage execution of Gheorghe Doja, the leader of the peasant revolt of 1514. In Mocioni Square also known as the Küttl Square, can be found the Romanian Orthodox Church of Josefin, built between 1931 and 1936, styled after the Hagia Sophia Church in Constantinople, and behind it the Fiatska Houses, in the Secession style. If you take Ady Endre Street, which starts from the square, you will end up at the Iron Bridge over the Bega river, allegedly built by Gustave Eiffel (1871), although the experts have established that this is just another urban legend. Yet more legends surround the Turkish House at 2, Evliya Çelebi street, dating it would seem, from the 16th to17th centuries: it is said to have been used as a summer residence by the Timişoara Pasha or as a harem or that it is connected to the Citadel by an underground passage.

BUZIAŞ

This climatic health resort, dating back almost 200 years, located 35km east of Timişoara, was where Europe's first municipal swimming pool filled with effervescent mineral water opened in 1874. In the 20-hectare park there is a 50-metre-high wooden column, in the Turkish-Byzantine style, unique in Romania. Also look out for the plane-restaurant, brought here in 1978, if you fancy a cup of coffee in an original setting; the experience is unique – guaranteed!

ARAD

An old city on the Mureş River, 50km from the Hungarian border, Arad has been attested in the historical record since 1028, and in 1131 was mentioned in the *Vienna Illuminated Chronicle*. It was under Turkish ruling from 1551 to 1687-91 (the city north of the Mureş river) and 1716 respectively (the city south of the Mureş River), and in the 18th century it was part of the Habsburg Empire.

The **Citadel of Arad**, dating from the 16th century, rebuilt between 1698 and 1701 by Austrian military engineer Filipp Ferdinand Harsch, during the time of Prince Eugene of Savoy, has a host of Baroque buildings from the Habsburg period. It is laid out in the Vauban style,

Photo: *Administrative Palace, Arad*

with six sides, three layers of earthworks and a moat filled with water. Unfortunately, the impressive 90-hectare complex, sited on a bend in the Mureș River, is not open to visitors and continues to be used as a military garrison managed by the Ministry of Defence.

The most striking edifice in Arad is the **Palace of Culture** (1911-1913), in George Enescu Square, which combines a variety of architectural styles (neoclassical, Renaissance, Gothic). The grand 300-room construction is home to the State Philharmonic and several sections of the Arad Museum Complex.

The **Administrative Palace**, at 75, Revolution Avenue, built between 1872 and 1875 in the neo-Renaissance style, now houses City Hall, the Prefecture and Arad County Council. The clock in the 54-metre-high tower was brought from Switzerland in 1878; every hour on the hour it chimes Beethoven's Ode to Joy. On the same avenue, you will also find it worth your while to have a look at the National Bank (1906), at no. 72, the Cenad Palace (1894), at no. 73, the Palace of Financial Affairs (1896), at no. 77, and the Neumann Palace (1891), at no. 78. The brick facade of the Lutheran Evangelical Church, at no. 61,

dating back to 1906, has lent it the name Red Church. The Roman-Catholic Church of the Minorites, at no. 96A, was built between 1902 and 1903. At no. 103, the Ioan Slavici State Theatre, in the Baroque style, dates back to 1874. Nearby, on Gh. Lazăr Street, the neoclassical **Old Theatre** (1817) survives, but in a serious state of disrepair. It is the oldest theatre in Romania.

A stroll through the centre will convince you that the charm of the city resides in its superb buildings, which bear the hallmark of various architectural styles: neo-Renaissance, neoclassical, Baroque, Secession etc.

The former Water Tower (1896), at 9A Ceaikovski Street, is now an art gallery.

Look out for the **Padlock House** (1815), on Tribunul Dobra Street, which once belonged to the ironsmiths' guild; in a niche on the corner was once found the Guilds Trunk, dating from as early as 1827, which is currently exhibited on the second floor of the Art Museum. In the walls of the **Cannonball House** (c. 1800), on Calea Timișorii, seventeen cannonballs fired from the citadel towers during the 1848 Revolutions can still be seen.

The statue (1729) dedicated to Saint John of Nepomuk, the patron saint of Arad, is sited at the junction of Episcopiei Street and Desseanu Street. The Holy Trinity monument on Calea Timișorii, was erected in 1746 to commemorate the victims of the 1738-40 plague. A statue of Saint Florian has stood since 1869 at the junction of Adam Muller Guttenbrunn Street and Zimbrul Street, in the New Arad district, which was inhabited in the 18th and 19th centuries by the German minority. Arad was also home to a beautiful Roman-Catholic Baroque chapel dedicated to St. Florian (1753), which was demolished in 1977 to make room for a Securitate headquarters.

Covering an area of 40 hectares on the banks of the Mureș River is the N**eptun Municipal Swimming Pool**, which consists of 5 swimming pools, summer gardens, restaurants, and 500 camping huts.

Photo: *Palace of Culture, Arad*

North-west of the city, at the end of Dunărea Street can be found the church of the Gai Monastery, founded in 1762 by Serbian Bishop Sinisie Jivanovici.

In a forest on the Mureş River, in Bodrog Vechi village, 15km west of Arad, you can visit the **Hodoş-Bodrog Monastery**, which dates from the early 12th century (1135). It is thought to be one of the oldest places of worship in the country.

DID YOU KNOW?

According to legend, the Hodoş-Bodrog Monastery was founded after a massive bull named Hodoş discovered an icon of the Theotokos and a bucket full of gold coins in a spot next to a stream where he had been grubbing with his horns for days on end. The bull was slaughtered for having gored a shepherdess to death and the gold coins were used to build the church. The money ran out after only three sides of the façade had been plastered, with the north facade yet to be completed, since the plaster bought with other money kept crumbling. In the altar you can find preserved to this day the icon and the horns of Hodoş the bull, in a glass casket.

Macea Castle (25km from Arad), built in 1724 by the boyar Mihai Cernovici, is now home to an Ethnographic Museum, Botanical Museum and Museum of Romanian Caricatures. In 1990 the castle grounds were converted into the botanical garden of the Vasile Goldiş University in Arad.

The pilgrims say that the water of the stream flowing through the forest where the **Feredeu Hermitage** is tucked away, near the commune of Şiria, 30km north-east of Arad, has healing powers.

Lipova, a small settlement on the left bank of the Mureş River, 30km away from Arad, was first attested as early as the 12th century. In the 15th and 16th centuries it was a major centre for the crafts, with numerous guilds. Union Square, where the old burg used to stand, has been turned into a park. It is here that you can find the Orthodox Church of the Dormition of the Theotokos. It has a Baroque facade, but within it has a Byzantine-style narthex, dating from the 14th century, comprising half the nave; the frescoes in the old nave, close to the entrance, date from the 15th century. The Old Romanian School, built in the early 19th century, has many Baroque features. From the time of Turkish rule (1552-1595, 1613-1718) has been preserved an astonishing Turkish Bazaar (17th century): a commercial centre with an arcade resting on eight pilasters. The Misici manor house (19th century), at 21 Nicolae Bălcescu Street, is now the City Museum. Three kilometres from the city, on the Şistarovăţ Stream, 138m above sea level, you can find the **Lipova Baths**, a climatic and health resort with mineral springs that are good for digestive and cardiovascular conditions.

Erected in the time of Béla IV (1235-1270), rebuilt in 1245, and fortified in the 15th century by Iancu of Hunedoara, the **Şoimoş Citadel**, north of the Mureş River, atop Cioaca Tăutului, 129m above sea level, overlooks the old road leading into the heart of Transylvania. Between 1552 and 1699, this stone citadel played a vital role in the fight against the Ottomans. After 1788 it was abandoned and gradually became derelict.

CRIȘANA

ORADEA

Oradea, the largest city of the Romanian province of Crișana, in time became an important commercial centre. Its growth was boosted by its location, at the crossroads between Western, Central and South-Eastern Europe. Situated just 12km from the border, Oradea is the main entry gateway to Romania from Western Europe.

The period of Austrian rule was beneficial from every point of view, as it was then that the city's most beautiful buildings were constructed.

According to the Vienna Illuminated Chronicle, the pentagonal Oradea Citadel, surrounded by a moat filled with water, was founded in the 11th century by King Ladislau I of Hungary (1077-1095), but its current form owes much to its reconstruction in the 16th century, in the Italian style. Since 2010, the 150,000-square-metre complex has undergone major restoration work and is due to re-open to tourists in 2015. The enceint will house a Citadel Museum, Art Gallery, Centre for Religious Studies, Multi-denominational Museum, City Museum, and Centre for Excellence in Culture and the Arts.

Union Square (originally Ladislau Square) bordered by the City Hall, St. Ladislau Church, Eastern Catholic Church of the Holy Hierarch Nicholas, Eastern Catholic Bishop's Palace, Moon Church, and the Black Eagle Palace. In its centre there is a statue of Michael the Brave.

The symbol of Oradea and a landmark of Secession style architecture in Romania, the **Black Eagle Palace** (1907-1909) was designed by Budapest architects Jakab Dezső and Komor Marcell. The complex, built on the site of the earlier Black Eagle and Zoldfa (the Green Tree) inns, is made up of two wings joined by a superb glass-covered, Y-shaped passage, with entrances from Independence Street, Vasile Alecsandri Street and Union Square. The passage has a stained-glass window depicting a black

eagle, now a symbol of the city, made in Neumann Karoly's Oradea workshop in 1909. The most impressive of its facades overlooks Union square; it is asymmetrical and typical of the Secession style. The complex now houses a hotel, cinema, bank, clubs, coffee shops and restaurants.

The 50-metre tower of the **City Hall Palace**, built between 1902 and 1903 and designed by architect Kálmán Rimanóczy, dominates the square.

The **St. Ladislau Church**, built between 1721 and 1741, features an altarpiece made by Friedrich Silcher in 1863, which shows Saint Ladislau handing a bunch of keys to the Bishop of Oradea.

The **Orthodox Cathedral of the Dormition** of the Theotokos is also known as the **Moon Church** because its spire houses a clock with a working mechanism (1793) that indicates the phases of the moon. The sphere of the moon makes one complete rotation every 28 days. The church was erected between 1784 and 1790 in a style that combines the Baroque and the neoclassical.

The **Moskovits Palace** (1905), at 1, Vasile Alecsandri Street, designed by architect Kálmán Rimánoczy Jr., is notable for its facade decorated with ceramic tiles

Photo: *Black Eagle Palace, Oradea*

in yellows and blues and using the *sgrafitto* technique for the work scenes.

The **Roth House**, at 3, Vasile Alecsandri Street, built between 1902 and 1906 in the Secession style, uses bricks on its façade, joined together in straight and curved lines. Across the street, at no. 4, you can admire the Art Nouveau facade of the Deutsch K. I. Glassblowing Shop (1906-1910), decorated with floral reliefs inspired by traditional embroidery.

The **Ullmann Palace** (1913), on 1 December Square, whose architecture was inspired by the Viennese Secession style, was designed by architect Lőbll Ferenc, who was commissioned by Ullmann Sándor, a member of one of the city's leading Jewish families. The ornaments on the facade represent Jewish ceremonial items: the menorah (the seven-branched candelabrum) guarded by the lions of Judah, floral and geometric motifs. The ground floor is decorated with blue-green tiles.

The **Stern Palace**, at 10, Republicii Avenue, built between 1904 and 1905, has a frieze under the eaves that features folk art motifs, executed in coloured plaster.

The architecture of the **Apollo Palace** (1912-1914), at 12, Republicii Avenue, combines the Berlin Secessionist style and German Imperial heraldry. The decorations – stucco, figurines and ironwork – are striking. The ground floor is now the Unic Store, and on the last floor with its huge skylights there are artists' studios.

The massive dome of the **Zion Neolog Synagogue** (or the Zion Temple), built between 1877 and 1878 in Moorish style and designed by architect David Busch, on the bank of the Crişul Repede river, is visible from afar.

Cross the Crişul Repede to Ferdinand Square. It is bordered by the Queen Maria State Theatre, the Bazaar, the Astoria Hotel, the Transylvania Hotel, the Levay Palace and the Poynar House, which are in various styles: neoclassical, neo-Renaissance, Secession, Eclectic. It is a miniature open-air museum of architecture. The theatre, built between 1899 and 1900 by Viennese company Fellner and Helmer, is guarded by statues of the Muses of tragedy (Melpomene) and comedy (Thalia).

The **Roman-Catholic Basilica of the Assumption of the Virgin Mary** was built between 1752 and 1780. The main nave is 70m long and between 30 and 40m wide, and its walls are covered in Vaşcău marble; the altarpiece is made of Carrara marble. In the church is kept the casket with the relics of Saint Ladislau; there is a statue of the saint next to the side door, while another bronze statue stands outside the church. Do not miss the Christmas concerts, when the organ donated by Empress Maria Theresa of Austria in 1780 takes centre stage. In 1991, Pope John Paul II granted it the title of minor basilica. Along with the Canons Line (a 250-metre-long gallery, made up of 57 arcades

Photo: *Elegant buildings on the bank of Crişu Repede, Oradea*

connecting 10 buildings) and the Roman-Catholic Bishop's Palace (which until 2014 housed the Museum of the Criş River Land, before it moved to the Citadel) it forms the Baroque Complex of Oradea, the largest of its kind in Romania.

Stroll or cycle up to the Ciuperca (Mushroom) Restaurant on the top of **Cat Hill**, where you will get a panoramic view of the city.

Close to Oradea (8-10km) lie two of the most famous health resorts in Romania: **Băile Felix** and **Băile 1 Mai**. The thermal waters found here are rich in oligometals, bicarbonates, calcium, and sodium at temperatures ranging from 43 to 49°C. Next to Băile 1 Mai can be found the Water Lily Lake, home to three protected species: the Egyptian white water lily (*Nymphaea lotus var. thermalis*), a relic of the tertiary period, the *Scardinius erytrophtalmus racovitzai*, a species of rudd, and the *Melanopsis pareyssi* a species of snail. Băile Felix is home to a wooden church dating back to 1785, brought there from the Brusturi village.

SATU MARE

Visitors to Satu Mare will be surprised by the diversity of the city's architecture. Here, you can admire a Roman-Catholic Cathedral (1786-1798), the neoclassical Bishop's Palace (1805-1851), a Reformed Church (the Chains Church), built between 1793 and 1802 in the Baroque style, the Vácsay House (1798, 1840), in the Baroque and neo-Gothic styles, the White House (1912), the Dacia Hotel (1902), in the Secession style, and an Orthodox Cathedral (1932-1937), in the eclectic style. The 47-metre-high Firemen's Tower (📷 Tue-Sun: 4pm-9pm) provides wonderful views of the city.

Satu Mare was created in 1721, when two citadels on the banks of the Someş River merged: Sătmar and Mintiu. They had been linked by a wooden bridge in 1715. Sătmar dates back to as early as the 10th century, when is was part of Menumorut's voivodeship; later, after the river was diverted, the fortress became an island. Mintiu was founded by German settlers in the middle of the 12th century.

In 1481 at **Ardud**, 18km from Satu Mare, Bartolomeu Dragfi, the nephew of the Moldavian ruler Dragoş Vodă erected a four-tower stone citadel, on the ruins of which a second citadel was founded, two hundred years later.

Thirty-five kilometres from Satu Mare, on the right bank of the Someş River, look out for the archaeological site of the Dacian ovens at Medieşu Aurit, where over 150 unique ovens, almost 2,000 years old, were unearthed between 2009 and 2010. Six ovens, two metres in diameter, have been restored.

Photo: *Dacia Hotel, Satu Mare*

Maramureș

previous pages: Luminația *(the Day of the Dead)*, *celebrated on 1st of November*
Left: *Ieud village, guarded by snowy peaks*

Maramureş

Nestling between mountain massifs with peaks of over 1,500m, including the Rodna, Ţibleş and Gutâi, Maramureş is, as an old song says, "an ancient land with men like none other". The villages here, dotted along the meandering courses of the Tisza, Mara, Iza, Cosău and Vişeu rivers, are unique. Year after year they are flooded with tourists seeking the archaic and enthralling atmosphere of the olden days. They all wish to see the majestic Maramureş gates and wooden churches, to take part in archaic traditions, such as *Tânjaua de pe Mara* (an agrarian celebration on Mara Mountain, revolving around richly adorned cattle yokes) and *Ruptul Sterpelor* (the Separation of the Barren Ewes, a pastoral tradition), to drink *horinca* (plum brandy) and eat "three-fingers-thick" fatback, to admire the villagers' folk costumes, to take a ride on the steam train along the Vaser Valley, and to visit the Merry Cemetery of Săpânţa.

The myriad modes of woodworking are best observed in Maramureş. It is a fact: this region of northern Romania is famed for the wonderful woodworking culture that flourishes here. The locals' gates, painstakingly carved with decorative motifs, including suns, the Tree of Life, the Cross, geometric shapes, birds, snakes and anthropomorphic figures, are remarkable examples of rustic art. You can find the most beautiful wooden gates in Nănești, Bârsana, Oncești, Budești, Vadu Izei, Desești, Săpânţa and Giulești. Compared with their larger stone counterparts, small wooden churches, such as are found in Maramureş, suggest a different conception of space. Expressions of local spirituality, the wooden churches of Şurdești, Botiza, Călinești and Bogdan Vodă, with their soaring, slender spires, seem to transcend the transient nature of the material from which they are built. The whole village gathers around the church on Sunday and feast days. Such occasions are good opportunities to admire a parade of traditional Maramureş costumes.

The communities here have preserved many items of traditional household machinery: the whirlpool, for washing rugs, windmills, brandy stills, grain crushers, and oilseed presses. They have by no means become redundant or museum pieces: before every major religious feast, when each house is thoroughly cleaned, the women of the village gather at the *vâltoare* – the village "washing machine" – to launder their hand-woven carpets and other thick wool linen. The ingenious piece of equipment called *horincie* (a brandy still) is designed for making the famous local *horincă* (plum brandy, "sixty-fire water"), twice distilled, which the locals will, without fail, invite you to partake in as soon as you cross their threshold.

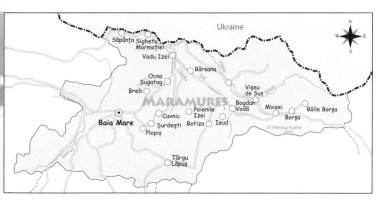

Photo: *Waiting for the guests, in Botiza village*

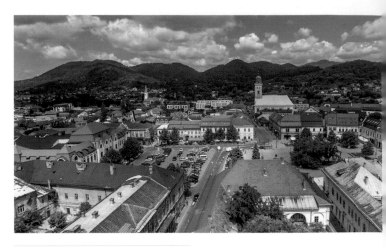

BAIA MARE

Baia Mare, in the foothills of the Gutâi Mountains, attested as *Civitas Rivuli Dominarum*, an important mining town, as early as 1329, was granted the right to build defensive walls and bastions in 1469. Of the then fortifications only the Butchers' Bastion survives.

The old centre is dominated by the 50-metre-high Stephen Tower, built between 1445 and 1468 to celebrate Iancu of Hunedoara's victory in the Battle of Ialomița. The square, bordered with numerous recently restored Baroque buildings, is a favourite promenade with the locals.

Iancu of Hunedoara built a castle in Baia Mare for his wife, Elizabeth, which was completed in 1468 by Matthias Corvinus. Only an annex of the castle, the Iancu of Hunedoara House, has been preserved. There are other city buildings reminiscent of its long past: the Roman-Catholic Church of St. Anthony, the Baroque Church of the Holy Trinity, once part of a Jesuit monastery (1717-1720), a wooden church dating from 1630, built by master builders from Chechiș village, which in 1939 was moved to the open-air Ethnographic Museum on Dealul Florilor, the former Minorite monastery (1734), the Mint House (1734-1738), home to the archaeology and history sections of the Maramureș County Museum, the Reformed Church (1792), and the former Casino (1834).

THE WOODEN CHURCHES LISTED AS UNESCO SITES

The churches of Maramureș are unique not only for their magnificent woodcarvings, but also for their architectural technique and the harmony of their proportions, which achieve perfection. Some of them have been listed as UNESCO World Heritage sites, including the wooden churches of Poienile Izei (1604), Budești – Josani (1643), Ieud Hill (17th century), Bârsana (1720), Desești (1770), from the historical Land of Maramureș, Șurdești (1767) and Plopiș (1792), in Țara Chioarului, and Rogoz (1663), in Țara Lăpușului.

The **Ieud Hill Church** (the Nativity of the Theotokos), which dates back to the 17th century, has murals painted by Alexandru Ponehalschi. In its loft was discovered the *Ieud Codex*, the oldest body of laws in Romanian (1391). It preserves a collection of old icons on wood from the 17th to 18th centuries, a collection of icons from Nicula (the first centre for icons on glass in Transylvania), priceless books and documents, and rugs made using natural dyes.

The **Saint Nicholas Church in Budeşti – Josani** was built in 1643 on the site of an earlier church from the 15th century. The church, made of massive wood beams resting on a stone foundation, was painted in harmoniously combined warm, bright colours around the year 1762 by Alexandru Ponehalschi, one of the most active mural painters in Maramureş. Unfortunately, the murals have been preserved intact only on the south and west walls of the narthex. The paintings on the icon screen are also by Ponehalschi.

The **Saint Parascheva Church in Poienile Izei** dates from the 17th century. The nave is rectangular and the porch is on the west side. It has a double-hem roof, and the spire above the narthex, housing three bells, has a belvedere covered by a helm roof with extended eaves and a tall cross on top. Unlike other churches, the altar is four-sided, like in the olden days. The murals, painted in 1794, are noteworthy for their eclectic style, which combines traditional iconographic elements and other motifs specific to the period.

The **Saint Parascheva Church in Deseşti** was built in 1717 (in 1770, according to some). Its architecture follows a more traditional line: the way the wood beams are joined together, the balanced shapes and volumes and the overall harmony of the ensemble give an impression of simplicity and elegance. What makes the site original are the rafters in the upper part, which support the roof truss, extended and shaped like steps. The church preserves valuable murals, painted in 1780 by Radu Munteanu and Gheorghe Vişoveanul.

The **Church of the Entrance of the Theotokos into the Temple in Bârsana** (1720) is a typical example of Maramureş architecture. It is notable for its small size, rectangular plan, five-sided apse, bell tower above the narthex, and double-hem roof. The church was painted in 1806 by two local painters; the murals show Baroque touches.

The 17th-century **Church of the Holy Archangels Michael and Gabriel in Rogoz**, a village on the Lăpuş River, was built in 1663, and rebuilt in 1717. The church is one of the most interesting in Maramureş. The nave is rectangular in form, the narthex features apses, and the altar is seven-sided. The bell tower has four small towers at its corners. Under the eaves there are numerous brackets carved in the shape of horse heads.

Photo: *Ieud village, at sunrise*

The **Church of the Holy Archangels Michael and Gabriel in Plopiş** was built in the 18th century by Ioan Macarie and the murals were painted in 1811 by Stephen of Şişeşti. The church has a three-lobed nave vault, unique among the wooden churches of Maramureş.

The **Church of the Holy Archangels Michael and Gabriel in Şurdeşti**, a village in Cavnic Valley, was built in 1767 and the murals were painted in 1783 by Stephen of Şişeşti. It is reckoned to be the tallest wooden structure in Romania and even Europe, thanks to its 54-metre spire. The porch has two rows of superposed arcades, on the ground floor and the upper floor. The icon screen is remarkable for its polychrome, gilded, carved Baroque elements and its icons painted on a gold ground.

SĂPÂNŢA

At Săpânţa, 18km from Sighetu-Marmaţiei, can be found the best-known *in situ* exhibit of the Museum of Maramureş: the house of Stan Ion Pătraş, the founder of the nearby cemetery, which is unique, thanks to the ironic and casual way in which he viewed death. In his courtyard you can still find his workshop, where one of his apprentices carries on his craft. Over almost 80 years, the Merry Cemetery of Săpânţa has been enriched with 800 carved wooden crosses painted in "Săpânţa blue". They are decorated with naive paintings in strong, undiluted colours, and unpretentious yet witty epitaphs, which sum up the life of the deceased with a dose of humour.

The wooden portals of Maramureş

Separating two worlds (the exterior and the interior), the portal functions as both a threshold and a means of representation. A mark of the social and economic status of the family and invested with protective powers, the traditional portals of Maramureş are remarkable for their monumentality and intricate woodcarvings. They rest on from two to six columns connected by a *fruntar* (upper beam) and capped with a shingle roof. The woodcarvings are invested with magical powers: the twisted rope and wolf's tooth protect from evil; the Tree of Life symbolises plenty and eternal life; the rosettes are a symbol of the Sun and God; and the zoomorphic and anthropomorphic figures each have their own mythical meanings. The most beautiful portals can be found in the villages of, Bârsana, Onceşti, Vadu Izei, Deseşti, and Budeşti.

DID YOU KNOW?

Vâltoarea, *a hydraulic installation, specific to Maramureş, which harnesses centrifugal force, is the village "washing machine", around which the women gather to clean their blankets, rugs and other thick wool and linen.*

Photo: *The Church of the Holy Archangels Michael and Gabriel in Şurdeşti*

***Tânjaua de pe Mara* (the Mara Mountain Yoke, a rural festival at which are displayed richly adorned cattle yokess)**

In the first half of May, Hoteni hosts the *Tânjaua de pe Mara*, a festival dedicated to the most hardworking villager: the first man who goes out to plough. He is paraded through the village to his field, where one of the village elders wishes him a good harvest, and then to the river, where he is sprinkled, for "good luck and plenty / And for good brown soil again". The girls are sprinkled too and the parade proceeds to the feted man's house, where there is dancing into the small hours of the night to the accompaniment of the *ceteră* (traditional violin), *zongoră* (a type of guitar) and *dobă* (a two-skinned drum made by artisans). A custom similar to the *Hoteni Tânjaua* is *Udătoriul* (the Dipping), preserved in Şurdeşti (Ţara Chioarului).

***Ruptul Sterpelor* (the Separation of the Barren Ewes)**

In May, the local traditional calendar marks yet another ancient feast, *Ruptul Sterpelor*, at which is celebrated the readying of the sheepfolds for summer and the amount of milk produced by each flock is weighed to establish how much cheese, soft cheese and whey each villager will receive for the period his sheep remain on the mountain. After the sheep are sprinkled with holy water and the milk is weighed, the celebration begins. People eat traditional foods (*balmoş* – sheep milk cheese boiled in milk or butter with maize flour – and lamb stew), drink *horincă* (plum brandy) and listen to folk music. In the past it was celebrated with more simplicity and religious piety, as shepherding was the main activity of the traditional community. Nowadays, however, it is becoming excessively touristy and festive.

THE VASER VALLEY

From Vişeu de Sus you can set off up the Vaser Valley (62km). For 42 kilometres of the valley there is a narrow-gauge forest railway, built in 1932, along which runs an old-fashioned steam engine with a train of wagons for hauling timber. Since 2000 the train has also had passengers carriages. The historical train puffs its way through the steep mountain valley and wild forests, passing through the tunnels bored through the solid rock and stopping at Novăţ, Novicior, Bardiu, Cozia, Botizu, Şuligu, Făina, Măcârlău, Lostun, Ivăşcoaia and Comanu train stations. A ride on the train has become one of the most famous attractions in Maramureş. It is an amazing opportunity for nature lovers to explore the hidden reaches of the Maramureş Mountains, seeing Vinderel Lake and the Mihăilescu Peak on the way, travelling to the Tomnatec Sehleanu narcissus meadow near Repedea village and up as far at the Toroiaga Peak (1,930m) and Prislop Pass (1,416m), on the other side of which lies Bukowina.

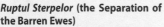

Photos: Tânjaua de pe Mara *and* Ruptul Sterpelor, *two ancient agrarian feasts from Maramureş*

THE GUTÂI MOUNTAINS

With peaks of up to 1,450m, these mountains feature extremely diverse landscapes and several spectacular nature reserves, including Creasta Cocoşului (Cockerel's Crest), an extinct volcano, which is an excellent climbing spot, and Cheile Tătarului (Tartar's Gorges), which cut a furrow through the andesite and are dotted with small clusters of forests. On the south side of the Gutâi Mountains, on the shore of Bodi Lake, you can find the Mogoşa resort, with its excellent ski slope, and on a plateau surrounded by pine trees, on the south-west side, is the Izvoare climatic and ski resort.

THE RODNA MOUNTAINS

Northern Maramureş is guarded by the ridges of the Rodna Mountains, famous for their glacial cirques and lakes: Pietrosul Mare (2,303m), Ineu (2,279m), Buhăescu Mare (2,225m), Puzdre (2,188m), Bătrâna (1,710m), Nedeia Ţăranului (1,857m), Galaţu (2,048m), Găgălău (2,159m) and Omului (2,135m). These tall, sheer mountains are dotted with glacial lakes, including the beautiful Lala Mare, Lala Mică, Iezer, Buhăescu and Repedea, and more than 800 caves (Peştera Zânelor, Izvorul Albastru al Izei, Izbucul Izei etc.). The Rodna Mountains, part of which is included in the national park of the same name, is one of the most important alpine tourism areas in the country.

In their foothills, along the Vişeu Valley, can be found the **Băile Borşa resort**, well known for its mineral waters rich in iron, calcium and magnesium. Twelve kilometres separate it from the Borşa complex, popular among winter sports aficionados, who can enjoy its numerous ski slopes. From here you get unforgettable views of the Pietrosul Rodnei, Piatra Albă, Buhăescu Mare and Buhăescu Mic, Repedea, Cormaia peaks and the Horses Mountain. A chairlift service will take you to Ştiol Grove. Nearby, the **Horses Waterfall** (90m), with the highest drop in Romania, puts on a stunning show of plunging, splashing waters.

SIGHETU MARMAŢIEI

The historical Land of Maramureş barely had any urban environment until the mid-20th century. The only town that has been here for centuries is Sighetu Marmaţiei, at the confluence of the Tisza and Iza rivers, first attested in 1326.

The fully preserved Old City, a veritable gallery of architecture in the Baroque, Secession and Eclectic styles, testifies to its past importance and once thriving economic life.

A stone's throw away from Freedom Square stands the Memorial to the Victims of Communism, housed in the prison built by the Austro-Hungarians in 1897. In 1950, the communists imprisoned the country's elite here: politicians, economists, army officers, professors, bishops, many of whom perished in the extremely harsh conditions.

Photo: *Horses Waterfall*

Sighetu Marmaţiei preserves another memorial to dark times in the past: the Holocaust Monument, which commemorates the 12,500 Jews from the town who were deported to concentration camps by the Horthy regime in 1944. Of the eight synagogues that existed in the town before the Second World War, only one remains. Nearby, writer and philosopher Elie Wiesel lived as a young child. He survived the Auschwitz-Birkenau concentration camp, where he was sent with his family in May 1944. The Wiesel House is now home to the Museum of Jewish Culture and Civilisation in Maramureş. Together with the history, archaeology, natural sciences and ethnographic sections of the Museum of Maramureş, it pieces together the bigger picture of the historical, cultural and spiritual heritage of this region and its rich past.

THE IZA VALLEY
Located 5km from Sighetu Marmaţiei, **Vadu Izei**, first attested in 1383, is famous for its monumental wood portals, carved by Vasile Apan and Gheorghe Borodi. You can visit the former in his workshop at no. 605, where he continues to carve icons, wooden ladles, seals, spoons etc., all decorated with geometric motifs. The settlement has a very rich choice of farm holiday cottages.

Thirteen kilometres to the south sits **Bârsana**, with its famous church (➤163) listed as a UNESCO Heritage Site, and a beautiful monastery, recently built a few kilometres away. The monastery has a 57-metre-high wooden Maramureş church, visited by thousands of tourists. Folk artist Ioan Bârsan has turned his homestead, at no. 605, into a Museum of Folk Culture.

Further south you can find **Glod**, with its wooden church, seven whirlpools, several brandy stills and a sulphur mineral spring (Borcutul de sub Stâncă).

At Şieu, Rozavlea and Poienile Izei you can admire other wooden churches and monumental gates, intricately carved with traditional motifs.

Turning off Iza Valley, we head out to **Botiza**, located in a picturesque setting in the foothills of the Ţibleşul Mountains. Here you can visit the watermill and the saltwater spring or set off on a trip to Dănilă's Rocks or the mineral springs of Saxon's Valley. Father Isidor Berbecaru, the founder of the new church, built between 1975 and 1978, promotes local tourism, and in the 1970s his wife Victoria revived the tradition of weaving naturally dyed wool rugs, in her workshop, which can be found at no. 748. Other local women (Iulia Corău, at no. 222, Ilişca Manţa, at no. 435) carry on this old craft.

Photo: *Blessing of Easter foods at the Botiza church*

Recommendations and Useful Information

Previous page: *Women's Cave*

Tours, trips and other holiday activities

MOUNTAINEERING

Climbing the peaks of the Carpathians is one of the most thrilling experiences you can have in Romania. The ranges you can choose from are the Bucegi Mountains (Omu Peak, 2,504m), Piatra Craiului Mountains (Piscu Baciului Peak, 2,237m), Făgăraş Mountains (Moldoveanu Peak, 2,544m), Retezat Mountains (Peleaga Peak, 2,509m), Metaliferi Mountains (Poieniţa Peak, 1,437m), Rodna Mountains (Pietrosu Peak, 2,303m), Southern Carpathians (Cucurbăta Mare Peak, 1,849m) and Ceahlău Mountains (Ocolaşul Mare Peak, 1,907m). Tourist guides and maps with detailed routes are available at the information centres. For those unwilling to go it alone, the travel agencies offer guided tours, with various activities included (such as rock climbing – abseiling).

SKIING

Romania has 151 certified ski slopes, totalling 135km in length. The most popular can be found in the resorts of Poiana Braşov (➤116), Predeal (➤47), Azuga (➤47), Straja, Arieşeni – Vârtop, Parâng, Semenic (➤143) etc. They have various degrees of difficulty (easy, intermediate, advanced) and are generally equipped with ski lifts, chairlifts and cable cars.

CYCLING

A bicycle ride along the forest roads or paths in the heart of the Romanian Carpathians is a unique experience, combining the satisfactions of outdoor sport with the joy of being close to nature. Among the mountain bike (MTB) routes with a low degree of difficulty is the one connecting Predeal (➤47) and Buşteni (➤46), passing through Cabana Susai, Azuga and Valea Cerbului, and the route across the plateau of Baiului Mountain (departure point: Sinaia, arrival point: Azuga). Those in love with scenic landscapes can try the Zărneşti – Râşnov – Poiana Braşov – Braşov route, rated intermediate. If you have a head for adventure and are looking for an adrenaline-packed challenge, then try the Predeal – Zărneşti – Dâmbovicioara – Măgura – Braşov route or the one over Piatra Craiului.

In 2014, The Buila – Vânturărita National Park Administration issued an interactive map for cyclists, with 13 routes (10 for mountain biking and 3 for cycle tourism), containing detailed information on route lengths, average and maximum climbing grades, differences in altitude, and elevation points along the way.

BIRD-WATCHING

Undoubtedly, the best place in Romania for bird-watching is the Danube Delta (➤85), home to almost 300 bird species (of which 44 species are sedentary and 132 migratory), and the best time to go is between the late spring and mid-autumn. Many travel agencies offer tours of the Fortuna, Sireasa, Nebunu and Băclăneşti Mari lakes and the surrounding channels. Here, you can watch the great white and the Dalmatian pelican, cormorants, little and great egrets, grey, purple and yellow-crowned night herons, little bitterns, red-necked grebes, common kingfishers, white-tailed eagles, Eurasian coots, black-winged stilts, Eurasian spoonbills, ibises, northern lapwings, and many more. The best known of the one hundred bird colonies in the Danube Delta Biosphere Reserve is at Roşca-Buhaiova, which has the highest density of great white pelicans (*Pelecanus onocrotalus*) in Europe. From October/November to mid-March, the delta is the wintering place for several bird species that nest within the Arctic Circle or in Siberia.

RAFTING

The most spectacular rafting routes in Romania are along the Jiu River (between Livezeni and Bumbeşti Jiu), Cerna River (upstream of the Cerna Gorges), Nera River (between Şopotul Nou and Valea Beuşniţei), Crişul Repede River (from Bulz or Bucea up to Vadu Crişului), Mureş (Topliţa-Deda Canyon), Bistriţa River (upstream of Vatra Dornei as far as Poiana Teiului) and the Arieş River (between Albac and Turda), with its frothy waters, boulder-jumbled narrow channels and countless bends. A river less known to rafters is the Buzău, which has two routes, upstream and downstream of Siriu Lake; it is the nearest to Bucharest. The best

time for rafting is from late spring to early summer, when the water is at its most turbulent. Travel agencies specialising in this adventure sport include equipment in their fees: rafting boat, paddles, life jacket, neoprene suit, paddling boots, helmet, as well as training and authorised guides. The fee does not include transportation, board and lodging.

ZIPLINING

Get your kicks on the zip line, at speeds of 10 to 20m/s, in the Cheişoara, Râşnoava Gorges, the Şapte Scări Canyon, and also Black Sea beach resorts.

PARAGLIDING

Paragliding has become one of the most popular adventure sports in Romania. The glide lasts around 15 to 20 minutes and rides are available in many areas across the country, particularly near Braşov (Postăvaru – Poiana Braşov, Bunloc, Postăvaru or Codlea) and Sibiu (Bâlea, Păltiniş, Tocile – Sadu).

HOT AIR BALLOONING

There are several websites (www.balonzbor. ro, www.balloony.ro, www.balonro.ro, www.balon.home.ro, www.inchiriere-balon.go.ro, www.inchirierebalon.home. ro, www.balloony.ro, www.balon-aer-cald.ro) that offer recreational hot air balloon rides, around Bucharest (Clinceni, Mihăileşti), Braşov, Bran, and Timişoara, as well as on the Black Sea coast. Rides last for around one hour, and the balloon can reach altitudes of around 1,000m.

HORSE RIDING

Several horse riding clubs and stud farms offer recreational horse riding: Clubul Piccadilly (Bucharest), Hipocan Corbeanca (Bucharest), Equestria (Ţâncăbeşti, Ilfov), Panicel Complex (Râşnov, Braşov), the Dream Horse Estate (Botoşani), Mangalia Stud, Rădăuţi Stud, Rodeo (Tomeşti, Jassy), Scorillo (Curteni, Sântana de Mureş).

Attractions for Children

NATURAL PHENOMENA

Mud Volcanoes ➤61
The Sphinx and the Old Ladies Rocks of Bucegi ➤46-47
The Trovants Museum ➤63

CAVES

Bears Cave ➤133
Women's Cave ➤64
Polovragi Cave ➤63
Comarnic Cave ➤143

SALT MINES

Slănic Prahova ➤47

Praid

> ✉ 44 Gării Street, Praid, Harghita county
> 🕐 Daily: 8am-4pm 💲 2 Lei (children), 22 Lei (adults)

The Praid salt mine, 120m deep within the core of the Gurghiului Mountains, Harghita County, resembles a miniature city. It has a popular adventure park (Club Aventura).

Turda

> www.salinaturda.eu
> ✉ 7 Aleea Durgăului, Turda
> 📞 0364.260940
> 🕐 Daily: 9am-4pm
> 💲 10 Lei (children), 20 Lei (adults)

After improvements lasting two years and costing six million Euros, the Turda Salt Mine re-opened in January 2010. It comprises the former Iosif, Terezia and Rudolf mines, with treatment facilities, an amphitheatre, sports grounds and a Ferris wheel.

WATERFALLS

Horses Waterfall (Borşa resort) ➤166
Beuşniţa Waterfall ➤146
Capra Waterfall ➤55

ADVENTURE PARKS

Edenland

> www.edenland.ro
> ✉ Cantonului Street, Baloteşti
> 📞 0733-365263 💲 30-40 Lei (children), 50 Lei (adults) for 3 hours 🚌 Free transportation from Piaţa Presei Libere with Edenland buses (departures times: 10am, 12 pm, 2pm and 4pm from the Parking situated at the end of tram 41 line); microbus 551 (station: Spitalul SRI)

Located 20km from Bucharest, Edenland has eleven treetop trails, with varying degrees of difficulty. Other attractions: archery, airsoft, paintball, pendulum jump (15m in height), bike rental for rides through the forest, and tree houses that provide accommodation at 290 lei/ 2 persons.

Comana Adventure Park

> www.parcaventuracomana.ro
> ✉ 607 Gellu NaumStreet, Comana village, Giurgiu county 🕐 Daily: 9am-7pm
> 💲 50 Lei (3 hours)

The adventure park in Comana (➤41), 35km from Bucharest, has four tree climbing routes for children and three for adults, of progressive difficulty (easy, intermediate and advanced), a zip line over the lake, a bike rental service, boats and kayaks, powered paragliding and angling facilities. It also organises horse and carriage rides through the Comana Forest as far as Walnut Well (allegedly the spot where Vlad the Impaler met his end) or as far as Comana Monastery.

AMUSEMENT PARK

Children's Town, Tineretului Park
Children's Town is the most modern amusement park in the Capital, with bumper cars, a merry-go-round, a roller coaster, a water channel, a gym and a 150-metre-high Ferris wheel.

WATER PARKS

Aqua Magic Mamaia

> 📞 0241.831183
> 💲 Jun and Sep: 60 Lei (adults), 20 Lei (children).
> Jul and Aug: 80 Lei (adults), 30 Lei (children)

The first water park in the country (since 2003), Aqua Magic has an area of about 30,000 square metres, facilities for 3,000 visitors, and 14 special attractions. The children's area consists of two swimming pools: Waterplayground and Babypool, with special water slides for the little ones, while the adult area has the following attractions: Relax Pool, Jacuzzi, Lazy River, Space Bowl, Multislide, River Ride, Mega Pipe, Twister, Kamikaze, Turbo Slide and Black Hole.

Divertiland

> www.divertiland.ro
> 💲 Adults: 40 Lei (weekdays), 65 Lei (weekend).
> Children: 30 Lei (weekdays), 50 Lei (weekend).

The largest water park in Romania, Divertiland opened in 2012. It is 13 km from Bucharest, near the Bucharest – Piteşti road, and has facilities for 3,500 visitors. Among its attractions there are 22 water slides, the only wave pool in Bucharest (1,200 square metres of waves), the Arena del Sol (3,000 square metres, with beach chairs and a strand), an area for children aged three to twelve (Los Petitos), a slow-flowing river, and an island.

Braşov Water Paradise

> www.paradisulacvatic.ro
> ✉ 2F-2G Griviţei Bd., Braşov
> 🕐 Mon: 2-10pm, Tue-Fri: 11am-10pm, Sat-Sun: 10am-10pm 💲 25 Lei (children), 55 Lei (adults)

Established in July 2007, the Braşov Water Paradise covers an area of 12,000 square metres, and has facilities for 2,000 people. It includes six indoor pools, two outdoor pools, water slides, saunas, a jacuzzi, relaxation cave, a gym, an indoor football pitch, a beach volleyball court, a restaurant and outdoor dining areas.

Aqua Park President, Băile Felix

> www.aquapark-felix.ro
> 💲 45 Lei (adults), 20 Lei (children)

Aqua Park is part of the President Hotel and uses thermal water from the Băile Felix resort (➤155). It has 13 indoor pools, five outdoor pools, one wave pool, indoor and outdoor slides, a steam bath, a Finnish sauna, a relaxation area, pool tables, bowling, miniature football, and a restaurant with an outdoor dining area.

AQUARIA AND DOLPHINARIA

Constanţa Aquarium

> ✉ 1 Elisabeta Bd. (next to the Casino), Constanţa
> 🕐 Daily: 9am-4pm 💲 10 Lei (children), 20 Lei (adults)

Located on the Black Sea shore, next to the Casino, the Constanța Aquarium (➤74) opened on 1 May 1958. It is divided into three sections: marine fishes, freshwater fishes and exotic fishes, with 100 fish species and sea wildlife, from various parts of the world. The species most popular with the little ones are the stingray, red scorpion fish, starfish, greater pipefish and the straight-nosed pipefish, tompot blenny and the tentacled blenny.

Constanța Dolphinarium

> www.delfinariu.ro
> ✉ 255, Mamaia Bd, Constanța
> 🕑 Mon-Fri: 8am-4pm, Sat-Sun: 9am-5pm (Sept-May)
> Dolphinarium shows – Mon-Fri: 11am, 1pm, 3pm, Sat-Sun: 11am, 1pm, 4pm.
> Planetarium shows – Mon-Fri: 10:30am, 11:30a,, 1:30 pm, 3:30pm.
> 💲 Single ticket for the Dolphinarium, Micro-reserve and exotic birds, Planetarium: 50 Lei (adults), 25 Lei (children).
> Ticket for Aquarium: 20 Lei, 10 Lei (children)

The Constanța Museum for Natural Sciences (➤74) has several sections (a Planetarium, an exotic birds exhibition and a dolphinarium). The main attraction is the show put on by the dolphins, sea lions and the penguins.

Tulcea Aquarium

> www.icemtl.ro
> ✉ 1,14 Noiembrie Street, Tulcea 🕑 Tue-Sun: 9am-6pm 💲 5 Lei (children), 15 Lei (adults)

The Danube Delta Eco-tourist Centre includes an Aquarium with 27 pools filled with 100 tonnes of water, home to 24 species of fish indigenous to the Danube Delta and Black Sea, 23 species of reef fish, eight species of marine invertebrates and six species of corals from Indonesia.

TOURS AND RIDES

Ride the narrow-gauge steam train along the Vaser Valley (➤165) or from Moldovița to Argel (➤101).
Take a flight on a hot air balloon ➤171.

CITADELS AND CASTLES

Râșnov Citaded ➤118
Neamț Citaded ➤106
Făgăraș Citaded ➤119
Peleș Castle ➤46
Bran Castle ➤60
Hunyadi Castle ➤135

MUSEUMS

Grigore Antipa Museum of Natural History, Bucharest

> www.antipa.ro
> ✉ 1, Kiseleff Avenue, Bucharest 🕑 Tue-Sun: 10am-8pm (summer), 10am-6pm (winter)
> 💲 20 Lei (5 Lei, children). (Free for children during holidays)

The Antipa Museum holds almost two million exhibits in its zoology, geology, ecology, oceanography and palaeontology sections. After the overhaul of 2008-2011, which saw an investment of twelve million Euros, the revamped museum has an interactive media format utilising state-of-the-art technology (holograms, interactive screens etc.). The star of the show is the skeleton of a giant *Deinotherium gigantissimum*, an ancestor of the elephant, unearthed by researcher Gregoriu Ștefănescu near Mânzați village, Vaslui County. The species became extinct about 2.5 million years ago, after the Ice Age.

The museum frequently offers inter-disciplinary programmes designed for children (for instance, the Holy Molly creative thinking workshops, the Mad Scientists' Club, Learn to be Healthy, Rocked by the Deinotherium, Night at the Museum etc.).

The Sibiu Steam Locomotive Museum

> ✉ 22 Dorobanților Street 🕑 Daily: 8am-4pm

Created in 1994, the museum has a collection of 35 steam locomotives manufactured between 1885 and 1958 at the Reșița and Malaxa plants in Bucharest, as well as by German Henschel, Borsig, and Schwartzkopff in Germany and Baldwin in the United States.

Calendar of Festivals and Cultural Events

• January
Feast of the Epiphany

On the Feast of the Epiphany (6 January) the waters are blessed, being thus imbued with miraculous powers. It is said that whoever takes a plunge in river, lake or sea at Epiphany will be cured of ailments. In southern Romania, in the villages along the Danube and in Dobruja, there is also the tradition of Sprinkling the Horses (➤82).

• February
Fărşang ➤138

A carnival celebrated by the Saxons of Transylvania after Meatfare Sunday.

Parada Lolelor (Parade of the Lole)➤131

A custom, kept by the villages along the Hârtibaciului Valley, as part of which winter is buried (Sibiu).

Ziua Cucilor (The Cuckoo Day)

A celebration kept by the Bulgarian community of Brăneşti, 20km east of Bucharest, on the first Monday after Meatfare Sunday. The only carnival in the south of the country.

Paştele Cailor (Horse Easter)

The Bulgarian community of the Matei Voievod district in Tîrgovişte holds a horse parade on the first Saturday of Great Lent.

Florii (Palm Sunday, Flowers Day)

Palm Sunday falls on the Sunday before Easter. In Romania, on this day the Orthodox celebrate girls who are named after flowers. In the Bulgarian villages of Aluniş, Măgurele and Brăneşti, girls of to 12 years in age sing *Lăzăriţa*, a song that is pre-Christian in origins, as part of a ritual that symbolises the rebirth of nature.

• March
Mărţişor (a diminutive of March)

The tradition of *mărţişor*, which is Slavonic in origin, goes back to when March was the first month of the year. Men used to give women *mărţişoare* (originally a plaited piece of red and white wool, to which a small silver coin was attached) to ward off evil and bring good luck.

The Almond-flower Festival of Gura Vadului (Tohani, Prahova)

In the foothills of the Carpathians, in an area blessed by a Mediterranean climate atypical for the region, almond trees have been grown for almost 200 years. When in bloom, they put on a unique show. The seven hectares of crop yield a tonne of almonds.

• April
Easter

Easter is one of the most important Orthodox feasts. The whole country, and Bukowina and Maramureş in particular, still observes the age-old customs: eggs are painted, *pasca* (a sweet cheese cake) and *cozonac* (sweet Easter bread) are baked, and in the evening the faithful attend the Resurrection service, when the gates of Heaven open, after which they bring home lighted Easter candles.

Blajini Easter (Sunday of St. Thomas)

The first Sunday after Easter is dedicated to the souls of departed loved ones and ancestors, the so-called *Blajini* (the Gentle Ones), who live in a land far away, where the Waters of the River Saturday flow into the heart of the Earth. The faithful go to church, commemorate the deceased, and give alms.

Junii Braşovului (The Young Men of Braşov)

A folk celebration held on the first weekend after Easter in Braşov (➤115).

The Tulip Symphony, Piteşti

The tulip, the symbol of the city of Piteşti, has its own festival, an occasion for exhibitions of flowers, parades, sports competitions, concerts and sound and light shows.

Blooming of the Fernleaf Peonies at Zău de Câmpie (Mureş)

The Zău de Câmpie Plant Reserve is the highest place in the world where fernleaf peonies bloom (*Paeonia Tenuifolia*). They can be admired from the end of April to the beginning of May.

• May

***Tânjaua de pe Mara* (the Mara Mountain Yoke) ➤165**

A rural festival held at Hoteni.

The Peony Festival at Comana

An outdoor festival, celebrated on the second Sunday in May, in the Padina Tătarului area, near the settlement of Vlad Ţepeş (commune of Mihai Bravu, Giurgiu County).

The Daffodil Festival

Held in the first half of May, in the floodplain of the Dâmbovnic river, at the edge of the Negraşi village in Argeş County, where there is a four-hectare reservation of starry daffodils – *Narcissus stellaris (ssp. radiiflorus)*, a relic of the Quaternary Age.

Lilac Festival

The flowering of the lilac is an occasion for celebrations at Ponoarele (➤64).

• June

White Sunday (Descent of the Holy Spirit)

Forty days after Easter, on Pentecost Sunday, Romanians in the south of the country dance the Horseman dance (➤68), part of a healing ritual.

Midsummer (Drăgaica-Litha)

An old tradition celebrated on 24 June, the St. John's Day, around the summer solstice. On this day people gather yellow bedstraw flowers, which they make into a wreath to protect their houses against evil and diseases.

• July

The Maidens' Fair on Găina Mountain

An ancient pastoral feast held on the Sunday nearest Saint Elijah's Day (20 July), on a meadow atop of the mountain, at an altitude of 1,467m.

• September

The descent of the sheep from the mountains

An old pastoral feast, celebrated in the settlements of Mărginimea Sibiului(➤128).

Wine Making Festival

A festival dedicated to wine, held in Pietroasele, Buzău. An ox-wagon carries baskets full of grapes, which are later trodden by barefoot young women dressed in traditional costumes. The festival marks the beginning of the grape harvest.

George Enescu Festival

Held every two years, the internationally acclaimed Georges Enesco Festival brings together some of the world's best philharmonic orchestras and soloists in Palace Hall, the Athenaeum (➤31) and Radio Hall. The latest festival was held in 2015.

• October

The National Theatre Festival (NTF)

The best theatre productions from all over the country are presented on the stage of the National Theatre in Bucharest. In the last three years, theatrical companies from abroad have also been invited to perform.

• November

The Day of the Dead (*Luminaţia*)

On the night of 1 November, thousands of candles are lit by the faithful in cemeteries across Transylvania, burning bright until the break of dawn.

• December

Christmas

The same as everywhere else in the world, children in Romania breathlessly wait for Santa Claus. In the countryside, carolling bands of merrymakers, carrying the *Sorcova* (crafted from coloured paper or rags, to resemble a flowering branch) and singing *Pluguşorul* (the Little Plough, a song wishing good luck, happiness and success), dressed in colourful costumes (as bears, goats and deer) roam the village, dancing in rituals meant to bring fertility and plenty.

The best Christmas market can be found at Sibiu (➤123).

Useful Information

TRANSPORTATION

• How to get to Romania

Many airline companies (Tarom, Air France, KLM, Alitalia etc.) have flights to and from Romania's capital, Bucharest. There are airports in other cities as well: Cluj-Napoca, Timişoara, Sibiu, Oradea, Arad, Târgu Mureş, Bacău and Craiova, to which Air Berlin, Austrian Airlines and the low-cost Blue Air and Wizz Air airliners schedule flights.

• Getting around the country
By train

Romanian Railways (CFR, www.cfr.ro) operates an extended railway network, which covers the entire country. There are three types of trains: Regio – R (the slowest and most affordable), InterRegio – IR (average speed) and InterCity – IC (the fastest and most expensive). For train timetables, go to www.cfrcalatori.ro.

By bus

Many transportation companies operate services between the major cities of Romania. To consult the timetables, go to www.autogari.ro website.

TIME ZONE

Romania is in the EEST zone, two hours ahead of Greenwich Mean Time (GMT+2). Under the 1997 Convention, summer time (GMT+3) begins on the last Sunday of March and ends on the last Sunday of October.

CLIMATE

Romania has a temperate climate. The mean summer temperature is 22-24°C, but can reach 38°C. In winter, the mean temperature is around -3°C.

The best time to visit Romania is between late March and early June and from early September to late October, when the temperature is warm and rainfall rare.

The best season for ski lovers is from December to mid-March, and for those wishing to bask in the sun on a Black Sea beach, from mid-June to mid-September.

CURRENCY

The national currency is *leu* ("lion", currency code LEI), subdivided into 100 *bani*.

The banknotes in circulation have faces values of 1, 5, 10, 50, 100 and 500 lei. The coins in circulation have face values of 1, 5, 10 and 50 bani.

When this guide went to press, 1 Romanian leu was worth 0.22 Euros.

LANGUAGE

The official language of Romania is Romanian, a Romance language, spoken by 89% of the population. Seven per cent of the population (particularly in Transylvania) speak Hungarian, and 1.5% speak German.

TELECOMMUNICATIONS

To call Romania from abroad, dial international access code 00 or +, country code 40, and the city code (21, for Bucharest), followed by the number.

If you want to make a long-distance call within Romania, dial the code of the county first, followed by the number.

Useful Phone numbers

Emergency no:	112
Police:	021.955, 021.9545
Fire Brigade:	021.981
Ambulance:	021.961
Gendarmes:	021.956
Info railway:	021.952
Consumer Protection:	021.9551

USEFUL WEBSITES

• GENERAL
www.mae.ro
The first-time visitors will find useful travelling advice and a list of foreign embassies in Bucharest at the website of the Ministry for Foreign Affairs.

www.romaniatourism.com
The Ministry of Tourism website provides information on the main attractions in Romania.

• TRANSPORTATION
www.tarom.ro

Details on flights operated by the national airline company.

www.cfr.ro
Romanian Railways train timetables.

www.autogari.ro
The most effective online bus booking system, with almost 10,000 national and international routes.

TOURIST OFFICES

• Bucharest
www.en.seebucharest.ro
✉ Piaţa Universităţii metro station passage
☎ 021.3055500 (interior 1003)
🕓 Mon-Fri: 9am-6pm, Sat: 10am-1pm

• Braşov
www.brasovtourism.eu
✉ 30 Piaţa Sfatului ☎ 0268.419078

• Sibiu
www.turism.sibiu.ro
✉ 7 Piaţa Mare ☎ 0269.208913

• Sighişoara
✉ 6 Piaţa Muzeului – Cetate
☎ 078 115 511

• Iaşi
www.turism-iasi.ro
✉ 12 Piaţa Unirii ☎ 0232.261990

• Cluj-Napoca
www.visitcluj.ro
www.visitclujnapoca.ro
✉ 6-8 Bd. Eroilor ☎ 0264.452244

• Timişoara
www.timisoara-info.ro
✉ 2 Piaţa Alba Iulia ☎ 0256.437973

• Constanţa
www.ccina.ro
✉ 185A Alexandru Lăpuşneanu Bd.
☎ 0241.555000

• Sinaia
www.primariasinaia.ro
✉ 47 Carol I Bd ☎ 0244.315656